D1558653

Pantry Shelf Sampler COOKBOOK Grace Additon

Gannett Books

Guy Gannett Publishing Co.
Portland/Maine

Published by Gannett Books, Guy Gannett Publishing Co., 390 Congress Street, Portland, Maine 04104, December, 1983.

First edition printed in the United States of America by Gannett Graphics, Augusta, Maine 04330, December, 1983.

Library of Congress Catalog Card # 83-081301.

ISBN # 0-930096-44-4.

ACKNOWLEDGEMENTS

A note of appreciation is extended to Susan Jack for her editing expertise and to Barbara Sharood for her clever stitchery design which is the cover of this book. And my warm gratitude to all the cooks who shared their prized recipes.

DEDICATION

This book is dedicated to my loved ones.

FOREWORD

"It will be a family kind of cookbook," Grace remarked. It has to be. I watched Grace and Don Additon's sons and daughter grow up. Over the years they each delivered our *Maine Sunday Telegram*. As long as I wrote my food column in the *Telegram* they were especially interested in what I had to say.

They told me about their mother a long time ago. When I retired from writing Cooking Down East and their mother became the food columnist for the *Maine Sunday Telegram* their joy knew no bounds.

At last the recipes Grace had been using in her own family were to be shared. Not only was this a joy in Grace's family but to the readers of her column. In turn, you sent your family recipes to her and they became a part of her columns, also.

Naturally, the answer had to be a cookbook. Grace's cookbook. I like thinking of the fun she had choosing what would go into her cookbook. I wish I might have peeked over her shoulder.

So much to be mindful about. New ideas that will save money, provide good nutrition and make for tasty eating. No one questions the fact that food prepared in your own kitchen and served at your own table will bring the family closer together.

So I walked into Grace's kitchen one fall morning to learn what she was up to. "I'm a family cook," she told me again. We know her recipes are reliable. That is what we look for when we read food columns. It is a must when we own a new cookbook. It is what you will find in Grace's book.

The anticipation has been great. It is in its use that Grace's cookbook will become an integral part of our lives. With great pride we welcome Grace to the family of Maine Cookbook writers. It is a special group. Look at your own shelves of cookbooks. Not too many Maine individuals have written cookbooks. True, we own church, grange, lodge and club cookbooks, all Maine produced.

So it is a rare privilege to write your own cookbook. I am sure the cookbook authors in Maine welcome you, Grace, as I do. We need you to bring another Maine story into our homes.

It will be one of the most rewarding experiences in your life, Grace. Bless You!

Marjorie Standish

Introduction

Cookbooks, like people, are similar; yet, each is unique with individual personality and charm. My aim is a cookbook unlike any other as I attempt to preserve our food heritage as well as present the contemporary culinary style which is part of our daily lives. The Pantry Shelf Sampler, a melting pot of old and new flavors, reflects both the background of our people and the natural food resources of the area.

New Englanders take great pride in the family recipes which have been handed down from one generation to another and this cookbook boasts many of these old-time specialties — reputable dishes like Bean Soup and Indian Pudding that have come into their own.

Within these pages is a collection of 400 kitchen-tested recipes which I have accumulated during my years as homemaker, food columnist, and dietitian. Many of the recipes have been contributed by the good cooks in my family, some are from friends — folks from far and near and from all walks of life; others are from column cooks who have shared their treasures for the past ten years.

Some of the recipes are new; more, variations of familiar dishes made easy with convenience foods, but most are my version of regional favorites. A few have been developed in my own kitchen; yet, more important, ALL recipes, yours and mine, have won the enthusiastic approval of taste-testers.

The recipes have been written with both seasoned and novice cooks in mind. All methods are easy to follow and careful attention has been given to instructions as well as measurements. The portions are based on "average" servings; hence, heartier appetites may require 1½ to 2 portions as a serving.

For best results, measure all ingredients exactly. When a recipe reads "sifted flour," then you know that sifting the flour is necessary before measuring. When unqualified or the recipe indicates just "all-purpose flour," you need only stir the flour gently to *lighten it before measuring. To avoid being confused with baking powder, the ingredient baking soda is referred to as "soda."*

My background — I was born country, but I claim no credit for that — reflects my cooking style. It's basically simple with an eye to nutrition as well as economy. I love food and cooking is a joy and has been for as long as I can remember . . . from the early days back on the farm, throughout the years that homemaking was my one and only interest, right up to the present time. Cooking is my profession; it's also my hobby. My reward is my family's good health and lots of good eating!

The decision to write a cookbook was made twenty-five years ago when a number of newly-married friends, lacking in kitchen expertise, sought cooking advice and instruction. As food columnist for the Maine Sunday Telegram, *cooks not only have consulted me about food-related matters, but have discovered that my recipes can be trusted. Scores of readers have encouraged me to put the recipes in book form. So — to all my cooking friends who have helped make this book a reality — THANKS!*

Although the recipes within are only a sampling of Yankee cooking, your dining table offers you a cook's tour of the region; and, hopefully, you will agree that my choices do indeed savor the flavor of New England. May this Sampler bring you as much pleasure as I have had sharing it with you. ENJOY!

Grace Additon

Augusta, Maine
September, 1983

TABLE OF CONTENTS

Chapter 1

What better way to savor the flavor of New England than with a hot, tantalizing soup, stew or chowder! Nutritious, economical and adaptable, soups have Yankee appeal. Our philosophy of "Don't throw it away, throw it in the soup kettle" has made soups the mainstay of country cooking.

Out of necessity, our forebears discovered the nutritive value of soup-making — it meant survival. Eventually, however, thrifty housewives introduced the flavor of land and sea in creative combinations for a culinary excellence which has become a trademark of Yankee cookery.

At the turn of the century a pot of bubbling soup, along with the old black woodstove, was a common scene in provincial kitchens. Gradually, however, a more "efficient" range replaced the iron monster and canned soups became fashionable.

While commercial soups have a definite place on the pantry shelf — their convenience is a boon to the busy cook and scores of recipes throughout this book make use of them — soup-making is a mark of economy. It is neither a difficult nor time-consuming procedure.

The recipes in this chapter are a sampler of the soups, stews and chowders basic to the region. Some span decades and bring a touch of nostalgia, while others are contemporaries of old-time favorites. In no way are the ingredients and seasonings restrictive. They are intended only as a guide. With a bit of creativity you will discover that our favorites are easily adjusted to your family's liking. Soon "Soup's On" will be a welcomed meal call!

Soups, Stews & Chowders

OYSTER BISQUE

Add corn and a dash of basil for a variation of an old favorite!

   2 **tablespoons butter or margarine**
   ⅓ **cup chopped onion**
   2 **tablespoons chopped green pepper**
   2 **tablespoons all-purpose flour**
   1 **teaspoon salt**
     Dash pepper
   1 **pint shucked fresh oysters with liquor**
   1 **7-ounce can whole-kernel corn, undrained**
   ⅔ **cup (5⅓-ounce can) evaporated milk or light cream**
1⅓ **cups milk**
   1 **tablespoon butter**

In a 2-quart saucepan melt 2 tablespoons butter or margarine. Add onion and green pepper; cook till tender but not brown. Blend in flour and seasonings.

Check oysters for bits of shell; add oysters with liquor and un-drained corn to saucepan. Simmer over low heat for 10 minutes or just till edges of oysters begin to curl. Stir in evaporated milk or cream and milk. Heat but DO NOT boil! Add butter and additional salt and pepper, if necessary. Serve very hot with oyster crackers. Makes about 5 cups.

Variation:

Oyster Stew

Follow recipe for Oyster Bisque except — omit onion, green pepper and whole-kernel corn. Makes 2 generous servings.

DO NOT confuse evaporated milk with sweetened condensed milk. The latter is a whole milk concentrate with a large amount of sugar added. They CANNOT be used interchangeably!

TOMATO BISQUE

From the kitchen of a seasoned cook comes a recipe for an old-fashioned soup — so-called because its color resembles lobster bisque.

    3 cups milk
    ½ cup dry bread or cracker crumbs
      Slice of onion
    1 16-ounce can or 2 cups cooked tomatoes
    1 teaspoon sugar
    2½ tablespoons butter
    1 teaspoon salt
      Dash pepper

In a large saucepan scald milk with crumbs and slice of onion. Remove onion; put mixture through a sieve or whirl in blender. Set aside.

In same saucepan bring tomatoes and sugar to a boil; reduce heat and simmer for 10 minutes. Coarsely blend or chop tomatoes into small pieces. Reheat tomato mixture.

Return milk to saucepan; add butter, salt and pepper. Heat but DO NOT boil! Serve with crisp crackers. Makes 5 cups.

FISH CHOWDER

A traditional New England chowder! Tastes even better when allowed to "ripen" to blend the flavors!

    ¼ cup diced salt pork (rind removed)
    1 large onion, peeled and chopped
    3 cups diced peeled raw potato
    1½ cups fish stock or water
    1½ pounds skinless haddock or cod fillets
    1 5⅓-ounce can evaporated milk
    2 cups milk
    1 teaspoon salt
    ⅛ teaspoon pepper
    2 tablespoons butter

In a large saucepan or Dutch oven fry salt pork until crisp. Remove and reserve for garnish. Add onion to drippings and cook till tender, about 5 minutes. Add potatoes and fish stock or water. Cover and cook for 10 minutes or until potatoes are partially cooked.

Lay fish on top of potatoes. Simmer, covered, 10 minutes or until fish can be separated into flakes with a fork. Remove any bones. Stir in milk; season with salt and pepper. Allow to ripen in refrigerator for a day or two. Reheat but DO NOT allow to boil. Add butter. Garnish with pork pieces, if desired. Makes 6 servings.

For chowders, do not thaw frozen fish!

OLD-FASHIONED CORN CHOWDER

This creamy all-time favorite takes the chill out of New England's cold winter weather. It's even tastier if allowed to "ripen" over very low heat for at least 1 hour. Serve piping hot in large bowls with a slice of pizza!

> 4 strips bacon
> 1 cup chopped onion (2 medium)
> 4 cups diced peeled raw potato
> 1 cup boiling water
> 1 teaspoon salt
> 1 16-ounce can cream-style corn
> 1 16-ounce can whole-kernel corn, undrained
> 1 13-ounce can evaporated milk
> 1 cup milk
> 2 tablespoons butter
> ⅛ teaspoon pepper

In a deep kettle or Dutch oven cook bacon till crisp. Remove and set aside.

Add onion to bacon drippings; cook until tender but not brown. Add potatoes, water and salt. Simmer, covered, 10 minutes or until potatoes are partially cooked. Add corn; simmer 10 minutes longer.

Stir in milk and butter. Season with pepper and more salt, if needed. Heat, but DO NOT boil! Serve piping hot with crumbled bacon atop each serving. Flavor improves with reheating. Makes 6 to 8 servings.

CREAM OF ASPARAGUS SOUP

A taste of springtime in a bowl!

      1 **pound fresh asparagus**
      1 **small onion, peeled and chopped**
   1½ **cups chicken broth**
      2 **tablespoons butter or margarine**
      2 **tablespoons all-purpose flour**
      1 **teaspoon salt**
    ¼ **teaspoon pepper**
    ½ **cup light cream**
   1½ **cups milk**

Wash asparagus; remove tough lower portions of the stalks. Simmer asparagus in a small amount of boiling salted water till tips are tender. Drain, reserving liquid. Remove tips from stalks; set aside.

Cut stalks into pieces and add to saucepan with onion; add reserved water and chicken broth to make about 2 cups liquid. Simmer, covered, 30 minutes. Put mixture through a sieve or whirl in a blender till smooth.

Melt butter or margarine in saucepan; blend in flour and seasonings. Add soup purée. Cook and stir 5 minutes. Add cream and enough milk to make a desired consistency. Heat but DO NOT boil! Season with additional salt and pepper, if needed. Place tips in soup bowls; pour hot soup over. Serve with a dollop of dairy sour cream, if desired. Makes 6 servings.

Variation:

Cream of Broccoli Soup

Follow recipe for Cream of Asparagus Soup except — substitute fresh broccoli for asparagus.

BEAN SOUP

Take your choice — serve this hearty soup as a meatless meal or add bits of cooked ham to make it even more tempting!

1 cup dry navy beans or small white beans
2 quarts beef stock or 3 beef bouillon cubes and 2
  quarts water
1 large onion, peeled and chopped
1 cup sliced celery
1 clove garlic, peeled and minced
1 tablespoon cooking oil
2 tablespoons snipped fresh parsley
1 16-ounce can tomatoes or 1 pint home-canned
  tomatoes
2 medium carrots, peeled and thinly sliced
½ teaspoon dried basil, crushed
½ teaspoon salt
⅛ teaspoon pepper
2 small unpeeled zucchini, sliced (2 cups)
1 cup shredded cabbage
1 cup frozen cut green beans
1 cup frozen green peas
  Grated Parmesan cheese

In a large kettle or Dutch oven combine beans and beef stock. Bring to a boil; boil gently for 2 minutes. Cover kettle and remove from heat. Let stand for 1 hour. Simmer, stirring occasionally, for 1½ hours.

In a medium skillet cook onion, celery and garlic in hot oil for 5 minutes or till vegetables are tender but not brown. Add mixture to beans with parsley, tomatoes, carrots, basil, salt and pepper. Cover and simmer for 15 minutes.

Add zucchini, cabbage, green beans and peas. Simmer, covered, for about 20 minutes or till vegetables are tender. Taste soup to correct seasoning; add salt and pepper, if needed. Serve piping hot with a generous sprinkling of grated cheese. Makes 3 quarts.

Chop celery leaves and add to soups and stews.

CHEESE SOUP

Folks with an inordinate passion for cheese will love this one!

3 cups chicken broth or stock
1 small onion, peeled and chopped
1 stalk celery with leaves, chopped
1 small carrot, peeled and chopped
2 tablespoons cornstarch
2 tablespoons cold water
1 cup (4-ounce pkg.) shredded sharp Cheddar cheese
⅛ teaspoon white pepper
⅛ teaspoon nutmeg
   Salt, if needed
1 egg yolk
½ cup light cream

In medium saucepan combine chicken broth, onion, celery and carrot; bring to a boil. Reduce heat and simmer, covered, for 45 minutes.

Strain mixture through a fine sieve; discard vegetables. Return broth to saucepan. Mix together cornstarch and cold water; stir into soup and cook until mixture thickens slightly.

Add cheese; cook, stirring, till cheese melts. Stir in pepper, nutmeg, and salt, if needed.

Combine egg yolk and cream; mix well and stir ½ cup hot soup into this mixture. Add mixture to saucepan, stirring rapidly. Cook for 2 minutes, but DO NOT boil. Serve hot. Makes 4 servings.

Keep heat low when adding cheese to soups or sauces; cook, stirring constantly, until cheese melts. With excessive heat and prolonged cooking, cheese will form strings and toughen.

Tightly cover leftover cooked rice and refrigerate — up to a week; or freeze — up to six months. Use in recipes calling for cooked rice or add to soups and stews.

CHICKEN-RICE SOUP

Nutritious and satisfying — the soup that nurtured our youngsters through all the childhood illnesses.

- 4 cups well-seasoned chicken broth
- 2 chicken-flavored bouillon cubes
- 2 medium carrots, peeled and diced
- 1 small onion, peeled and diced
- ½ green pepper, seeded and diced
- 1 stalk celery with leaves, chopped
- ¼ cup long-grain rice
- 1 cup diced cooked chicken
  Salt and pepper

In a large saucepan combine broth, bouillon cubes, carrots, onion, green pepper, celery and rice. Bring to a boil; reduce heat and simmer, covered, for 20 to 25 minutes or till rice is tender.

Add cooked chicken. Simmer to heat chicken. Taste soup to check seasoning. Add salt and pepper, if needed. Serve piping hot. Makes 4 to 6 servings.

HAMBURGER SOUP

Perfect dish for carefree cooking! For greater enjoyment, add hot whole wheat rolls to your menu.

- 1 pound ground beef
- 1 large onion, peeled and chopped
- 1 tablespoon butter or margarine
- 1 16-ounce can tomatoes or 1 pint home-canned tomatoes, cut-up
- 3 medium carrots, peeled and sliced
- 2 medium potatoes, peeled and cubed
- ½ cup chopped celery with leaves
- 3 cups beef stock or 3 beef-flavored bouillon cubes dissolved in 3 cups hot water
- 1½ teaspoons salt
- ¼ teaspoon pepper
- ¼ teaspoon dried oregano, crushed

1 16-ounce can cut green beans
Grated Parmesan or Romano cheese

In a large kettle or Dutch oven lightly brown ground beef and onion in butter or margarine, stirring to break up chunks of meat; drain off excess fat.

Add tomatoes, carrots, potatoes, celery, beef stock and seasonings. Bring to a boil; simmer, covered, for 15 to 20 minutes or till vegetables are tender. Add undrained green beans; simmer 15 minutes longer. Taste soup for seasoning; add salt if necessary. Serve piping hot with a sprinkling of grated cheese. Makes 6 to 8 servings.

30-MINUTE MINESTRONE

Good old-fashioned flavor in 30 minutes! Cooks having shelves stocked with home-canned vegetables might want to use a little ingenuity and make pot-luck minestrone.

1 tablespoon cooking oil
1 cup chopped onion
1 cup thinly sliced celery with leaves
1 16-ounce can diced carrots, undrained
2 10½-ounce cans beef broth
1 soup can water
1 16-ounce can tomatoes or 1 pint home-canned
   tomatoes
1 16-ounce can chick peas or kidney beans
1 16-ounce can baked beans or pork and beans
½ teaspoon salt
½ teaspoon dried basil, crushed
   Dash pepper
1 12-ounce can luncheon meat cut into strips
   4-ounces uncooked spaghetti broken into 3- or 4-inch
   lengths (1 cup)
   Grated Parmesan or Romano cheese

Heat oil in a large kettle or Dutch oven. Add onion and celery; cook for 2 or 3 minutes or till tender. Add carrots, beef broth, water, tomatoes, chick peas, baked beans, salt, basil and pepper.

Bring to a boil; simmer, stirring frequently, for 10 minutes.

Add luncheon meat strips and spaghetti. Simmer, stirring occasionally, for 7 to 8 minutes or till spaghetti is just tender. Serve piping hot with a sprinkling of grated cheese. Makes 6 to 8 servings.

There is a fine line of distinction between soups and stews. The ingredients in both are similar, except the vegetables and meats in stews are cut in larger pieces or chunks. Stews are cooked in less liquid and are thickened. They may be eaten with a fork.

FRENCH ONION SOUP

Holiday fare! Advance preparation enhances the flavor and eases the last-minute work load. Reheat slowly prior to serving.

> **3 medium yellow onions, peeled and thinly sliced (1 pound)**
> **2 tablespoons butter or margarine**
> **2 cups beef broth or stock**
> **1 teaspoon Worcestershire sauce**
> **¼ teaspoon salt**
> **Dash pepper**
> **4 slices French bread or hard rolls**
> **½ cup grated Parmesan cheese**

In a heavy saucepan cook onions in melted butter or margarine, stirring frequently, for 20 minutes or till deep golden brown. Add broth or stock and Worcestershire sauce. Bring to a boil and season to taste with salt and pepper. Simmer, covered, 30 minutes, stirring occasionally. (If desired, cover and refrigerate soup for 2 or 3 days to develop flavor.)

Cut bread or rolls into cubes and dry in a slow oven to make croûtons.

Serve soup piping hot topped with croûtons and a generous sprinkling of grated cheese. Makes 4 servings.

OLD-FASHIONED PEA SOUP

Some like it thick; some like it thin. My family likes a hot, well-seasoned pea soup with chunks of meat . . . ham, frankfurters or Polish sausage. And they wouldn't forgive me if I forgot the cornbread!

  1 pound (2 cups) dry yellow or green split peas
  8 cups water
  1 meaty ham bone
  1 cup coarsely chopped onion
  1 cup coarsely chopped celery
  1 cup coarsely sliced carrots
  ¼ teaspoon garlic salt
  ¼ teaspoon dried marjoram, crushed
  ¼ teaspoon pepper
  1 bay leaf
  ½ to 1½ teaspoons salt

Wash peas. In large kettle combine peas and water. Bring to a boil and boil gently for 2 minutes. Remove from heat. Let soak for 1 hour.

Add ham bone, onion, celery, carrots, garlic salt, marjoram, pepper and bay leaf. Bring to a boil. Reduce heat and simmer, covered, for 2 hours or until peas are soft. Stir occasionally.

Remove ham bone and cut off meat; discard bay leaf. Put vegetable mixture through a food mill, blender or sieve. Dice meat and return to soup. Cook over very low heat for 20 to 30 minutes, stirring occasionally. Add salt to taste, and enjoy. Makes about 2 quarts.

Remove fat from a hot soup or stew with pieces of paper toweling. Or, cool and refrigerate the dish, then lift off the solidified fat!

When a recipe requires 1 cup chicken or beef stock or broth, you may use canned broth or 1 bouillon cube and 1 cup water.

SAUSAGE AND VEGETABLE SOUP

An economical main-dish soup — hearty and nutritious!

    4 cups shredded cabbage
    4 medium carrots, peeled and sliced
    3 medium potatoes, peeled and cubed
    3 stalks celery with leaves, chopped
    1 large onion, peeled and thinly sliced
    2 quarts water or vegetable stock
    1 8-ounce can tomato sauce
    2 tablespoons vinegar
    1 tablespoon salt
    ½ teaspoon dried thyme, crushed
    ¼ teaspoon pepper
    4 beef-flavored bouillon cubes
    1 pound Polish sausage, cut in ¼-inch slices

In large kettle or Dutch oven combine cabbage, carrots, potatoes, celery and onion. Stir in water or stock, tomato sauce, vinegar, seasonings and bouillon cubes. Bring to a boil. Reduce heat
and stir in sausage.

Simmer, covered, for 35 to 45 minutes or until vegetables are
tender. Flavor of soup improves with reheating. Freezes well, too.
Makes 12 servings.

FRESH VEGETABLE SOUP

Great soup for using odds and ends from the vegetable patch.
Add vegetables to suit your fancy; just don't overcook them!

    2 tablespoons butter or margarine
    1 large onion, peeled and sliced crosswise
    3 medium ripe tomatoes, peeled and quartered
 1½ teaspoons salt
    ¼ teaspoon sugar
    ⅛ teaspoon pepper
 2½ cups beef broth
    2 medium carrots, peeled and sliced
    2 stalks celery with leaves, thinly sliced
    1 large potato, peeled and cubed

1 cup green beans, cut into ¾-inch lengths
1 cup corn, cut from cob
1 medium zucchini, thinly sliced
1 tablespoon snipped fresh parsley
Grated Parmesan cheese

In large kettle or Dutch oven melt butter or margarine. Add onion and cook until golden but not brown. Add tomatoes; season with salt, sugar and pepper. Cover and cook for 10 minutes.

Stir in beef broth, carrots, celery, potato, green beans and corn. Cover and cook for 20 minutes. Stir in zucchini and snipped parsley. Simmer for 10 minutes longer or until vegetables are tender. Add more liquid if necessary and season to taste with salt and pepper. Sprinkle each serving with grated cheese. Makes 6 servings.

Note:

Add ½ teaspoon dried oregano, crushed and ¼ teaspoon dried marjoram, crushed with the seasonings for a more flavorful soup.

CABBAGE PATCH STEW

A delightful stew which received an honorable mention in a local recipe contest!

1½ pounds stew beef
2 tablespoons cooking oil
1 large onion, peeled and thinly sliced
1 2-pound cabbage, coarsely shredded (about 10 cups)
2 pints home-canned tomatoes or 1 29-ounce can tomatoes
2½ cups beef broth, tomato juice or water
2 teaspoons salt
1 teaspoon caraway seed
1 teaspoon paprika
½ teaspoon pepper
3 tablespoons sugar
Juice of 1 lemon (3 tablespoons)

Trim excess fat from beef; cut into ¾-inch cubes.

In large kettle or Dutch oven heat cooking oil; add beef cubes and brown well on all sides. Add onion and cook till golden. Stir in cabbage, tomatoes, beef broth or other liquid, salt, caraway seed, paprika and pepper. Bring to a boil. Reduce heat and simmer, covered, 2 hours. Stir occasionally.

In a heavy skillet melt sugar to an amber-colored syrup, stirring constantly. Add to soup with lemon juice. Simmer 20 minutes longer. Taste and correct seasoning, if necessary. Serve with crusty hard rolls and butter. Makes 8 to 10 servings.

HERB STEW

From a 4-H'er with a flair for cooking comes this recipe for an old-fashioned soup with a hearty flavor. The beef is simmered in tomato juice while the herb bouquet enhances, yet produces a subtle flavor.

¼ **cup all-purpose flour**
2 **pounds beef stew meat, cut into 1-inch cubes**
1 **tablespoon cooking oil**
2 **teaspoons salt**
¼ **teaspoon pepper**
1 **clove garlic, peeled and minced**
4 **cups tomato juice**
1 **cup boiling water**
2 **tablespoons brown sugar**
¾ **teaspoon dried thyme**
¾ **teaspoon dried rosemary**
½ **teaspoon dried marjoram**
8 **small onions, peeled and cut up**
6 **medium potatoes, peeled and cubed (4 cups)**
4 **medium carrots, peeled and sliced (2 cups)**
1 **10-ounce package frozen peas**

Place flour in plastic bag. Add beef cubes and shake well to coat with flour.

In large kettle or Dutch oven, brown beef cubes in hot oil. Add salt, pepper, garlic, tomato juice, water and brown sugar. Tie herbs in a small nylon or cheesecloth bag. Add to kettle. Bring to a boil; reduce heat. Cover and simmer for 1 hour, stirring occasionally.

Remove herb bag. Add onions, potatoes and carrots. Cover; simmer 30 minutes longer or till meat and vegetables are tender. Stir in peas during last 10 minutes of cooking time. Makes 10 servings.

KRAUT AND FRANK STEW

Great fare for a quick lunch or light supper! This stew takes no more than an hour from start to serving time.

>   1 pound frankfurters, cut into 1-inch lengths
>   1 tablespoon butter or margarine
>   1 large onion, peeled and sliced
>   1 medium green pepper, diced
>   1 16-ounce can or 1 pint home-canned tomatoes, cut up
>   3 medium carrots, peeled and thinly sliced
>   3 medium potatoes, peeled and cubed
>   2 tablespoons packed brown sugar
>   1 teaspoon salt
>   1 teaspoon dried basil, crushed
>   ½ teaspoon caraway seed
>   ¼ teaspoon pepper
>   2 cups water
>   1 16-ounce can (2 cups) sauerkraut, drained

In large saucepan brown frankfurters in butter or margarine; remove with a slotted spoon. Set aside.

Add onion and green pepper to drippings in pan; cook till tender. Add undrained tomatoes, carrots, potatoes, brown sugar, salt, basil, caraway seed and pepper. Stir in water. Simmer, covered, for 35 to 40 minutes or till vegetables are tender. Stir occasionally. Add sauerkraut and franks. Simmer 10 minutes. Makes 6 servings.

Chapter 2

There's no doubt about New England's place in the world of sea-food. Known internationally for the delectable fish and shellfish harvested right off our shores, New England is the land of oyster stew, clam chowder, and the ultimate in epicurean dining — lobster!

When our forefathers settled in the region, they were blessed with an abundance of delicacies from the sea. Soon skillful cooks created a multitude of tasty and satisfying dishes which have become the hallmark of Yankee cuisine.

Thanks to quick-freezing process and modern transportation, the appreciation and cookery of seafood is no longer limited to coastal regions. Near and far, it's the choice of many cooks for special occasions and home entertaining.

Contrary to the commentary of at least one regional alien depicting life along the coast — "Where I understand people have lobster pots rather than lawns!" — seafood is not a Yankee's daily fare. I grew up in a household with a lawn, a lobster pot and a grandfather who was an expert in shellfish cookery. The similarity ends right there! Our lobster pot was portable. Every summer the highlight of school vacation was an old-fashioned clambake along the Maine coast. How well I remember that old black pot filled with delicacies Grampie had foraged from the sea and wrapped in seaweed over blazing driftwood to produce steam and an aroma of the sea itself!

Although feasting on bounty from the sea is a gastronomic delight for natives and visitors alike, a traditional clambake does have geographical limitations. Rather than share a "recipe" for this pleasant memory of yesteryear, I present a collection of dishes which promises pleasurable eating for folks in every corner of the globe. Reflecting Yankee tastes, these unpretentious recipes are representative of those enjoyed in the past as well as today.

Fish & Shellfish

BAKED HADDOCK WITH SOUR CREAM

It's super-tasting, easy-to-fix and a prize-winner in a state recipe contest. Maple syrup enhances without overpowering the delicate flavor of fish!

    1½ **pounds fresh haddock or other skinless fish fillets**
     1 **cup dairy sour cream**
    ¼ **cup fine dry bread crumbs or cornflake crumbs**
     1 **teaspoon salt**
     2 **teaspoons pure maple syrup**
     1 **teaspoon lemon or lime juice**
       Paprika

Wipe fish with damp cloth; place in a well-buttered 10x6x1½-inch baking dish.

In small bowl combine sour cream, bread crumbs or cornflake crumbs, salt, maple syrup and lemon or lime juice; blend well. Spread over fish.

Bake in a 400-degree oven for 25 minutes or till fish flakes easily when tested with a fork and sour cream is lightly browned. Sprinkle with paprika. Makes 4 to 6 servings.

BAKED SPANISH FISH FILLETS

Described by a good cook as "easy to make, economical and fine enough to serve guests." For fewer servings, use an 8-ounce can tomato sauce and halve remaining ingredients. Take it easy on the cloves, too!

    ¼ **cup butter or margarine**
     1 **cup finely chopped onion**
     1 **clove garlic, peeled and minced**
    ½ **cup finely chopped celery**
     1 **15-ounce can tomato sauce**
    ⅛ **teaspoon ground cloves**
     1 **bay leaf**
    1½ **cups finely shredded raw carrot**
    ¾ **cup chicken broth**
    ½ **teaspoon salt**

Dash pepper
2 pounds fresh or partially thawed frozen flounder
fillets or other fish
Freshly snipped parsley

Melt butter or margarine in heavy saucepan. Add onion, garlic and celery; sauté until onion is tender, but not brown. Add tomato sauce, cloves, bay leaf, carrot, chicken broth, salt and pepper. Cover; simmer for 30 minutes.

Butter a shallow 2-quart baking dish. Wipe fish with a damp cloth; pat dry. Sprinkle fillets lightly with additional salt and pepper. Roll up and secure with a toothpick. Arrange in baking dish. Pour sauce over and around fish.

Bake in a 350-degree oven for 30 minutes or till fish flakes easily when tested with a fork. Sprinkle with snipped parsley. Makes 6 servings.

CRISPY FISH FILLETS

Better than what you might expect at a fish fry!

1 pound fresh or partially thawed frozen fish fillets
¼ cup all-purpose flour
½ teaspoon salt
1 egg yolk
2 tablespoons water
1 tablespoon cooking oil
1 egg white, stiffly beaten
¼ cup all-purpose flour
Cooking oil or shortening for deep-fat frying

Wipe fish with a damp cloth and pat dry. Cut into serving-size pieces.

In medium bowl combine flour and salt. Make a well in center; add egg yolk, water and 1 tablespoon cooking oil. Stir with a wooden spoon until batter is smooth. Fold in egg white.

In shallow dish dip fish in remaining ¼ cup flour, then in batter. Deep-fat fry fish, a few pieces at a time, in oil or shortening heated to 375 degrees for 3 to 5 minutes or till golden brown. Drain. Sprinkle with vinegar, if desired. Pass the tartar sauce. Makes 3 to 4 servings.

CRISPY HADDOCK FILLETS

A meal-in-minutes!

>   1½ pounds fresh haddock or other skinless fillets
>   ⅓ cup milk
>   1 teaspoon salt
>   ⅛ teaspoon pepper
>   ¾ cup crushed cornflakes (3 cups cereal)
>   2 tablespoons butter or margarine, melted

Wipe fillets with a damp cloth; cut into serving-size pieces. In a small bowl combine milk, salt and pepper. Dip fish into milk mixture; then roll in crushed flakes.

Place in a single layer on a greased baking sheet. Drizzle melted butter or margarine over tops.

Bake, without turning, in a 450-degree oven for 15 minutes or till fish flakes easily when tested with a fork. Pass the tartar sauce. Makes 4 servings.

Note:

To coat fish evenly with crumbs, place a portion of the crumbs and a piece of fish in a plastic bag; shake well. Repeat till all pieces are coated.

FISH CAKES

Cooks from past generations used salted cod — soaked, drained and cooked — to make their fish cakes. However, this contemporary version is less bothersome, although milder in flavor. Fish cakes can be made from scratch or from leftover cooked fish and mashed potato. Early pioneers served them crispy brown with baked beans on Sunday morning. We also like them for lunch or light suppers!

>   4 medium potatoes, peeled
>   1 tablespoon butter or margarine
>   1 teaspoon salt
>   ⅛ teaspoon pepper
>   1 egg
>   1 pound skinless cod or haddock fillets
>   2 to 4 tablespoons bacon drippings or other fat

Cook potatoes in a small amount of boiling salted water till tender; drain well. Mash — makes about 2 cups. Add butter, salt and pepper. Cool. Add egg and beat well.

Meanwhile, rinse fish; simmer in a small amount of water just till fish flakes easily. Drain, reserving stock for future use.

Carefully check fish for bones; mash. Add to potato mixture; blend well. Shape with wet hands into 12 patties. Place on a plate, separating layers with wax paper. Chill until ready to fry.

In a large skillet heat bacon drippings or other fat till hot. Add patties and fry till golden brown. Turn and brown top side. Makes 12 three-inch patties.

LIGHTHOUSE FISH PUFFS

This impressive dish is well worth the extra effort it takes to prepare. The thin fillets are coiled and filled with crabmeat dressing — another winner from a seafood contest!

    1½ pounds skinless thin fish fillets (sole, haddock or
        cod)
    ¾ cup fresh or canned crabmeat
    1 tablespoon butter or margarine
    1 cup fresh mushrooms, thinly sliced
    2 tablespoons finely chopped onion
    2 tablespoons all-purpose flour
    ½ teaspoon salt
    ¼ teaspoon dried savory, crushed
    ¼ teaspoon dried thyme, crushed
        Dash cayenne pepper
    ½ cup light cream
        Juice of 1 lemon (3 tablespoons)
    ½ cup fine dry seasoned bread crumbs
    2 tablespoons butter or margarine, melted

Wipe fish with a damp cloth; pat dry. Slice fish into long strips (3 or 4 inches) and coil inside 8 buttered muffin or custard cups. Sprinkle fish lightly with salt and pepper. Set aside. Remove cartilage from crabmeat; flake.

In a small saucepan melt butter or margarine. Add mushrooms and onion; cook for 5 minutes or till tender. Blend in flour and seasonings. Slowly stir in cream and cook, stirring constantly, until mixture thickens. Add crabmeat and 1 tablespoon of the lemon juice.

Divide mixture evenly among "puffs" in cups. Drizzle remaining lemon juice atop. Bake in a 350-degree oven for 20 minutes or till fish is firm.

In a small bowl combine crumbs and melted butter or margarine; mix well. Remove fish from oven and sprinkle each "puff" with a tablespoon of crumb mixture. Return to oven and bake until crumbs are nicely browned, about 5 minutes; or, broil 4 inches from heat until crumbs are golden. Serve with tartar sauce. Makes 4 to 6 servings.

When buying fish, estimate 1 pound whole or round fish per serving; ½ pound dressed fish and ⅓ pound fillets, steaks and sticks for each serving.

Fish is done the moment the sheen goes off the flesh.

SOUFFLÉ-TOPPED FISH

The creation of a competitive cook which received first place in a seafood recipe contest!

> 2 to 2½ pounds skinless fresh or partially thawed
>   frozen fish fillets
>   Salt and pepper
> ½ cup mayonnaise or salad dressing
> ¼ cup sweet or dill pickle relish
> 2 tablespoons snipped fresh parsley
> 1 tablespoon lemon juice
> ¼ teaspoon salt
>   Dash pepper
> 2 egg whites

Wipe fish with a damp cloth; pat dry. Cut into serving-size portions. Arrange fish in a single layer on a lightly greased rack in a broiler pan or in a shallow baking pan. Sprinkle with salt and pepper.

In small bowl combine mayonnaise, relish, parsley, lemon juice, ¼ teaspoon salt and a dash of pepper; blend well.

In another bowl beat egg whites until stiff but not dry. Fold into mayonnaise mixture.

Broil fish, 4 inches from heat, for 6 to 10 minutes or until almost cooked through. Spread sauce evenly over tops of fish. Return to broiler; broil until sauce is puffed and lightly browned. Serve immediately. Makes 6 servings.

CRABMEAT CASSEROLE

An old standby that goes to many family gatherings: buffets, barbecues and potlucks.

> **2 cups Medium White Sauce (recipe on page 97)**
> **1 cup shredded sharp Cheddar cheese**
> **2 egg yolks**
> **1 6 or 6½-ounce can crabmeat, drained and cartilage removed or 8 ounces fresh or frozen crabmeat, thawed and well-drained**
> **2 slices bread, crusts removed and cubed**
> **½ cup soft bread crumbs**
> **1 tablespoon butter or margarine, melted**

Prepare medium white sauce. Add shredded cheese to white sauce; stir till cheese melts. Remove from heat.

In small bowl beat egg yolks with a fork. Slowly stir a small amount of hot cheese sauce into yolks. Return mixture to remaining cheese sauce; cook till blended, stirring constantly, about 1 minute. Stir in crabmeat and bread cubes. Season to taste with salt and pepper.

Turn mixture into buttered 1½-quart casserole. Combine bread crumbs with melted butter or margarine. Spread crumbs evenly atop casserole.

Bake in a 350-degree oven for 30 minutes or till hot and bubbly and nicely browned on top. Makes 6 servings.

CRAB QUICHE

Quiche buffs and seafood addicts will approve of this one!

    1 9-inch unbaked pie shell
    1 cup shredded Swiss cheese
    1 6 or 6½-ounce can crabmeat, drained and cartilage
      removed or 8 ounces fresh or frozen crabmeat,
      thawed and well-drained
    1 small onion, finely chopped
    3 eggs
    1 cup light cream or half-and-half
    ½ teaspoon salt
    ¼ teaspoon dry mustard
      Dash nutmeg
    ¼ cup slivered almonds

Line unpricked pie shell with a 12-inch square of aluminum foil; fill with dried beans. Bake in a 425-degree oven for 5 to 7 minutes. Carefully remove foil with beans; continue to bake shell for 3 minutes longer. Prick any air bubbles.

Spread cheese evenly over bottom of pie shell. Arrange crabmeat, then onion over cheese.

In bowl beat eggs till light. Beat in cream or half-and-half, salt, mustard, and nutmeg. Pour over mixture in shell. Top with almonds. Bake in a 350-degree oven for 40 minutes or till center is firm. Let stand 10 minutes before cutting. Makes 6 servings.

CLAM CASSEROLE

An indispensable recipe for every cook's repertoire. This one is good either as a side dish or for a light supper. It's easy to tote to a community supper, too!

    2 eggs
    2 6½-ounce cans minced clams, undrained
    1 cup fine cracker crumbs (24 saltines)
 1½ cups milk
    ¼ cup butter or margarine, melted
    2 tablespoons minced onion
    ½ teaspoon salt

In mixing bowl beat eggs lightly. Stir in clams with juice, crackers and milk. Add butter or margarine, onion and salt; mix well. Pour mixture into buttered 1½-quart casserole.

Bake in a 325-degree oven for 60 minutes or till knife inserted just off center comes out clean. Serve warm or cold. Makes 6 servings.

NEW ENGLAND STEAMED CLAMS

A New England tradition: steamer clams, melted butter, fresh corn-on-the-cob — and ravenous appetites!

4 dozen soft-shelled or steamer clams
½ cup boiling water
Melted butter

Clean clams to get rid of grit and mud by scrubbing with a stiff brush or rinsing thoroughly. Place in a large kettle and add boiling water; cover and return to boiling point. Reduce heat and steam gently for about 8 minutes or till clams open. Drain clams, reserving liquid. Strain liquid.

Serve clams hot in the shells with a side dish of melted butter for dunking clams and a glass of clam liquid. Makes 2 servings.

BOILED MAINE LOBSTER

Rejoice! 'Tis a feast fit for a king or queen.

1¼ to 2-pound lobster per person
Water
2 or 3 tablespoons salt

In a large kettle add water to a depth of about 3 inches. Add salt; bring to a rapid boil. Quickly plunge live lobster, head first, into the water. Cover and bring to the boiling point. Steam gently for 15 to 20 minutes, depending on size of lobster. Remove from water and lay on its back to drain; wipe dry.

To serve hot, place whole lobster on a large plate with a side dish of melted butter; or, serve cold with mayonnaise.

To use in dishes calling for lobster meat, place lobster on its back and split lengthwise with a sharp knife. Discard sac under the head (stomach) and back vein (intestinal tract). Crack claws. Remove meat from body and claws: cut meat into chunks.

Note:
> The green material, the liver or tamalley, is edible just as the red spawn or coral is.

LOBSTER CASSEROLE

A nifty way to s-t-r-e-t-c-h 1½ cups lobster meat into 4 servings!

> 1½ cups lobster meat, cut into chunks
> 1 cup soft bread crumbs, crusts removed
> 1 cup light cream
> 1 egg, well beaten
> 2 tablespoons butter or margarine, melted
> 1 tablespoon lemon juice
> 1 teaspoon prepared mustard
> ½ teaspoon grated onion
> ½ teaspoon salt
>   Dash pepper
> ¼ cup fine butter cracker crumbs
> 1 tablespoon melted butter or margarine

In a large bowl combine lobster meat, soft bread crumbs, cream, egg, 2 tablespoons butter or margarine, lemon juice, mustard, grated onion and seasonings. Mix lightly with a fork. Turn mixture into a buttered 1-quart baking dish or casserole.

In a small bowl combine dry crumbs and 1 tablespoon melted butter or margarine; mix well. Spread mixture evenly over top of casserole. Bake in a 350-degree oven for 25 to 30 minutes or till hot and top is lightly browned. Makes 4 servings.

Variation:

Fish or Crabmeat Casserole

Substitute 1½ cups cooked fish or crabmeat for the lobster.

SCALLOPED OYSTERS

Without the scalloped oysters, Christmas would not be Christmas. As a matter of fact, seafood addicts claim that this is the hallmark of holiday dining!

1 pint shucked fresh oysters
1 cup fine cracker crumbs
½ cup fine dry bread crumbs
½ cup butter or margarine, melted
½ teaspoon salt
⅛ teaspoon pepper
3 tablespoons light cream
1 tablespoon dry sherry

Drain oysters; remove shell particles. Strain liquor; reserve. In small bowl combine cracker and bread crumbs; stir in melted butter or margarine. Spread one-third of the crumbs in bottom of a buttered shallow baking dish. Arrange half of oysters over crumbs; sprinkle with salt and pepper. Add another third of the crumbs, then remaining oysters. Sprinkle remaining crumbs over top.

Blend together reserved oyster liquor, light cream and sherry. With a knife, carefully poke holes down through layers; pour cream mixture into holes. Dot top with butter.

Bake in a 400-degree oven for 20 minutes or till hot and top is lightly browned. Makes 4 to 6 servings.

Note:
    No more than two layers of oysters should be used as top and bottom layers
    will be overdone while center layer will be undercooked.

Don't ruin the flavor of oysters by overcooking. Cook just enough to heat through.

Shucked oysters have been removed from the shells; they have a sweet, mild odor and are packed in little or no liquid.

DOWN EAST SCALLOP CASSEROLE

A wonderful make-ahead casserole. For full enjoyment, make this dish early in the day and refrigerate to blend flavors.

1 pound sea scallops, quartered
3 tablespoons butter or margarine
2 tablespoons diced green pepper
2 tablespoons finely chopped onion
¼ cup all-purpose flour
1 teaspoon dry mustard
1½ cups milk (or preferably part cream)
1 cup shredded Cheddar cheese
½ cup condensed tomato soup
¼ cup sliced stuffed olives
½ cup fine dry bread crumbs
2 tablespoons butter or margarine, melted

Put scallops in a saucepan; barely cover with water and bring slowly to boiling point. Drain well and set aside.

In same saucepan melt 3 tablespoons butter or margarine; add green pepper and onion. Cook and stir till onion is tender but not brown. Add flour and mustard, stirring constantly. Gradually add milk and lower heat to simmer; cook and stir till mixture is thick and smooth.

Add cheese, stirring till melted; stir in soup and olives. Season with salt and pepper, if needed. Add drained scallops. Turn mixture into a buttered 1½-quart casserole.

Combine bread crumbs with melted butter or margarine. Sprinkle evenly over top of casserole. Bake in a 350-degree oven for 20 to 25 minutes or till hot and bubbly and crumbs are nicely browned. Makes 4 to 6 servings.

SCALLOPS AU GRATIN

The inspiration of a coastal cook for a delectable taste of the sea. Although it may not be a budget dish, it certainly is worthy of an occasional splurge!

2 pounds fresh sea scallops

¼ **cup butter or margarine**
2 **cups diced green pepper (2 medium)**
2 **cups chopped celery**
1 **cup chopped onion**
3 **cups soft bread crumbs (4 slices)**
1 **teaspoon salt**
¼ **teaspoon pepper**
2 **cups light cream**
1 **cup shredded sharp Cheddar cheese**

Rinse scallops and drain; place scallops in a large saucepan and add water to barely cover; bring to a boil, uncovered. Remove from heat; drain. Set aside.

In same saucepan melt butter or margarine; add green pepper, celery and onion. Cook until vegetables are tender but not brown.

Combine scallops, bread crumbs, salt and pepper with sautéed vegetable mixture; toss. Place in a buttered 3-quart casserole. Pour cream over scallop mixture. Sprinkle cheese evenly over top.

Bake in a 350-degree oven for 30 minutes or till bubbly and scallops are tender. Makes 8 servings.

SCALLOPS AND MUSHROOM CASSEROLE

Two favorites in a white sauce. It definitely is a dish for the sophisticated palate!

1 **pound scallops**
2 **cups well-seasoned Medium White Sauce (recipe on page 97)**
¼ **cup butter or margarine**
½ **pound fresh mushrooms, sliced**
1 **cup chopped celery**
¼ **cup finely chopped onion**
¼ **cup finely chopped green pepper**
⅛ **teaspoon dried basil, crushed**
½ **cup fine cracker crumbs**
2 **tablespoons butter or margarine, melted**
¼ **cup shredded sharp Cheddar cheese**

Rinse scallops; drain. If large cut in half across grain. Set aside. Make medium white sauce. Melt ¼ cup butter or margarine in large saucepan; add mushrooms, celery, onion, green pepper and basil. Cook, stirring, over medium heat till mushrooms are tender but not soft.

Add scallops to mushroom mixture; mix well. Cook over low heat, stirring frequently, for 5 minutes. Stir in white sauce and mix thoroughly. Pour mixture into buttered 1½-quart casserole.

Combine cracker crumbs with melted butter or margarine; mix in cheese. Sprinkle evenly over top of casserole. Bake in a 350-degree oven for 25 minutes or till hot and golden brown. Makes 4 servings.

Fresh bay scallops — up to ½-inch in diameter — or the larger sea scallops are purchased cleaned and removed from shells.

SCALLOP NEWBURG

A family favorite from a coastal cook who says she divides the mixture between two casseroles, bakes both; serves one and freezes the second for future enjoyment. Reheat in a slow oven.

>   **2 pounds scallops**
>   **1 10¾-ounce can condensed cream of shrimp soup**
>   **1 10¾-ounce can condensed cream of mushroom soup**
>   **1 8-ounce can sliced mushrooms, drained**
>   **¼ cup dry sherry**
>   **½ teaspoon garlic salt**
>   **½ cup fine dry seasoned bread crumbs**
>   **2 tablespoons butter or margarine, melted**
>   **1 tablespoon snipped fresh parsley**

Rinse scallops; drain well and cut into ½-inch pieces. In large bowl combine scallops, soups, mushrooms, sherry and garlic salt. Turn mixture into a buttered 3-quart casserole.

Combine bread crumbs and melted butter or margarine. Spread evenly atop casserole. Bake, uncovered, in a 325-degree oven for 50 to 60 minutes or till hot and bubbly. Sprinkle parsley over top. Serve over fluffy hot rice or in patty shells. Makes 8 to 10 servings.

BLAINE HOUSE SEAFOOD CASSEROLE

This scrumptious dish from the governor's mansion is the ultimate in epicurean dining. Its consistency is similar to bread pudding, but rich and so-o-o satisfying. For elegant dining, serve in coquille shells with fresh green peas to accompany it.

And why 21 servings? "Because that is the number of guests which can be seated at the state dining room table, "points out the governor's cook.

      1 **pound lobster meat**
      1 **pound scallops**
      1 **pound crabmeat or shelled shrimp**
      ¾ **cup butter or margarine (1½ sticks)**
      ¾ **cup all-purpose flour**
    2¼ **teaspoons dry mustard**
     15 **slices white bread**
      3 **pints all-purpose cream**
        Salt and paprika
      ½ **cup dry sherry**
    1½ **cups fine butter cracker crumbs**
      6 **tablespoons butter or margarine, melted**

Cut lobster meat into large cubes; cut large scallops in half across grain; remove bits of shell from crabmeat.

In large skillet melt butter or margarine. Add seafood; sauté stirring, until tender, about 5 minutes. DO NOT OVERCOOK! Sprinkle flour and dry mustard over seafood. Add as much cream as skillet will hold. Cook and stir till mixture thickens.

Remove crusts from bread; save for another occasion. Break bread into large bowl; add remaining cream. Stir in seafood mixture. Season to taste with salt and paprika. Add sherry or equal amounts of sherry and brandy. Turn mixture into large buttered roasting pan or two 13x9x2-inch baking pans.

In medium bowl mix cracker crumbs with melted butter or margarine. Sprinkle a generous layer atop casserole. Bake in a 325-degree oven for 40 to 45 minutes or until hot and bubbly. Makes 21 servings.

CRAB AND SHRIMP CASSEROLE

A country cousin who grew up cooking for five brothers shares this easy-to-prepare casserole. It's delightful!

        1 tablespoon butter or margarine
        1 cup chopped celery
        ½ cup finely chopped onion
        ½ cup diced green pepper
        1 cup fresh crabmeat, flaked (see note)
        1 cup cooked small shrimp
        ½ teaspoon salt
        1 teaspoon Worcestershire sauce
        ¾ cup mayonnaise or salad dressing
        1 cup soft bread crumbs
        1 tablespoon butter or margarine, melted

In skillet melt 1 tablespoon butter or margarine; add celery, onion and green pepper. Sauté until vegetables are tender but not brown. Remove from heat.

Stir in crabmeat, shrimp, salt, Worcestershire sauce and mayonnaise. Place mixture in a buttered 1-quart casserole.

Combine crumbs with melted butter or margarine. Sprinkle evenly atop casserole. Bake in a 350-degree oven for 30 minutes or till hot and bubbly. Makes 4 to 6 servings.

Note:
> If desired, use 6 to 6½-ounce can crabmeat, drained and cartilage removed, and 4¼-ounce can shrimp, drained.

HAM AND SHRIMP JAMBALAYA

A Yankee's version of a quick-and-easy Southern dish!

        1 pound raw shrimp in shells or 1 cup cooked shrimp
        2 tablespoons butter or margarine
        ½ cup chopped onion
        ½ cup diced green pepper
        1 clove garlic, peeled and minced
        1 10¾-ounce can condensed tomato soup
        ⅓ cup water

¼ teaspoon dried oregano, crushed
¼ teaspoon salt
  Dash pepper
1½ cups cooked rice
 1 cup diced cooked ham
 2 tablespoons toasted slivered almonds

Shell and clean raw shrimp; pat dry. Melt butter or margarine in a medium saucepan. Add onion, green pepper and garlic; cook, stirring occasionally, till vegetables are tender but not brown. Add tomato soup, water, oregano, salt and pepper; mix well. Stir in rice, ham and shrimp. Turn mixture into a buttered 1½-quart casserole.

Bake, uncovered, in a 350-degree oven for 30 to 35 minutes or till hot and bubbly. Sprinkle with nuts. Makes 6 servings.

SHRIMP AND MUSHROOM QUICHE

A winner from a cook whose specialty is seafood cookery!

 1 9-inch unbaked pie shell
 1 4¼-ounce can small shrimp
 2 tablespoons butter or margarine
 1 cup sliced fresh mushrooms or 1 4-ounce can
   mushroom stems and pieces, drained
 1 cup shredded Swiss or Cheddar cheese
 3 eggs
 1 cup dairy sour cream
 ½ teaspoon salt
   Dash pepper
 1 tablespoon snipped fresh parsley

Line unpricked pie shell with a piece of foil; then weight it down with dried beans. Bake in a 425-degree oven for 5 to 7 minutes. Carefully remove foil with beans and continue baking for 3 minutes longer.

Meanwhile drain shrimp; reserve liquid. In skillet melt butter or margarine; add mushrooms and cook till tender, about 3 minutes. Combine mushrooms, shrimp and cheese. Spread evenly over bottom of warm pie shell.

In a bowl beat eggs lightly; beat in reserved liquid from shrimp, sour cream, salt, pepper and parsley. Pour over mixture in pie shell. Bake in a 350-degree oven for 40 minutes or till filling is firm in center. Serve warm. Makes 6 servings.

STEAMING "GREEN" SHRIMP IN SHELLS

1½ pounds fresh or frozen raw shrimp in shells
1 quart water
¼ cup salt

In a large kettle, for each 1½ pounds shrimp bring 1 quart water and ¼ cup salt to a rapid boil; add washed shrimp. Cover and bring water to a boil. Reduce heat and simmer for 2 or 3 minutes or till shells turn red. Drain and cool. Pull off head if not already removed and peel off shell; if necessary, remove dark vein along back of shrimp. Chill and serve in salads or in cocktails.

Green shrimp is the term used to describe raw or uncooked shrimp!

One pound green shrimp yields about 7½-ounces or 1 cup cleaned and peeled shrimp.

TO PEEL AND CLEAN "GREEN" SHRIMP

With a slight twist of the fingers, remove heads. Twist off tail end and pull out meat. Rinse meat and use in any dish that requires further cooking.

When cooking peeled raw shrimp, cook in ½ cup boiling water to which 1 teaspoon salt and 1 teaspoon vinegar or lemon juice have been added for about 45 seconds or just till shrimp lose glossiness and curl up. DO NOT OVERCOOK! Drain and cool.

DEACON'S DELIGHT

Tuna and noodles in a creamy cheese sauce are perfect partners for a casual family meal . . . a recipe from a reputable family cook! Serve with a tossed green salad.

1 8-ounce package wide egg noodles
1 10¾-ounce can condensed cream of mushroom soup
1 6½ or 7-ounce can tuna packed in oil, undrained and
   flaked
¼ cup chopped onion
¼ cup chopped green pepper
1 13-ounce can evaporated milk (1⅔ cups)
2 cups (8-ounce pkg.) American cheese or process
   cheese spread, cubed
¾ cup crushed cornflakes
1½ tablespoons butter or margarine, melted

Cook noodles in boiling, salted water till tender; drain. Combine soup, undrained tuna, onion, green pepper, evaporated milk and cheese cubes. Carefully stir in noodles. Turn mixture into a buttered 2-quart or 12x8x2-inch baking dish.

Mix together cornflake crumbs and melted butter or margarine; sprinkle evenly over top. Bake in a 400-degree oven for 20 to 25 minutes or till hot and bubbly. Makes 6 to 8 servings.

Peeled and cleaned shrimp are headless shrimp — either raw or cooked — with shell and intestinal vein removed!

Coquilles are shell-shaped baking dishes used for individual servings.

TUNA-IN-A-LOAF

*A recipe from a cooking contest works magic with a can of tuna
. . . an impressive budget-dish!*

> 3 egg yolks
> 1 12½-ounce can tuna, drained and flaked (or 2
>   6½-ounce cans tuna)
> 1 10¾-ounce can condensed cream of celery soup
> 1 cup fine cracker crumbs
> ¼ cup finely chopped onion
> 1 tablespoon snipped fresh parsley
>   Dash pepper
> 1 tablespoon lemon juice
> 3 egg whites
> 3 or 4 thin lemon slices

In large bowl beat egg yolks lightly with a fork; add tuna, soup,
cracker crumbs, onion, parsley, pepper and lemon juice; mix well.

In medium bowl beat egg whites till stiff and glossy. Fold into
tuna mixture.

Line the bottom of a buttered 9x5x3-inch loaf pan with lemon
slices. Spoon tuna mixture atop. Bake in a 350-degree oven for 45
to 50 minutes or till center of loaf is firm. Invert onto warm platter. Garnish with sprigs of parsley and additional lemon slices, if
desired. Makes 6 servings.

Variation:

Salmon-in-a-Loaf

Follow recipe for Tuna-in-a-Loaf except — substitute 1 16-
ounce can pink or red salmon, discarding skin and bones, for
tuna.

The redder the flesh of canned salmon, the higher the price!

TUNA NOODLE SUPREME

An old favorite with an Italian accent. Mushrooms and ripe olives add elegance!

   4 ounces (3 cups) medium or wide noodles
   1 small onion, peeled and finely chopped
   1 tablespoon butter or margarine
   1 10¾-ounce can condensed cream of mushroom soup
   ⅔ cup light cream (see note)
   ⅓ cup grated Parmesan cheese
   1 6½ or 7-ounce can tuna, drained
   1 4-ounce can sliced mushrooms, drained
   ¼ cup sliced ripe olives
   2 tablespoons snipped fresh parsley
   2 teaspoons lemon juice

Cook noodles in boiling, salted water till tender; drain. There should be about 2 cups of cooked noodles.

In skillet cook onion in butter or margarine till tender but not brown. Add soup, cream and cheese; heat and stir.

Break tuna into chunks; add to soup mixture with mushrooms, olive slices, parsley, lemon juice and noodles. Mix well. Pour into buttered 2-quart casserole. Sprinkle with additional Parmesan cheese and paprika. Bake in a 350-degree oven for 25 to 30 minutes or till hot and bubbly. Garnish with a sprig or two of parsley and olive slices. Makes 6 servings.

Note:
   If desired, substitute a small can of evaporated milk (5⅓-ounces) for light cream.

Tuna prices are determined by type and the pack. Albacore or "white meat" tuna is more costly than light tuna.

Tuna packed in water contains about 100 less calories per can than oil-packed tuna.

TARTAR SAUCE

To accompany your fish and seafood dishes!

> **1 cup mayonnaise**
> **2 tablespoons sweet pickle relish, drained**
> **1 tablespoon grated onion**
> **1 tablespoon snipped fresh parsley**
>   **Dash cayenne pepper**
> **1 teaspoon vinegar**

In small bowl combine mayonnaise, relish, onion, parsley, pepper and vinegar; mix well. Chill. Makes 1¼ cups.

To insure good flavor and quality, use commercial packaged frozen fish within 3 months after purchasing!

To thaw frozen fish, flash thaw by leaving package at room temperature for 15 minutes or under running cold water just long enough to separate fillets.

Cooking Notes

Chapter 3

Poultry has been long recognized for both nutritive value and diversity. It's an excellent source of protein, digestible and low in fat as well as calories. It's economical, easy to prepare and family-pleasing.

Poultry provides a lot of pleasurable year-round eating at our house just as, no doubt, it does at yours. My folder of chicken recipes bulges with dishes to suit every occasion and flavors to please every member of the family. Poultry is perfect for picnics, parties and plain everyday enjoyment.

Historians tell us that this heritage food was introduced to the New World by early settlers who included chickens among their valued possessions. During my childhood, chicken was reserved for Sunday dinners and holidays; how Mama prepared her bird depended on whether it was a retired egg producer or the overly confident baron of the barnyard. Her creations, as I recall, were always a mouth-watering culinary experience.

Since the forties poultry consumption per capita has more than doubled; and, thanks to an innovative and progressive poultry industry, today's cook has unlimited opportunities for poultry cookery. It adapts to stewing, roasting, broiling, frying and grilling . . . not to mention the countless dishes for cooked poultry. Best of all, it remains one of our best buys for protein. Poultry costs little more and in some instances less than it did forty years ago.

As you leaf through the pages of chicken specialties, you will discover that simplicity is the key. While some recipes have been changed to suit contemporary tastes and methods of cooking, others, such as Old-Fashioned Chicken Pie, are the same good old dishes America grew up on. So -- "put a chicken in your pot" and may you have satisfaction in being a "good pervider" for your family!

Poultry & Eggs

CHICKEN BREASTS SAUTERNE

A company dish from a Midwestern home economist! For those who wish not to imbibe, replace the wine with chicken broth.

- 2 16-ounce cans French-style green beans, drained
- 3 whole large chicken breasts, skinned and halved lengthwise
- ½ teaspoon seasoned salt
  Paprika
- 1 10¾-ounce can condensed cream of mushroom soup
- ⅓ cup Sauterne or dry white wine
- 1 cup shredded Cheddar or American cheese
- 2 tablespoons chopped pimiento
- 1 tablespoon dried parsley flakes

Place green beans in a buttered 2½-quart baking dish or casserole. Arrange chicken atop beans, meaty side up. Sprinkle with seasoned salt and paprika.

Combine soup and wine; pour over chicken. Sprinkle cheese, pimiento and parsley evenly atop.

Bake, covered, in a 325-degree oven for 1¼ hours or till chicken is tender. Remove cover and continue to bake for 15 minutes. Serve with hot fluffy cooked rice. Spoon sauce over chicken and pass remaining sauce. Makes 6 servings

CHICKEN REUBEN BAKE

Sauerkraut addicts will approve wholeheartedly of this combination — chicken, sauerkraut and Swiss cheese. The dish is a blue ribbon winner from a national chicken cook-off!

- 4 whole chicken breasts, halved, skinned and boned
- ¼ teaspoon salt
- ⅛ teaspoon pepper
- 1 16-ounce can sauerkraut, drained and excess liquid pressed out
- 4 4x6-inch slices natural Swiss cheese
- 1¼ cups bottled Thousand Island dressing

Place chicken breasts in a single layer in a buttered, shallow baking dish. Sprinkle with salt and pepper. Place sauerkraut over chicken and top with Swiss cheese. Pour dressing evenly over all. Cover dish with foil.

Bake in a 325-degree oven for 1½ hours or till chicken is tender. Garnish with sprigs of parsley, if desired. Makes 8 servings.

Note:
> To make fewer servings, use an 8-ounce can sauerkraut and halve remaining ingredients. Arrange in a buttered 10x6x1½-inch baking dish. Makes 3 or 4 servings.

COUNTRY CHICKEN STEW

Hearty family fare for a cold winter night. This creamy chicken-vegetable stew is easy-to-make and economical, too!

    2½ to 3 pound broiler-fryer chicken, cut-up
    1 tablespoon cooking oil
    1 10¾-ounce can condensed cream of chicken soup
    1¼ cups water
    3 stalks celery, cut in ½-inch lengths
    1 medium onion, peeled and quartered
    1 teaspoon salt
    1 teaspoon dried thyme, crushed
    4 medium carrots, peeled and cut in 1-inch slices
    3 medium potatoes, peeled and quartered

In large kettle or Dutch oven brown chicken in hot oil, turning once. Drain off fat.

Combine soup and water; pour over chicken. Add celery, onion, salt and thyme. Cover and simmer for 30 minutes, stirring occasionally. Skim fat. Add carrots and potatoes. Cook 30 minutes longer or until vegetables and chicken are tender. Makes 6 servings.

❖❖❖❖❖❖❖❖❖❖❖❖❖❖❖❖❖❖❖❖❖❖❖❖

If desired, substitute an equal amount of chicken broth or apple juice in dishes calling for white wine.

❖❖❖❖❖❖❖❖❖❖❖❖❖❖❖❖❖❖❖❖❖❖❖❖

FORGET-IT CHICKEN

*A dish for the family worthy of its name. You fix it and forget it
. . . until serving time!*

> 1 cup long-grain brown rice
> 1 10¾-ounce can condensed cream of mushroom soup
> 1 4-ounce can mushroom stems and pieces, undrained
> 1 envelope dry onion soup mix
> 2 cups chicken broth or water
> 3 large whole chicken breasts, skinned, halved
>   lengthwise and boned
>   Paprika

Place rice in a 13x9x2-inch baking pan. Combine mushroom
soup, mushrooms and onion soup mix; stir in chicken broth or
water. Pour mixture over rice. Arrange chicken breasts atop.
Sprinkle lightly with paprika. Cover with a piece of aluminum foil.
   Bake in a 325-degree oven for 1½ hours or till chicken and rice
are tender. Serve with a green vegetable. Makes 6 servings.

MARINATED CHICKEN BREASTS

*A Southern gentleman's recipe! The oil and vinegar marinade
imparts a delightful flavor whether the chicken is broiled or
grilled.*

> 3 whole chicken breasts, halved lengthwise (see note)
> ¼ cup salad oil
> ¼ cup wine vinegar
> 2 teaspoons sugar
> 1 teaspoon dry mustard
> 1 teaspoon salt
> ½ teaspoon pepper
> ½ teaspoon dried tarragon, crushed
> ¼ teaspoon dried rosemary, crushed
> 1 clove garlic, peeled and minced

Place chicken in a heavy plastic bag; set bag in a shallow dish.
   In a jar with a tight-fitting lid combine salad oil, vinegar, sugar,
dry mustard, salt, pepper, tarragon, rosemary and garlic. Cover

and shake vigorously to blend ingredients.

Pour marinade over chicken; twist-tie bag. Refrigerate for several hours or overnight, turning bag occasionally.

Drain chicken, reserving marinade. Broil or grill chicken, turning occasionally and brushing frequently with marinade, about 35 to 45 minutes or till meat is tender and skin is crisp. Delicious with Pecan Pilaf (recipe on page 117). Makes 6 servings.

Note:

> If desired, a 2½ to 3-pound cut-up chicken may be used as a substitute for chicken breasts. Makes 4 servings.

NANCY'S CHICKEN MAHARANI

Inspired by a creative cook, this impressive dish won a cash prize in a national contest. It consists of boneless chicken breasts filled with cheeses and topped with chutney . . . a perfect entrée for entertaining!

> **2 cups shredded Cheddar cheese (room temperature)**
> **1 8-ounce package cream cheese, softened**
> **4 whole chicken breasts, halved, skinned and boned**
> **2 teaspoons lemon juice**
> **1 teaspoon salt**
> **⅛ teaspoon pepper**
> **2 tablespoons cooking oil**
> **1 10-ounce jar chutney, chopped**

In small bowl mix together cheeses until light and fluffy. Chill until firm.

Smooth out chicken breasts on wooden board. Flatten each breast to ¼-inch thickness using the side of a heavy knife or wooden mallet. Rub with lemon juice, salt and pepper.

Place a portion of cheese mixture in center of each piece of chicken, leaving a ½-inch edge all around. Roll up, tucking sides in like an envelope and secure with wooden picks. Place in shallow baking pan. Brush each breast on all sides with cooking oil.

Bake, uncovered, in a 350-degree oven for 40 minutes. Remove picks. Spoon chutney over chicken. Bake at 350 degrees for 20 minutes longer or until chicken is fork-tender and sauce is warm.

Serve over hot, fluffy cooked rice and garnish with sprigs of parsley. Makes 8 servings.

Note:
Prepare this dish in advance and refrigerate until cooking time. The cheese filling hardens and keeps from bubbling out during baking.

OVEN-FRIED CHICKEN

Fried chicken, Southern-style, is hard to beat; but oven-fried chicken is less fuss, less mess and, best of all, delicious!

  ¼ **cup butter or margarine**
  ½ **cup all-purpose flour**
  1 **teaspoon salt**
  ½ **teaspoon paprika**
  ¼ **teaspoon pepper**
  12 **chicken drumsticks or thighs**

Place butter or margarine in a 15x10x1-inch jelly roll pan. Melt in a 400-degree oven.

Meanwhile, combine flour, salt, paprika and pepper in a heavy plastic bag; mix well. Add chicken pieces, two at a time, and shake to coat evenly; roll in melted butter.

Arrange chicken, skin side down for thighs, without touching in a single layer in pan. Bake at 400 degrees for 30 minutes. Turn. Continue to bake for 20 to 25 minutes or till nicely browned and tender. Serve hot or cold. Makes 6 servings.

SIMMERED CHICKEN

The beginning of lots of good eating — use in any dish calling for cooked chicken or turkey. A practical note: allowing the chicken to cool slightly right in the broth makes it moist and flavorful.

  1 **large (about 3 pounds) broiler-fryer chicken, cut-up**
  2 **stalks celery with leaves, cut into chunks**
  1 **large onion, peeled and sliced**

1 **carrot, peeled and sliced**
1 **teaspoon salt**
¼ **teaspoon pepper**
3 **cups water**

In a large saucepan or Dutch oven place chicken, celery, onion, carrot and seasonings. Add water to barely cover, about 3 cups. Cover saucepan and simmer for 1 hour or till chicken is tender.

Remove chicken to platter. Cool slightly. Separate meat from bones, discarding skin and bones. Makes 2½ to 3 cups cooked chicken.

Strain broth through a fine sieve. Chill. Remove hardened fat. Makes 3 cups chicken broth.

Use chicken and broth in recipes calling for cooked chicken or chicken stock. If desired, freeze separately in 1- or 2-cup air-tight containers.

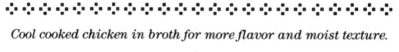

Cool cooked chicken in broth for more flavor and moist texture.

SWEET AND SOUR CHICKEN LEGS

This dish is ideal for a casual family dinner. Use it as part of a complete oven meal.

10 **to 12 chicken legs (about 5 pounds)**
1 **8-ounce bottle low-calorie Russian dressing**
1 **envelope dry onion soup mix**
1 **10-ounce jar apricot preserves**

Rinse chicken legs; pat dry with paper toweling. Remove skin, if desired. (Turn back leg skin and pull off like a glove.) Place close together in a shallow baking pan.

In small bowl combine Russian dressing, soup mix and preserves; blend well. Spread mixture evenly over chicken legs. Bake, uncovered, in a 350-degree oven for 1¼ hours or till chicken is fork-tender. Baste chicken occasionally with sauce. Makes 8 to 10 servings.

CHICKEN À LA KING

Served in patty shells, this good-tasting chicken mixture makes a nice company entrée; for family fare, serve the mixture over fluffy cooked rice or hot biscuits.

    1 cup sliced fresh mushrooms
    1 tablespoon finely chopped green pepper
    2 tablespoons butter or margarine
    4 tablespoons all-purpose flour
    ½ teaspoon salt
    ½ teaspoon celery salt
 1½ cups milk
    1 cup chicken broth
    2 cups cubed cooked chicken
    1 tablespoon snipped fresh parsley
    1 tablespoon chopped pimiento

In a large saucepan simmer mushrooms and green pepper in butter or margarine for 5 minutes. Stir in flour, salt and celery salt; cook 5 minutes longer.

Slowly stir in milk and chicken broth; cook and stir over medium heat till thickened and bubbly.

Add chicken, parsley and pimiento. Heat through; DO NOT boil. Makes 4 servings.

CHICKEN CHOW MEIN

An Oriental flavor in a saucepan!

    2 tablespoons butter or margarine
    1 medium onion, peeled and chopped
    1 cup sliced fresh mushrooms
    2 cups cubed cooked chicken
    1 14-ounce can chop suey vegetables, drained
    1 cup bias-cut celery
 1½ cups chicken broth
    2 tablespoons soy sauce
    1 teaspoon sugar
    2 tablespoons cornstarch
   ¼ cup cold water

In large saucepan melt butter or margarine. Add onion and mushrooms; cook till tender but not brown.

Add chicken, chop suey vegetables, celery, chicken broth, soy sauce and sugar. Simmer for 15 minutes.

Blend cornstarch and water. Stir into chicken mixture. Cook, stirring, until slightly thickened and clear. Serve over chow mein noodles or hot cooked rice and pass the soy sauce. Makes 4 servings.

CHICKEN DELIGHT CASSEROLE

Make this high protein casserole early in the day and refrigerate until dinnertime. It consists of chicken, cheese, milk and eggs.

> 4 slices bread
> 3 tablespoons mayonnaise
> 3 cups cubed cooked chicken or turkey
> 1¼ cups (4 ounces) sliced fresh mushrooms or 1 4-ounce can sliced mushrooms, drained
> 1 tablespoon butter or margarine
> ½ cup sliced water chestnuts
> 4 slices sharp process American cheese
> 2 eggs
> ½ cup milk
> 1 10¾-ounce can condensed cream of mushroom or celery soup
> ¼ teaspoon salt

Trim crusts from bread; arrange slices in a buttered 8-inch square baking dish. Spread with mayonnaise; cover with chicken or turkey.

Cook mushrooms in melted butter or margarine till tender. Add water chestnuts and heat through; sprinkle over chicken. (When using canned mushrooms, spread mushrooms and water chestnuts over chicken without heating.)

Cut cheese slices diagonally in half; arrange in 2 rows (points overlapping in opposite directions) over mushrooms and water chestnuts.

Mix together eggs, milk, soup and salt; beat till smooth. Pour over casserole. Cover. Chill at least 4 hours or overnight.

Bake, uncovered, in a 325-degree oven for 1 hour or till hot and nicely browned on top. Let stand 10 minutes before cutting into squares. Makes 6 servings.

CHICKEN DIVAN

An easy version of an old classic.

> 1 10-ounce package frozen broccoli spears
> 8 to 12 slices cooked chicken or turkey breast (12 ounces)
> 4 tablespoons grated Parmesan cheese
> 1½ cups medium white sauce
> 2 egg yolks
> Dash cayenne pepper

In saucepan cook broccoli in 2 or 3 tablespoons boiling salted water until almost done; drain.

Arrange chicken or turkey slices in bottom of a lightly buttered 10x6x1½-inch baking dish. Top with broccoli spears. Sprinkle with 2 tablespoons of the Parmesan cheese.

Make a white sauce using 3 tablespoons each of butter or margarine and all-purpose flour, ¾ teaspoon salt, dash of pepper and 1½ cups milk (see recipe on page 97).

In small bowl lightly beat egg yolks with a fork. Slowly add a small amount of hot sauce to yolks, stirring constantly. Return mixture to remaining sauce in pan; cook till blended, stirring constantly, about 1 minute. Add a dash of cayenne.

Spread mixture over broccoli spears. Sprinkle with remaining Parmesan cheese. Bake in a 350-degree oven for 25 to 30 minutes or till golden and lightly puffed. Makes 4 servings.

Store eggs, large end up, in the refrigerator. Eggs lose more quality in one day at room temperature than a week under refrigeration!

CREAMED CHICKEN AND MUSHROOMS

Popovers make this a show-off entrée for either a luncheon or brunch!

   ¼ cup butter or margarine
   1¼ cups sliced fresh mushrooms or 1 4-ounce can
      mushroom stems and pieces, drained
   ¼ cup all-purpose flour
   ½ teaspoon salt
   ⅛ teaspoon pepper
   1 cup chicken broth
   1 cup milk
   2 cups cubed cooked chicken or turkey
      Dash curry powder

In saucepan melt butter or margarine; add mushrooms and cook till tender. (When using canned mushrooms, cook lightly for 1 or 2 minutes.) Blend in flour, salt and pepper.

Add chicken broth and milk; cook, stirring constantly, until mixture is smooth and thick. Cook, stirring, 1 minute longer.

Stir in cooked chicken; heat till bubbly. Season to taste with curry powder and, if needed, more salt. Serve in hot popovers (recipe on page 159) or over hot toast points. Makes 6 servings.

OLD-FASHIONED CHICKEN PIE

A flaky pastry encases chunks of tender chicken in a creamy sauce. It's country cooking at its best and a favorite from childhood.

      Pastry for double-crust pie
   1½ cups chicken broth
   2 chicken-flavored bouillon cubes
   ⅓ cup all-purpose flour
   ½ cup milk
   ½ teaspoon salt
   ⅛ teaspoon pepper
   3 cups cubed cooked chicken or turkey
   ⅛ teaspoon curry powder (optional)
   1 egg yolk
   1 tablespoon water

Prepare pastry for double-crust pie. Fit half into a 9-inch pie plate. DO NOT prick. Set aside.

In medium saucepan bring chicken broth and bouillon cubes to a boil. Combine flour, milk, salt and pepper; blend well. Stirring constantly with a wire whisk, gradually add flour mixture to chicken broth. Simmer till mixture is smooth and thickened. Stir in chicken; season with curry powder, if desired.

Turn mixture into pastry-lined pie plate. Cover with top crust; trim edges. Flute or press edges with a fork. Snip 2 or 3 slits near center. Blend egg yolk and water; brush mixture over top crust.

Bake in a 425-degree oven for 20 to 25 minutes or until crust is golden and flaky. Makes 6 servings.

❖ ❖

As a safety precaution always use care and cleanliness in handling raw poultry or meat. Avoid cross-contamination to other foods by cleaning and sanitizing all cutting surfaces and tools.

❖ ❖ ❖ ❖ ❖ ❖ ❖ ❖ ❖

Completely cook poultry at one time; never partially cook and finish at another time.

❖ ❖

SCALLOPED CHICKEN SUPREME

By using convenience foods — frozen beans, canned soups and stuffing mix — much of the advance preparation has been done for you. This tasty casserole, ideal for either family or buffet table, is a boon to the busy cook!

    2 9-ounce packages frozen French-style green beans
    5 to 6 cups cubed cooked chicken or turkey
    2 10¾-ounce cans condensed cream of chicken soup
    1 pint (2 cups) dairy sour cream
    1 envelope dry onion soup mix
    1 8-ounce package herb seasoned stuffing mix
 1⅓ cups hot chicken broth
    ¼ cup butter or margarine, melted

In saucepan cook beans in small amount of boiling salted water for 3 minutes; drain. Spread beans evenly in bottom of a large buttered baking dish or 3-quart casserole. Top with chicken or turkey.

In medium bowl combine soup and sour cream; blend in dry onion soup mix. Pour mixture evenly over poultry.

Combine stuffing mix, hot chicken broth and melted butter or margarine; toss to mix. Spread mixture atop casserole.

Bake in a 350-degree oven for 45 minutes or till hot and bubbly and stuffing is lightly browned. Makes 10 servings.

SWISS TURKEY-HAM SUPREME

A super recipe for utilizing the holiday leftovers. Served with a green vegetable, it makes a delightful luncheon.

> 2 tablespoons butter or margarine
> 1 small onion, peeled and chopped
> 3 tablespoons all-purpose flour
> ¼ teaspoon salt
> ¼ teaspoon pepper
> 1 3-ounce can sliced mushrooms, undrained (⅔ cup)
> 1 cup light cream
> 2 tablespoons dry sherry
> 2 cups cubed cooked turkey
> 1 cup cubed cooked ham
> ⅔ cup sliced water chestnuts
> ½ cup shredded Swiss cheese
> 1½ cups soft bread crumbs
> 3 tablespoons butter or margarine, melted

Melt 2 tablespoons butter or margarine in skillet. Stir in onion; cook till tender but not brown. Blend in flour, salt and pepper. Add undrained mushrooms, cream and sherry. Cook and stir mixture over medium heat until thickened and bubbly. Stir in turkey, ham and water chestnuts. Check seasonings and, if necessary, add ¼ teaspoon salt.

Pour mixture into buttered 1½-quart casserole. Sprinkle cheese evenly over top. Combine crumbs and melted butter or margarine. Scatter around edge of casserole. Bake in a 400-degree oven for 25 minutes or till hot and lightly browned. Makes 6 servings.

ROAST TURKEY

A traditional New England favorite for the holidays!

14 to 16 pound fresh or thawed frozen turkey
Stuffing of your choice
Salt and pepper
Soft butter or cooking oil

Remove giblets; rinse and dry the turkey. Fill wishbone cavity lightly with stuffing. Close and fasten neck to body with a metal skewer. Season the body cavity with salt and pepper. Stuff body lightly as stuffing expands during cooking. (Any remaining stuffing may be baked in a covered casserole during last 45 minutes of roasting time; baste frequently with turkey drippings.) Sew or skewer the body opening. Tie legs together with a string and then tie string around the tail. Fold wing tips under the back.

Place turkey on a rack in a roasting pan. Rub breast of bird with butter or cooking oil. If desired, insert a meat thermometer without touching bone in center of inside thigh muscle. Roast in a 325-degree oven for 15 minutes per pound or till meat thermometer registers 180 to 185 degrees, basting bird occasionally with pan

When buying turkey, allow ¾ to 1 pound per serving for birds under 12 pounds; ½ to ¾ pound per serving for larger birds. For cooks who welcome leftovers for "pickings" as well as future meals, no bird is too large!

Thaw frozen turkeys in the refrigerator till pliable, allowing about 24 hours for each five pounds of bird. Leave the bird in its original wrapper and place in a shallow pan to catch the drips. Once thawed, cook the turkey immediately.

Stuff a turkey just before it goes in the oven. Never stuff it before refrigerating or freezing!

drippings. (It should take about 4 hours for a turkey this size. Or, if following a roasting guide, use this test: move the thigh joint up and down — it moves easily when poultry is cooked — or puncture the skin at joint to see if the juices run clear.) Let rest for 20 to 30 minutes before carving. Makes 16 servings with "pickings" for future meals.

Note:

For best results, lay the turkey on one side for the first hour of roasting; then on second side for next hour. Finally, finish roasting breast side up. If bird browns early in the roasting period, cover loosely with aluminum foil.

Variation:

Roast Chicken

Prepare chicken following directions for roasting a turkey except — roast in a 375-degree oven for 30 minutes per pound. A 3 to 4 pound chicken should take about 1½ to 2 hours. Baste occasionally with pan drippings. Cover loosely with aluminum foil if browning becomes excessive.

OLD-FASHIONED SAVORY STUFFING

It's savory and moist — just like grandma's!

⅓ cup butter or margarine
½ cup chopped celery with leaves
½ cup chopped onion
½ cup giblet stock or hot water
6 cups soft bread cubes
2 teaspoons poultry seasoning
1 teaspoon salt
¼ teaspoon pepper
1 egg, slightly beaten

In a small saucepan melt butter or margarine. Add celery and onion; cook slowly till tender. Pour mixture and giblet stock or hot water over bread cubes; toss lightly.

Add poultry seasoning, salt, pepper and egg; mix well. Makes about 1 quart stuffing or enough for 6 pounds poultry.

OYSTER DRESSING

A flavor of the sea to dress up fowl!

   ½ pint shucked fresh oysters or 1 8-ounce can whole
      oysters
   3 tablespoons butter or margarine
   1 tablespoon chopped onion
   1 tablespoon snipped fresh parsley
   ½ teaspoon poultry seasoning
   ½ teaspoon salt
   ⅛ teaspoon pepper
      Milk
   4 cups soft bread cubes
   1 egg, slightly beaten

   Drain oysters, reserving liquid. Chop large oysters, if desired.
Set aside.
   In a small saucepan melt butter or margarine. Add onion and
cook till tender. Add oysters; cook just till edges begin to curl.
Blend in parsley, poultry seasoning, salt and pepper.
   Add enough milk to reserved oyster liquid to make ½ cup; add
to saucepan. Pour mixture over bread cubes. Stir in egg; mix well.
Makes about 1 quart dressing or enough for 6 pounds poultry.

SAUSAGE DRESSING

This moist dressing is the favorite of a neighborhood cook.

   6 tablespoons butter or margarine
1½ cups chopped celery
   ½ cup chopped onion
   6 cups dry bread cubes
   3 tablespoons snipped fresh parsley
   1 teaspoon salt
   ¾ teaspoon pepper
   ¾ pound uncooked sausage meat
      Giblet stock or hot water

   In a small saucepan melt butter or margarine. Add celery and
onion; cook till tender. Pour mixture over bread cubes.

Add parsley, salt, pepper and sausage meat; mix well. Moisten lightly with giblet stock or hot water. (The dressing should be crumbly.) Makes enough for a 12 to 14 pound turkey.

TO COOK GIBLETS

Poultry giblets
1 small onion, peeled and sliced
1 stalk celery with leaves, cut in 1-inch pieces
¼ teaspoon salt
Water to cover

In a small saucepan place heart, gizzard and neck. Add onion, celery, salt and water to cover. Bring to a boil; reduce heat and simmer for 1 to 1½ hours for chicken giblets, 2 hours for turkey giblets or till tender. Add liver for the last 10 minutes of cooking time (20 minutes for turkey). Cool giblets in broth; remove and discard neck. Chop giblets finely. Use broth and chopped giblets for gravy or stuffing.

Use ½ cup of stuffing for each pound of ready-to-cook poultry. If leftovers are desired, allow ¾ to 1 cup stuffing per pound of poultry.

To stuff poultry, fill neck and body cavities lightly. DO NOT pack as stuffing expands in cooking!

Leftover gravy, broth and stuffing should all be placed in separate containers and refrigerated promptly. Use within a day or two. For longer storage, freeze leftovers in airtight containers.

GIBLET GRAVY

Promptly refrigerate any leftover broth or gravy and use within a day or two. Bring broth and gravy to a boil before eating.

　　¼ **cup pan drippings and butter**
　　¼ **cup all-purpose flour**
　　¼ **teaspoon salt**
　　　Dash pepper
　　2 **to 3 cups chicken stock or giblet broth**
　　½ **cup finely chopped cooked giblets**

Pour pan drippings into measuring cup; if necessary, add melted butter to make ¼ cup.

Return drippings to pan; stir in flour, salt and pepper. Cook over low heat, stirring constantly for 2 or 3 minutes or till flour turns dark golden. DO NOT let it burn! Slowly add liquid, scraping in all the crispies from edge and bottom of pan.

Strain gravy into medium saucepan. Cook, stirring constantly, until mixture comes to a boil and thickens. Stir in giblets. Simmer gently for 2 or 3 minutes. Season to taste with salt and pepper. Serve hot. Makes 2 to 3 cups.

To hard-cook eggs using the cold-water method, put eggs in a saucepan; add COLD water to cover. Bring water to a boil; immediately turn off heat. Cover pan and leave eggs on the burner for 15 to 20 minutes. Remove from water and place in cold water for 2 minutes.

To hard-cook eggs using the hot-water method, put eggs in a saucepan; add water to cover. Quickly bring to a boil; reduce heat and simmer, covered, for 15 to 20 minutes. Remove eggs from water and plunge into cold water.

PICKLED EGGS

*A taste of Amish cooking to tote to picnics, garnish salads or sa-
tisfy hunger pangs!*

  10 to 12 hard-cooked eggs, peeled
  1½ cups white vinegar
  2 tablespoons sugar
  1 teaspoon salt
  1 teaspoon whole peppercorns

Pack eggs snugly in a wide-mouth 1-quart jar. In a medium
saucepan combine vinegar, sugar, salt and peppercorns. Heat to
boiling, stirring constantly. Reduce heat and simmer, uncovered,
for 10 minutes.

Pour hot liquid over eggs. (Add additional vinegar if needed to
cover eggs.) Cool. Cover jar and refrigerate at least 5 days before
serving. Pickled eggs may be stored up to 2 weeks without change
in flavor or texture. Makes 10 to 12 servings.

PAPPY'S LOVE NESTS

*Created as a Sunday evening snack by a family man for his
four young children. Pappy claims this dish gets "the most mileage out of one egg" and says, "Be ready to make more than one —
for yourself!"*

For each serving:

  1 slice whole wheat or enriched white bread
  Mustard
  1 slice sharp process American cheese
  1 egg, separated
  Salt and pepper
  Dash bottled hot pepper sauce
  1 strip uncooked bacon

Place bread on an ungreased cookie sheet or in a shallow pan;
spread lightly with a dab of mustard. Make a 1-inch circle in center of cheese slice. This "well" prevents egg yolk from sliding.

Separate the egg and place yolk in the "well." Add salt, pepper and a dash of hot pepper sauce to the yolk.

In a small bowl beat egg white until light and fluffy. Place this fluff over bread, cheese and yolk. Cut strip of bacon in half and arrange on fluff. Bake in a 450-degree oven for 10 minutes or until fluff is golden brown and bacon is crisp. Makes 1 serving.

FLYING SAUCERS

Before the days of Golden Arches and fast foods, we had breakfast specials — right at home, and a contest to name one. Although the visual aspects of the dish were carefully considered, it may have been a timely interest that influenced the name of this family favorite. Whatever the sentiment, Dad gets the credit. Our children still request "Flying Saucers" on return visits and happy memories of days past flash through my mind each time I prepare this good-honest-family breakfast dish!

For each serving:

>   1 egg
>   1 slice whole wheat bread
>   Butter or margarine
>   1 slice salami
>   Salt and pepper
>   1 slice sharp process American cheese

Poach egg, uncovered, in boiling salted water for 3 to 5 minutes. Meanwhile, preheat broiler. Spread bread with soft butter or margarine. Place on cookie sheet and broil 3 to 4 inches from heat until toasted as desired.

Place salami on toast. Place poached egg on top of salami. Season with salt and pepper; dot with butter or margarine. Top with cheese, anchoring to egg with wooden pick. Broil until cheese begins to melt and is golden brown. (Salami curls up to resemble a flying saucer.) Makes 1 serving.

Cooking Notes

Chapter 4

A young bride preparing her first smoked pork shoulder was interrupted by a friend. Seeing the young woman cut a slice of meat from one end of the roast prompted the more seasoned cook to ask why. "Because my mother does," the bride answered authoritatively.

Apparently not fully satisfied with her answer, the bride later questioned her mother's wisdom. In turn the mother replied, "I've seen my mother do it!"

Fortunately, grandmother was able to provide the younger cooks with a valid reason for trimming the meat. "I had to make it fit my pot!"

Early New England housewives were resourceful women —they had to be. By combining cooking skills with ingenuity, they became adept at creating some wonderful combinations — old dishes with imperishable quality which have become synonomous with New England: baked beans, boiled dinners and pot roasts. Today, in kitchens throughout the region, contemporary cooks prepare these old specialties from yesteryear in much the same way our ancestors enjoyed them.

The recipes in this chapter are characterized by simplicity — both in techniques and ingredients, as well as economy. Dishes with ancestral roots go back to the earliest days while others have ethnic and contemporary influences. Experiment with seasonings to add your personal mark and when your Burgundy Beef or Tourtière turns out just right, may it make you a "maestro" of the culinary arts as far as your family is concerned!

Meats & Main Dishes

HINTS FOR BUYING AND COOKING MEAT

Most Americans plan at least one meal each day around meat, the most costly single item on the food list. Here are some hints to help make the most of your meat dollars.

1.   Think in terms of cost per serving or portion rather than cost per pound. Select cuts with the most meat for the least money.

2.   The amount of bone, gristle and fat varies greatly. "Specials" high in fat and waste may actually be costing you more than higher-priced leaner cuts. Cost-compare similar cuts.

3.   Identify cuts by appearance. Names of beef cuts may vary from one section of the country to another just as they may vary from one store to another. Bones are your best guide for identifying cuts of meat. In general, long bones (T-bones and ribs) indicate tender cuts while round bones (arm chuck) denote less tenderness.

4.   Choose the right cooking method for the cut. Consider tenderness, size and thickness.

5.   The key to successful meat cookery is to use medium to low temperatures and cook for as short a time as possible. A meat thermometer is the best way to determine when a roast is done. To test a steak for doneness, however, cut along the bone and check the interior color.

6.   For oven roasting, select a shallow pan as this allows the heat to circulate around the roast.

7.   Place meat on a rack (or bones if a rib roast) to keep the meat away from the drippings.

8.   There are two schools of thought about seasoning. Some experts say don't season before cooking; others maintain seasoning improves flavor. This is a personal choice as either way the seasonings penetrate very little below the surface.

9.   Allowing a roast to stand for 15 to 20 minutes before carving makes slicing easier.

10.   Allow longer cooking time for outdoor broiling on a breezy day. (Cooking time varies with the intensity of heat.)

11.   Frozen meat requires 1¼ to 1½ times as long to cook as thawed or fresh meat.

12.   Thaw frozen meat in the refrigerator; cook soon after thawing.

BRAISED BEEF AND MUSHROOMS

This Chinese style of cooking comes from a cook who knows how to make a little beef go a long way. Other less tender cuts of beef, such as flank steak, may be substituted. Assemble or prepare all ingredients BEFORE starting to cook, and this includes setting the table. Then cook, serve and enjoy!

> 1 **pound beef eye of round**
> 2 **tablespoons cooking oil**
> 1 **large onion, peeled and thinly sliced**
> 1½ **cups sliced fresh mushrooms**
> 1 **cup beef broth**
> 2 **tablespoons dry sherry**
> 1 **teaspoon sugar**
> 1 **teaspoon soy sauce**
> 1 **teaspoon gravy browning sauce**
> ¼ **teaspoon salt**
> ¼ **teaspoon garlic salt**
> ¼ **teaspoon ground ginger**
> 1 **tablespoon cornstarch**
> 1 **tablespoon cold water**

Freeze meat for 1 hour before slicing. When ready to cook, cut across grain in thin slices and then cut each slice into thirds.

Heat the oil in a large, heavy skillet or wok. Add beef and brown quickly on all sides. Add onion and mushrooms; cook for 2 to 3 minutes.

Add beef broth, sherry, sugar, soy sauce, gravy browning sauce, salt, garlic salt and ginger; mix lightly. Bring to a boil; reduce heat and simmer, uncovered, 30 minutes.

Combine cornstarch and water; add to skillet and stir till thickened. DO NOT boil! Serve over hot cooked rice. Makes 4 servings.

Partially frozen meat holds its shape and is easier to slice than fresh meat.

BURGUNDY BEEF

Although there are as many versions for simmering beef in wine as there are towns in New England, this one has been adapted from the recipes of two reputable male cooks. To quote one, "This is a good dish to experiment with!" Incidentally, oven-simmering is preferable to stove-top cooking as the heat is more uniform.

2 **pounds boneless beef chuck or round steak**
6 **strips bacon**
3 **tablespoons bacon fat**
3 **tablespoons all-purpose flour**
1 **cup beef stock or bouillon**
½ **cup Burgundy wine**
1 **bay leaf**
   Sprig fresh parsley
½ **teaspoon salt**
⅛ **teaspoon pepper**
½ **pound peeled small white onions**
¼ **pound small fresh mushrooms**

Cut steak into 1½-inch cubes; trim away excess fat.

In a heavy skillet fry bacon until crisp; drain, reserving drippings. Crumble and place bacon in 2½-quart casserole.

Set aside 3 tablespoons bacon fat; reheat fat remaining in skillet. Add beef cubes, a few pieces at a time, and brown well on all sides; place in casserole.

Blend flour with reserved bacon fat and add to skillet; cook and stir till browned. Remove pan from heat; stir in stock and wine. Return to heat and bring liquor to a boil. Simmer until thickened. Add bay leaf, parsley, salt and pepper.

Pour liquor over meat. Simmer, covered, in a 325-degree oven for 1½ hours. Add onions and mushrooms; continue cooking for 1 hour or until meat and vegetables are tender. Add salt and pepper to taste, if needed. Skim off excess fat and discard bay leaf. Serve over hot fluffy cooked rice or egg noodles. Sprinkle snipped parsley atop each serving. Makes 6 servings.

Note:

Frozen small whole onions may be used in this dish.

CHINESE PEPPER STEAK

An Oriental creation from a coastal cook to please a Western palate! Since speed is essential in stir-fried dishes, prepare all ingredients before you start to cook.

1½ **pounds boneless beef top of round steak**
¼ **cup cooking oil**
1 **clove garlic, peeled and minced**
1 **teaspoon salt**
1 **teaspoon ginger**
½ **teaspoon pepper**
3 **large green peppers, cored, seeded and cut into strips**
2 **large onions, peeled and thinly sliced**
½ **cup beef bouillon (see note)**
¼ **cup soy sauce**
½ **teaspoon sugar**
1 **tablespoon cornstarch**
¼ **cup cold water**

Freeze meat for 1½ to 2 hours before slicing. When ready to cook, cut across the grain into strips about ⅛-inch thick and 2-inches long.

Heat oil in large skillet. Add garlic, salt, ginger and pepper; sauté until garlic is golden. Add meat slices, a half at a time, and brown very lightly over high heat (about 2 minutes). Remove meat.

Add green peppers and onions to skillet. Sauté over moderate heat for 3 minutes.

Return meat to skillet. Add bouillon, soy sauce and sugar.

Blend cornstarch and cold water. Remove pan from heat and stir this mixture into the meat. Simmer, stirring, 2 minutes or until sauce is thickened. Serve on hot boiled rice. Makes 6 servings.

Note:
  For bouillon, dissolve 1 beef-flavored bouillon cube in ½ cup boiling water.

Stir-fry vegetables just till tender-crisp.

EASY BEEF-IN-A-POT

A fuss-free main dish that needs no last-minute attention.

2½ to 3 pounds beef stew meat, cut in 1-inch cubes
1 10¾-ounce can condensed cream of mushroom soup
½ envelope dry onion soup mix (¼ cup)
½ cup red wine (optional)

Place meat in a large casserole or bean pot. Combine mushroom soup, onion soup mix and wine; spread over meat. To retain steam, seal casserole or top of bean pot with a piece of aluminum foil. Cover.

Bake in a 325-degree oven for 3 hours or till meat is fork-tender. Skim off excess fat. Serve over hot cooked noodles. Makes 6 to 8 servings.

EASY ROUND STEAK DINNER

The long slow cooking gives this main dish marvelous flavor and tenderness, too.

2 pounds boneless beef round or shoulder steak
2 tablespoons drippings or cooking oil
1 teaspoon salt
¼ teaspoon pepper
1 large onion, peeled and thinly sliced
1 medium green pepper, seeded and cut into strips
1 10¾-ounce can condensed tomato soup

Trim excess fat from meat; cut meat into serving-size portions. Place trimmings in a heavy skillet and render over low heat until 2 tablespoons fat have accumulated. Remove and discard trimmings.

Brown meat on both sides in hot fat. Season with salt and pepper. Place in a 2-quart baking dish or casserole. Add onion to skillet; cook till tender. Place atop meat. Lay green pepper strips over onion. Cover all with tomato soup.

Cook, covered, in a 300-degree oven for 2½ to 3 hours or till meat is tender. Makes 6 servings.

NEW ENGLAND BOILED DINNER

With the first crisp autumn day comes thoughts of a cabbage and corned beef feast. To natives, it is known as a New England Boiled Dinner. SIMMER, don't boil the beef!

> 3 to 4 pounds corned beef round or brisket
> 1 large yellow turnip, peeled and cut into 6 slices
> 6 medium potatoes, peeled
> 6 medium onions, peeled
> 6 medium carrots, peeled
> 1 medium head cabbage, outer leaves removed and cut into 6 wedges
> 6 medium fresh beets or 1 16-ounce can sliced beets
> 1 tablespoon butter or margarine
>   Salt and pepper to taste

Wipe beef to remove brine on surface. Place in a large kettle or Dutch oven; barely cover with cold water and slowly bring to the boiling point. DO NOT boil! Remove scum and simmer, covered, 3 to 4 hours or till tender. (Allow 1 hour per pound of meat.)

About 30 minutes before meat is cooked, skim off fat. Add turnip; cook 10 to 15 minutes before adding potatoes, onions and carrots. Cook 15 to 20 minutes. Remove meat to platter and add cabbage wedges to kettle; cook 10 to 20 minutes or till all vegetables are tender.

Meanwhile wash beets; cook, covered, separately in a small amount of boiling salted water for 35 to 40 minutes or till tender. Slip off skins and slice. Add butter and season with salt and pepper. Keep warm. (Or, heat canned beets in liquid in a small saucepan.)

Slice beef thinly across grain. Place in center of a large warm platter. Surround meat in an attractive arrangement with vegetables. Serve beets separately. Makes 6 servings.

If desired, substitute an equal amount of beef broth in dishes calling for red wine.

YANKEE POT ROAST

This old-time favorite makes a superb family meal.

> 3 **pounds boneless beef chuck, bottom round or rump**
>   **roast**
> 2 **tablespoons beef drippings or cooking fat**
> 1 **teaspoon salt**
> ¼ **teaspoon pepper**
> 1 **medium onion, peeled and thinly sliced**
> 1 **medium carrot, peeled and sliced**
> 1 **stalk celery, sliced**
> 1 **cup water or beef broth**
> 4 **medium potatoes, peeled and halved**
> 4 **medium carrots, peeled and halved**
> 4 **medium onions, peeled**
> 3 **tablespoons all-purpose flour**
> ½ **cup cold water**

Trim excess fat from meat. Place trimmings in a heavy kettle or Dutch oven and render over low heat until 2 tablespoons fat have accumulated. Remove and discard trimmings.

Brown meat on all sides in hot fat. Season with salt and pepper. Add onion, carrot and celery; cook till onion is golden. Add water or beef broth. Cover and simmer for 3 to 3½ hours or till meat is tender, adding water as needed. (There should be never more than 1 inch of liquid in the kettle.)

One hour before meat is done, add potatoes, carrots and onions; continue cooking till tender. Remove meat and vegetables to platter.

Skim excess fat from pan juices. Blend flour with ½ cup cold water; add to pan. Cook and stir till thickened and bubbly. Season. Serve gravy with meat and vegetables. Makes 4 servings with leftover meat.

To marinate meat, place in a heavy plastic bag. Pour in the marinade and twist-tie bag. Place tie-end up in a shallow dish to catch unexpected leaks.

TERIYAKI MARINADE

Meat and marinade: a wonderful marriage. Marinating imparts a delicious flavor as well as tenderizes the meat. For a milder flavor, dilute soy sauce with a little water. Roast pork is good basted with this marinade, too.

⅔ **cup soy sauce**
¼ **cup salad oil**
4 **cloves garlic, peeled and minced**
2 **teaspoons ground ginger**
2 **teaspoons dry mustard**
2 **tablespoons molasses**

In a glass bowl or jar with a tight-fitting lid combine soy sauce, salad oil, garlic, ginger, dry mustard and molasses; mix well. Cover. Let stand at room temperature for 24 hours. Makes 1 cup marinade or enough for 2 to 3 pounds of meat.

STEAK TERIYAKI

Place a 2- to 2½-pound beef sirloin steak, cut ¾-inch thick, in a large shallow baking dish. Pour marinade over meat. Cover and marinate in refrigerator, turning occasionally, for 2 to 3 hours. Broil steak, turning and basting frequently with marinade, until cooked to desired doneness. Makes 6 servings.

RUMP ROAST TERIYAKI

Place a 3½- to 4-pound boneless rump roast in a plastic bag. Add marinade; twist and tie knot bag. Place knot side up in a deep bowl. Refrigerate for 24 hours or as long as 2 or 3 days, turning occasionally.

Remove meat from bag; reserve marinade. Place meat on a rack in a shallow pan. Roast, uncovered, in a 325-degree oven for 1¾ to 2 hours for medium doneness. Use marinade to baste meat during cooking process. Makes 8 to 10 servings.

CHICKEN TERIYAKI

Select a 2½- to 3-pound broiler-fryer chicken, cut into serving-size pieces. Rinse and pat dry. Marinate in refrigerator, turning occasionally, for 3 to 4 hours. Place pieces in a foil-lined pan, skin side up. Bake in a 325-degree oven for 1 hour or till chicken is tender. Baste frequently with marinade. Makes 4 servings.

BASIC ITALIAN SAUCE

A standby for cooks of every age. Seasoning is a personal matter.

    2 tablespoons cooking oil
    1 cup chopped onion (1 large)
    1 cup chopped celery
    ½ cup chopped green pepper
    2 cloves garlic, peeled and minced
    4 cups cooked tomatoes (2 16-ounce cans or 2 pints
        home-canned)
    1 29-ounce can tomato purée
    1 6-ounce can tomato paste
    1 cup tomato juice
    3 tablespoons snipped fresh parsley
   2½ teaspoons salt
    2 teaspoons sugar
    1 teaspoon dried oregano, crushed
    1 teaspoon dried basil, crushed
    ¼ teaspoon dried thyme, crushed
    ¼ teaspoon pepper
    ⅛ teaspoon cayenne pepper
    1 4-ounce can mushroom stems and pieces

Heat oil in a large kettle or Dutch oven. Add onion, celery, green pepper and garlic. Cook till vegetables are tender but not brown, about 5 minutes.

Place tomatoes (2 cups at a time) in blender container. Cover; blend till smooth. Add to vegetables with tomato purée, tomato paste and juice, parsley and seasonings. Simmer, uncovered, for 2 to 3 hours; stir occasionally. Add undrained mushrooms; simmer for 30 minutes longer or until sauce is of desired consistency. Makes about 2½ quarts.

Variation:

Italian Meat Sauce

In skillet lightly brown 2 pounds ground beef, stirring to break up chunks of meat. Spoon off excess fat. Add meat to Italian Sauce during last hour of cooking.

ITALIAN MEATBALLS

In Italian, the common name for meatballs is Polpette. This recipe is authentic . . . it is from an Italian chef!

> 1 **pound ground beef**
> 1 **cup soft bread crumbs**
> 2 **tablespoons grated Parmesan cheese**
> 1 **tablespoon dried parsley flakes**
> 1 **egg, well beaten**
> 1 **teaspoon salt**
> ¼ **teaspoon pepper**
> 1 **clove garlic, peeled and minced**
> 2 **tablespoons cooking oil**

In mixing bowl combine ground beef, bread crumbs, Parmesan cheese, parsley flakes, egg, salt, pepper and garlic; mix well. With wet hands, shape into 24 1-inch balls.

Heat oil in a large skillet. Add meatballs; brown slowly on all sides. Add to 1½-quarts Italian Sauce. Simmer for 30 minutes. Serve over hot cooked spaghetti; sprinkle grated Parmesan cheese atop each serving. Makes 6 servings.

To help meatballs retain their round shape, form into balls and place in a shallow pan. Bake, uncovered, in a 350-degree oven for 10 to 15 minutes or till lightly browned. Remove from pan with a slotted spoon.

BEST-EVER MEAT LOAF

A recipe from the parson's wife . . . and rightfully named! In addition to the basic meat loaf ingredients, this one includes shredded raw carrot, cheese and a yummy topping.

    2 eggs
    ⅔ cup milk
    2 teaspoons salt
    ¼ teaspoon pepper
    3 slices bread, crumbled
    1 onion, finely chopped
    1 cup shredded Cheddar cheese
    ½ cup shredded raw carrot
    1½ pounds lean ground beef
    ¼ cup packed brown sugar
    ¼ cup catsup
    1 tablespoon prepared mustard

In bowl beat eggs; add milk, salt, pepper and bread. Stir till bread disintegrates. Add onion, cheese, carrot and ground beef. Mix thoroughly. Pat into a 9x5x3-inch loaf pan.

Combine brown sugar, catsup and mustard; carefully spread over top of meat loaf. Bake in a 350-degree oven for 1¼ to 1½ hours. Let stand for 10 minutes before slicing. Makes 6 servings.

CHILI CON CARNE

A crowd pleaser! "Just find a bunch of bowls and people and watch the chili disappear." Go sparingly, at first, with the chili powder; you can always add extra.

    1 tablespoon butter or margarine
    1 pound lean ground beef
    1 medium onion, peeled and chopped
    1 16-ounce can red kidney beans (see note)
    1 16-ounce can tomatoes, cut up
    1 6-ounce can tomato paste
    1 tablespoon chili powder

   2 teaspoons sugar
   1 to 1½ teaspoons salt
   ⅛ teaspoon pepper
   Shredded Cheddar cheese

Melt butter or margarine in large skillet or Dutch oven. Add ground beef and onion; brown lightly, stirring to break up chunks of meat. Spoon off excess fat.

Drain kidney beans, reserving liquid. Add beans, tomatoes, tomato paste, chili powder, sugar, salt and pepper. Cover and simmer for 1 hour, stirring occasionally. Top each serving with shredded Cheddar cheese. Makes 4 servings.

Note:
   Reserved liquid from kidney beans may be stirred in to give chili the desired consistency.

HAMBURGER STROGANOFF

A less expensive version of an old classic, but awfully good!

   2 tablespoons butter or margarine
   1 small onion, peeled and chopped
   1 clove garlic, peeled and minced
   1 pound lean ground beef
   2 tablespoons all-purpose flour
   1 teaspoon salt
   ¼ teaspoon pepper
   1 4-ounce can sliced mushrooms, drained
   1 10¾-ounce can condensed cream of chicken soup
   1 cup dairy sour cream
   2 tablespoons snipped fresh parsley

In skillet melt butter or margarine; stir in onion and garlic, cooking until transparent. Add meat; cook and stir until meat is lightly browned. Drain off excess fat, if any. Sprinkle flour over meat; season with salt and pepper. Stir in mushrooms and soup. Simmer for 15 minutes, stirring occasionally.

Blend in sour cream. Heat through; DO NOT boil. Top with parsley. Serve over hot cooked noodles. Makes 4 servings.

LINDA'S SWEDISH MEATBALLS

Seasoning for this popular main dish comes from cream of mushroom soup and sour cream. Seasoned bread crumbs add zest.

> 1 pound ground beef
> 1 cup fine dry bread crumbs
> ½ cup milk
> 2 eggs, beaten
> 1 teaspoon salt
> ¼ teaspoon pepper
> 1½ tablespoons cooking oil
> 1 10¾-ounce can condensed cream of mushroom soup
> ½ cup water
> ½ cup dairy sour cream

In a large mixing bowl combine ground beef, bread crumbs, milk, eggs, salt and pepper; mix well. With wet hands, shape mixture into 1-inch balls.

Heat oil in a large skillet. Add meatballs; brown slowly on all sides. Pour off excess fat.

Mix together soup and water. Pour over meatballs. Cover and simmer for 10 minutes. Blend in sour cream. Heat through but DO NOT boil! Serve over hot cooked egg noodles. Makes 4 servings.

POLISH CABBAGE ROLLS

Also known as Golabki, this recipe from a high school chum is adaptable to oven or stove-top cooking. Personally, I like the oven method; it eliminates the cream . . . and extra calories!

> 1 small cabbage
> 1 egg
> 1 cup cooked rice
> 1 small onion, peeled and finely chopped
> 1 teaspoon salt
> ¼ teaspoon pepper
> 1½ pounds ground beef
> 1 12-ounce bottle chili sauce

1 cup light cream
¼ cup all-purpose flour

Remove outer wilted leaves of cabbage. Remove center core and rinse cabbage. Cook, covered, in a small amount of boiling salted water for 10 minutes or till just limp. Drain and set aside to cool.

In mixing bowl beat egg lightly; stir in rice, onion, salt and pepper. Add ground beef; mix well. Divide meat mixture into 12 equal portions.

Peel 12 leaves off cabbage, one at a time. Cut out the heavy center vein of each leaf. Place a meat portion on each leaf. Fold sides in like an envelope and roll ends over meat.

Stove-Top Method: Place rolls in a large saucepan, seam side down and close together. Pour chili sauce and 1 bottle water (or enough to barely cover) over rolls. Simmer for 2 hours.

Mix together cream and flour using a fork to avoid lumps. Add to cabbage rolls; shake down mixture by agitating pan. Simmer 10 minutes. DO NO boil! Makes 6 to 8 servings.

Oven Method: Place rolls in a lightly buttered 2-quart baking dish. Mix chili sauce and ½ cup water; pour over rolls. Bake, covered, in a 350-degree oven for 1¼ hours. Baste occasionally with sauce. Omit cream and flour. Good reheated, too!

PERSIAN LAMB KABOBS

A winner from another good country cook who developed the original recipe for a contest. Vary the ingredients with in-season vegetables.

> 1½ **pounds boneless lamb, cut into 1½-inch cubes**
> ½ **cup salad oil**
> ⅓ **cup wine vinegar**
> 2 **tablespoons honey**
> 1 **teaspoon salt**
> ½ **teaspoon pepper**
> 1 **teaspoon dried mint leaves, crushed**
> ½ **teaspoon dried rosemary, crushed**
> 2 **cloves garlic, peeled and minced**
> 2 **medium green peppers, cut in 1½-inch squares**
> 1 **16-ounce jar small onions, drained**

Place lamb cubes in a large bowl. In a jar with a tight-fitting lid combine oil, vinegar, honey, seasonings, herbs and garlic; cover and shake vigorously.

Pour mixture over lamb. Cover and marinate in regrigerator for several hours or overnight, turning occasionally.

Drain meat, reserving marinade. Thread meat and vegetables on skewers in following order: lamb, green pepper, lamb, onion. Repeat. Brush with marinade. Broil or grill 4 to 6 inches from heat for 15 to 20 minutes or till meat is cooked, turning skewers frequently and basting meat and vegetables occasionally with marinade. Makes 6 servings.

BARBECUED SPARERIBS

This tried-and-true recipe always receives a warm reception from my family. Allow ¾ to 1 pound spareribs per person; more rather than less, for hearty appetites. Any remaining are good reheated.

1 tablespoon butter or margarine
1 small onion, peeled and finely chopped
1 12-ounce bottle chili sauce
½ cup water
¼ cup lemon juice
2 tablespoons packed brown sugar
2 tablespoons vinegar
1 tablespoon Worcestershire sauce
½ teaspoon salt
¼ teaspoon paprika
3 pounds pork spareribs, cut into serving-size pieces

Melt butter or margarine in a medium saucepan. Add onion and cook until tender but not brown. Add chili sauce, water, lemon juice, brown sugar, vinegar, Worcestershire sauce, salt and paprika. Simmer, stirring occasionally, for 20 minutes.

Place ribs, meaty side down, in a shallow baking pan. Season lightly with salt and pepper. Cover loosely with aluminum foil and place in a 450-degree oven for 15 minutes.

Reduce oven temperature to 350 degrees and remove pan. Drain off excess fat. Turn ribs meaty side up. Pour barbecue sauce over meat and return pan to oven. Bake, uncovered, at 350 degrees for 1 hour or till meat is tender. Baste occasionally with sauce. Makes 4 to 5 servings.

PORK BUTT IN APPLE JUICE

A marvelously simple dish from a "born" cook! Country spare-ribs, blade steaks and boneless, rolled shoulder roast are all good choices for simmering in the oven.

1 4-pound pork shoulder butt roast
1 27-ounce can sauerkraut, drained
1 large bay leaf
4 cups apple juice
¼ cup packed brown sugar

Stove-Top Method: Place pork in a large kettle or Dutch oven; add sauerkraut and bay leaf. Mix together apple juice and brown sugar; pour over meat. Cover. Simmer 2½ to 3 hours or until meat is tender. Remove and discard bay leaf.

Thicken with a mixture of ¼ cup cold water and 2 tablespoons cornstarch, if desired. Cook and stir till liquid thickens. Makes 8 servings.

Oven Method: Follow directions for stove-top cooking except — cut roast in serving-size portions and place in a large casserole. Add about 3 cups apple juice. Bake in a 300-degree oven for 2 hours or till meat is tender.

❖ ❖

The fat normally trimmed from a smoked shoulder or ham may be cut away (before cooking the meat) and frozen — up to one month. "The fat adds zest to baked beans!"

To score pork, cut in ½-inch slices to rind, but not through it!

❖ ❖

PORK CHOPS RISOTTO

Wonderfully easy! One of my favorite dishes for staggering a meal or relinquishing clean-up to the kids! Add carrot sticks and a tossed green salad to complete the meal.

    6 pork loin chops, cut ½-inch thick
   ¾ teaspoon salt
   ¼ teaspoon pepper
   1 cup uncooked long-grain rice
  2½ cups hot water
   1 envelope onion soup mix
   1 large green pepper, cut into ¼-inch rings
    Chili sauce

Trim pork chops of outside fat, then slit edges of each 3 or 4 times. Sprinkle with salt and pepper.

In large skillet, over medium heat, cook trimmings until 2 tablespoons fat accumulate; discard trimmings. Slowly brown chops on both sides in hot fat; remove chops from pan and set aside.

Spread bottom of 13x9x2-inch baking pan with rice. Into drippings in skillet, pour the hot water; stir in onion soup mix. Bring to a boil, stirring to loosen brown particles from skillet. Pour over rice. Arrange pork chops atop and crown with rings of green pepper. Top with heaping teaspoonful of chili sauce in center of ring. Cover pan with a piece of aluminum foil. Bake in a 350-degree oven for 1¼ hours or till pork and rice are tender. Makes 6 servings.

TOURTIÈRE

A traditional French dish — "Pork Pies are served whenever the family gets together." For a filling that's more digestible, many cooks replace some of the pork with ground beef. Adjust the seasoning to suit your taste.

    Pastry for double-crust pie
  1½ pounds ground pork
   1 medium onion, peeled and diced
   1 teaspoon salt
   ¼ cup water

2 large potatoes, peeled
1 teaspoon sage or poultry seasoning
¼ teaspoon allspice
⅛ teaspoon cloves
⅛ teaspoon pepper
1 egg yolk
1 tablespoon water

Prepare pastry for double-crust pie. Fit half into a 9-inch pie plate. DO NOT prick. Set aside.

In medium saucepan combine ground pork, onion, salt and ¼ cup water; mix well. Simmer, covered, for 2 hours; stir occasionally. Skim off fat.

Cook potatoes in small amount of boiling salted water till tender; drain only if necessary. Combine potato and pork mixture. Mash with a masher until well blended. Add seasonings and salt to taste.

Spread mixture evenly in pastry-lined pie plate. Cover with top crust; trim edges. Flute or press edges with a fork. Snip 2 or 3 slits near center. Blend egg yolk with 1 tablespoon water; brush mixture over top crust.

Bake in a 425-degree oven for 20 to 25 minutes or until crust is golden and flaky. Makes 6 servings.

Freezing tip:
Bake pie in an oven-proof plate; underbrown. Cool, wrap and freeze. Reheat, frozen, in a 400-degree oven for 1½ hours or until heated through.

GABBY'S ITALIAN SAUSAGE SANDWICH

A food expert with Maine ties shares a "very simple, but very good sandwich recipe." It's especially flavorful with a combination of hot and sweet sausages. For summer enjoyment, add a tossed salad to the menu and pass the iced tea.

8 links Italian-style sausage
2 15-ounce cans tomato sauce
3 green peppers, seeded and cut into ½-inch strips
3 onions, sliced into rings and halved
⅛ teaspoon cinnamon
   Garlic salt to taste
¼ cup Burgundy wine (optional)

Cut sausages into ¾-inch lengths. Put in a cold skillet and sauté over moderate heat to reduce fat. Drain sausage on paper toweling; discard fat.

Place sausage pieces in a large saucepan; add tomato sauce, green peppers, onions, cinnamon, garlic salt to taste and, if desired, Burgundy wine. Simmer, covered, for 1 hour; stir occasionally. Serve on sliced hard rolls. Makes 4 to 6 servings.

Fresh sausage is not cured; cook thoroughly before eating.

ITALIAN SAUSAGES AND GREEN PEPPERS

A bit of Italian cookery from an ethnic couple. It's the kind of dish you get a craving for!

2 pounds hot or sweet Italian-style sausages
3 tablespoons cooking oil
3 green peppers, seeded and cut into strips
1 large onion, peeled and thinly sliced
1 cup sliced fresh mushrooms
½ teaspoon salt
Dash pepper

In heavy skillet cook sausages, covered, over low heat for 5 minutes. Remove fat as it accumulates and continue to cook, uncovered, until sausages are thoroughly cooked and browned, about 20 minutes. Turn occasionally with tongs; drain on paper toweling.

While sausages are cooking, heat oil in a large skillet. Add green peppers, onion and mushrooms. Cook, stirring frequently, for 5 to 8 minutes or till vegetables are tender but not brown.

Cut sausages in 1-inch lengths and add to mushroom mixture. Season with salt and pepper. Serve hot with fried rice and a green salad. Makes 6 servings.

SAUERKRAUT AND SAUSAGES

A combination of sauerkraut and apple juice, frankfurters and Polish sausage, this hearty dish takes but 10 minutes to prepare — then simmers for an hour. It's good reheated, too.

> 4 strips bacon
> 1 medium onion, peeled and sliced
> 1 2-pound package or 2 16-ounce cans sauerkraut,
>   rinsed and drained
> 1½ cups apple juice
> 1 tablespoon packed brown sugar
> 1 teaspoon salt
> ½ teaspoon caraway seed
> ¼ teaspoon pepper
> 1 bay leaf
> 1 pound kielbasa or Polish sausage, cut in 1½-inch
>   lengths
> 1 pound frankfurters, cut in 1½-inch lengths

In large kettle or Dutch oven cook bacon over medium heat until crisp. Remove bacon; drain and crumble. Remove all but 2 tablespoons of bacon drippings. Add onion and cook until tender but not brown.

Stir in sauerkraut, apple juice, brown sugar, salt, caraway seed and pepper. Add bay leaf, crumbled bacon, sausage and frankfurters. Cover and simmer, stirring occasionally, for 1 hour. Discard bay leaf. Serve with mustard and boiled parslied potatoes. Makes 8 servings.

Frankfurters, weiners or hot dogs — they are all the same product with different names.

Freezing of cured meats is NOT recommended as the seasonings added during curing hasten the development of rancidity.

VEAL PARMIGIANA

This renowned Italian dish may be made today for tomorrow's enjoyment. Boneless, skinless breasts of chicken — or chicken cutlets — may be substituted for the veal cutlets.

    1 **pound thin veal cutlets**
    ¼ **cup all-purpose flour**
    ¾ **teaspoon salt**
    ⅛ **teaspoon pepper**
    ¼ **cup butter or margarine**
    1 **medium onion, peeled and finely chopped**
    1 **clove garlic, peeled and minced**
    1 **8-ounce can tomato sauce**
    ½ **teaspoon sugar**
    ¼ **teaspoon dried rosemary, crushed**
    ¼ **teaspoon dried thyme, crushed**
   1½ **cups shredded mozzarella cheese**
    ¼ **cup grated Parmesan cheese**

Pound cutlets, if necessary, to a ¼-inch thickness. Dip in mixture of flour, salt and pepper, shaking off excess.

In a large skillet brown cutlets quickly on both sides in melted butter or margarine. Arrange in a lightly buttered shallow baking dish.

Add onion and garlic to skillet and cook, stirring, till golden. Stir in tomato sauce, sugar, rosemary and thyme. Bring mixture to a boil; reduce heat and simmer for 1 to 2 minutes.

Spoon ⅔ of sauce over veal. Arrange mozzarella cheese on top; spoon on remaining sauce. Sprinkle evenly with Parmesan cheese. Bake, uncovered, in a 350-degree oven for 25 to 30 minutes or till hot and bubbly. Makes 4 servings.

One cup dry beans makes 3 cups cooked beans.

To soak dry beans, use 2 or 3 cups of cold water for each 1 cup of beans.

OLD-FASHIONED BAKED BEANS

*Nothing fancy — just a promise of good eating for folks search-
ing for palatable home-baked beans. Although parboiling (the in-
itial cooking step) is optional, it does shorten the cooking time for
baking beans.*

> 2 pounds (4 cups) dry beans
> 1 medium onion, peeled
> ¾ pound lean salt pork
> ½ cup molasses
> ¼ cup sugar
> 1 tablespoon salt
> 2 teaspoons dry mustard
> ½ teaspoon pepper

Pick over beans, discarding any foreign matter. Rinse. Place in a
large kettle or bowl; cover with 3-quarts cold water and let stand
overnight. In morning bring beans to a boil; simmer for 10 minutes. Drain, reserving liquid.

Place whole onion in bottom of a 4-quart bean pot or casserole.
Add beans. Score pork by cutting ½-inch slashes in several places;
place on top of beans.

Combine molasses, sugar, salt, dry mustard and pepper with 2
cups of the reserved liquid; mix well. Pour over beans. Add as
much of the remaining liquid as needed to cover the beans. Cover.

Bake in a 300-degree oven for 6 hours or till tender. Check peri-
odically to add liquid or boiling water to keep beans covered. Uncover pot during last hour of baking. Makes 12 servings.

*To reduce foaming and boil-overs when parboiling beans, add
1 tablespoon butter or cooking oil to the pot.*

Chapter 5

The word "casserole" has a dual meaning. It refers to the utensil itself — a covered container with one or two handles — or the food mixture, generally a one-dish meal, cooked in a bake-and-serve dish. Since early America, the casserole or "covered dish" has been popular fare at public suppers, community gatherings and family reunions. Today, it is equally pleasing either as a casual one-meal dish or as elegant company fare.

Casseroles allow the cook to express ingenuity as well as individuality. With make-ahead qualities, they fit into the lifestyle of busy people. They balance the budget for thrifty cooks and utilize leftover food for hurry-up meals.

The aim of casserole cookery is to create attractive, delicious and nourishing dishes. With the simplest touches you make a good casserole a great one. There's practically no limit to the possibilities for adding flavorful and eye-appealing toppings: buttered crumbs and chips, slivered nuts and shredded cheese. Most casseroles are baked in a moderate oven so that the ingredients blend and heat slowly.

While this chapter could easily enlarge your repertoire of favorite meal-in-a-dish recipes, there are other delightful "covered dish" ideas incorporated among the chapters on meat, seafood and poultry; additional choices, such as Asparagus Quiche and Ham and Potatoes au Gratin, are provided in vegetable cookery. Let these recipes be the springboards of imagination for other creations. And, remember, whether you serve Chinese Pie as a simple at-home supper or tote a pan of Lasagne to a community meal, may you discover that what really counts is GOOD EATING!

Casseroles & Pasta

CHINESE PIE

"The very word calls up visions of my childhood," says the father of six who was introduced to this meal-in-a-dish by a great-aunt. His specialty is a favorite among his kids — and mine.

    1 tablespoon butter or margarine
    1 medium onion, peeled and chopped
  1½ pounds lean ground beef
       Salt and pepper
    1 16-ounce can cream-style corn
    1 cup cooked whole-kernel corn (optional)
    4 cups well-seasoned mashed potato
    ½ cup shredded Cheddar cheese
       Paprika

In a skillet melt butter or margarine; add onion, ground beef, ½ teaspoon salt and dash of pepper. Cook, stirring occasionally, until meat is lightly browned. Drain off excess fat.

Pour meat mixture into a buttered 2-quart casserole. Spread cream-style corn and, if desired, whole-kernel corn evenly over meat. Cover with mashed potato; sprinkle with shredded cheese and paprika.

Bake in a 375-degree oven for 20 to 25 minutes or till hot and bubbly. Makes 6 servings.

COMPANY CASSEROLE

This tasty, high protein dish includes cottage cheese, sour cream and Cheddar cheese. It's wonderful for a buffet table.

    8 ounces medium noodles
    1 tablespoon butter or margarine
    1 pound lean ground beef
    ¼ cup chopped onion
    1 clove garlic, peeled and minced
    2 8-ounce cans tomato sauce
    1 teaspoon salt
    ¼ teaspoon pepper
    1 cup dairy sour cream
    1 cup cream-style cottage cheese

¼ cup snipped fresh parsley
1 cup sliced, cooked carrots
1 cup shredded Cheddar cheese

Cook noodles in boiling, salted water till tender; drain. Melt butter or margarine in skillet; add ground beef, onion and garlic. Cook and stir until meat is lightly browned; drain off excess fat. Stir in tomato sauce, salt and pepper. Simmer, uncovered, for 5 minutes.

Combine sour cream, cottage cheese, parsley and carrots. Add to cooked noodles; mix well.

Place half of the cottage cheese mixture in a buttered 3-quart casserole. Top with meat mixture. Layer remaining cottage cheese mixture over meat. Sprinkle Cheddar cheese atop casserole. Bake in a 350-degree oven for 30 minutes or till hot and bubbly. Makes 8 to 10 servings.

CRUNCHY BEEF CASSEROLE

Use corkscrew macaroni, shells or bows and tote this one to your next community meal.

2 cups uncooked corkscrew macaroni
1 tablespoon butter or margarine
1 pound lean ground beef
1 10¾-ounce can condensed cream of mushroom soup
1 16-ounce can tomatoes
¾ cup shredded Cheddar cheese
¾ cup chopped green pepper
¾ teaspoon seasoned salt
1 3-ounce can French fried onion rings

Cook macaroni in large amount of boiling, salted water till tender. Drain; rinse in cold water.

Melt butter or margarine in skillet. Add meat; cook and stir until lightly browned. Spoon off excess fat.

Combine macaroni, soup, tomatoes, cheese, green pepper and seasoned salt with meat; mix well. Pour mixture into a buttered 2-quart casserole. Cover. Bake in a 350-degree oven for 30 minutes or till hot and bubbly. Uncover and scatter onion rings over top. Return to oven for 5 minutes. Makes 4 to 6 servings.

EASY STEW CASSEROLE

Reminiscent of grandmother's cooking! In days past the frugal housewife made her stew — in a bean pot — as a way of utilizing the oven heat on wash day. Old-fashioned Indian pudding made a compatible dessert then — just as it does today!

　2　pounds beef stew meat, cut in 1½-inch cubes
　6　medium carrots, peeled and cut in ¾-inch slices
　4　stalks celery, sliced in ½-inch pieces
　3　medium onions, peeled and sliced
　1　cup canned tomatoes or tomato juice
　½　cup fresh bread crumbs
　3　tablespoons quick-cooking tapioca
　1　tablespoon sugar
　1　tablespoon salt
　1　tablespoon Worcestershire sauce
　　　Mashed Potato Topping (recipe follows)
　½　cup shredded Cheddar or American cheese

In a 3-quart casserole combine stew meat, carrots, celery, onions, tomatoes or tomato juice, bread crumbs, tapioca, sugar, salt and Worcestershire sauce; mix well.

Bake, covered, in a 250-degree oven for 4 to 4½ hours. Top with Mashed Potato Topping. Sprinkle cheese atop potato. Return to oven for 30 minutes. Makes 8 servings.

Mashed Potato Topping

Peel and cook 5 medium potatoes. Mash while hot; add ½ cup milk and 1 beaten egg. Season to taste with salt and pepper. Arrange in a circle around edge of casserole.

To prevent pasta from sticking together, add 1 tablespoon of cooking oil to the kettle. Cook, uncovered, until tender, yet still firm. Drain immediately!

LASAGNE

A make-ahead meal from the gal next door. It's a great buffet dish!

1¼ pounds lean ground beef
1 medium onion, peeled and chopped
1 tablespoon butter or margarine
1 16-ounce can tomatoes
2 6-ounce cans tomato paste
1 tablespoon dried parsley flakes
1 tablespoon dried basil, crushed
1½ teaspoons salt
8 ounces lasagne or wide noodles
2 eggs, beaten
3 cups cream-style cottage cheese or ricotta cheese
½ cup grated Parmesan cheese
2 tablespoons dried parsley flakes
1 teaspoon salt
¼ teaspoon pepper
1 pound mozzarella cheese, thinly sliced or shredded

In large skillet lightly brown beef and onion in butter or margarine. Spoon off excess fat. Add tomatoes, tomato paste, parsley flakes, basil and 1½ teaspoons salt. Simmer, uncovered, for 30 minutes to blend flavors. Stir occasionally.

Cook noodles in large amount of boiling, salted water till tender (about 12 minutes). Drain in colander and rinse.

In large bowl beat eggs; add cottage cheese, Parmesan cheese, parsley, 1 teaspoon salt and ¼ teaspoon pepper; blend thoroughly.

In buttered 13x9x2-inch baking dish spread half the noodles; cover with half of the cottage cheese mixture, then half of mozzarella; top with half of the meat sauce. Repeat layers. If desired, sprinkle additional Parmesan cheese lightly over top of casserole.

Bake in a 350-degree oven for 40 to 45 minutes or until hot and bubbly. Let rest for 10 minutes before cutting into squares. Makes 8 servings.

Note:

Italian sausage meat may be substituted for ground beef.

MEATBALL STEW CASSEROLE

From a Down East cook comes a meal-in-dish recipe with end-less possibilities: Purists may precook fresh vegetables; others may substitute home-canned for commerically canned vegetables. Remember to save all the drained vegetable jucies for your next soup!

½ cup fine fresh bread crumbs
⅓ cup milk
1 egg
1 pound ground beef
1 teaspoon salt
½ teaspoon dried marjoram, crushed
½ teaspoon Worcestershire sauce
1 tablespoon butter or margarine
1 16-ounce can (2 cups) sliced carrots, drained
1 16-ounce can (2 cups) small boiled onions, drained
1 4-ounce can sliced mushrooms, drained
1 10¾-ounce can condensed cream of mushroom soup
½ teaspoon gravy browning sauce
¼ teaspoon nutmeg
1 10-ounce package (2 cups) frozen peas, thawed
3 cups well-seasoned hot mashed potatoes (see note)
1 cup shredded Cheddar cheese

In a large bowl combine bread crumbs and milk; let soak for 5 minutes. With a fork, beat in egg. Add ground beef, salt, marjoram and Worcestershire sauce; mix well. Form mixture into eighteen 1½-inch balls.

In a large skillet melt butter or margarine. Add meatballs and brown on all sides. Remove meatballs. To drippings in skillet add carrots, onions and mushrooms. Cook for 2 minutes. Add soup, gravy browning sauce and nutmeg; heat through.

Pour hot mushroom mixture into buttered 2½-quart casserole. Add peas, then arrange meatballs atop. Spoon potato around edge of casserole; sprinkle with shredded cheese.

Bake, uncovered, in a 400-degree oven for 25 minutes or till hot and bubbly. Makes 6 servings.

Note:
If desired, prepare a 4-ounce package of instant mashed potatoes, following package directions.

SOUTH-OF-THE-BORDER CASSEROLE

An emergency dish created from convenience foods! If desired, omit baking and instead simmer on top of the stove for 20 to 30 minutes. Serve corn chips on the side.

1 tablespoon butter or margarine
1 pound lean ground beef
1 medium onion, peeled and chopped
1 clove garlic, peeled and minced
1 16-ounce can tomatoes, cut up
1 16-ounce can red kidney beans
1 15-ounce can chili with no beans
1 teaspoon salt
¼ teaspoon pepper
1 6- or 7-ounce package corn chips (about 4 cups)
1 cup (4-ounce pkg.) shredded Cheddar cheese

Melt butter or margarine in large skillet; add ground beef, onion and garlic. Cook and stir until meat is lightly browned; drain off excess fat.

Stir in tomatoes, beans, chili, salt and pepper. Slowly bring to a boil. Simmer 5 minutes.

Place a layer of corn chips in bottom of a buttered 2½-quart casserole. Cover with half of the meat mixture. Add another layer of corn chips; top with remaining meat mixture. Sprinkle Cheddar cheese atop casserole. Bake in a 375-degree oven for 25 to 30 minutes or till hot and bubbly. Makes 6 to 8 servings.

As a general rule, macaroni and spaghetti double in volume with cooking; egg noodles yield slightly less volume.

To keep cooked spaghetti hot, drain and then place the colander over a pan containing a small amount of boiling water. To each 6 servings of spaghetti, add 3 or 4 tablespoons of butter to keep the strands from sticking together. Cover the colander.

BRUNCH CASSEROLE

Perfect for entertaining! Make it today for tomorrow's brunch!

½ cup ripe olive slices
6 hard-cooked eggs, peeled and sliced
1 cup diced ham
¼ cup chopped onion
¼ cup butter or margarine
⅓ cup all-purpose flour
1 teaspoon salt
⅛ teaspoon pepper
   Dash bottled hot pepper sauce
2 cups milk
1 tablespoon prepared mustard
1 cup soft bread crumbs (1½ slices)
3 tablespoons butter or margarine, melted

Arrange olive slices, egg slices and ham in a buttered 9-inch square baking dish or 1½-quart casserole.

In saucepan cook onion in butter or margarine till tender but not brown; blend in flour, salt, pepper and hot pepper sauce. Add milk all at once. Cook, stirring constantly, until mixture is thick and bubbly. Stir in mustard. Pour mixture over ham and eggs.

Combine soft bread crumbs and melted butter or margarine. Sprinkle crumb mixture atop casserole. Bake in a 375-degree oven for 20 to 25 minutes or till hot and crumbs are toasted. Makes 6 servings.

DOUBLE-GOOD MACARONI AND CHEESE

Thanks to another good cook for sharing this quick and easy variation of a family-pleasing dish. In her version cottage cheese and sour cream replace a basic cheese sauce.

8 ounces elbow macaroni
2 cups small curd cream-style
   cottage cheese (1 pound)
2 cups shredded Cheddar cheese (8-ounce pkg.)
¾ cup dairy sour cream

1 **egg, slightly beaten**
2 **teaspoons grated onion**
½ **cup chopped green pepper**
1 **teaspoon salt**
⅛ **teaspoon pepper**

Cook macaroni in boiling, salted water until tender, yet firm; drain well.

In large mixing bowl combine cottage cheese, Cheddar cheese, sour cream, egg, onion, green pepper, salt and pepper; mix well. Fold in cooked macaroni. Spoon into buttered 2-quart casserole or baking dish.

Bake in a 350-degree oven for 45 minutes or till hot and bubbly. Makes 6 to 8 servings.

FETTUCCINE

From an Italian household comes this recipe for tender pasta, made rich with butter, cream and grated cheese. And so-o-o good! Incidentally, fettuccine is the Italian name for noodles.

1 **pound medium egg noodles**
1 **cup butter or margarine**
½ **cup snipped fresh parsley**
1 **teaspoon chopped fresh basil**
  Dash garlic powder
  Dash pepper
½ **cup light cream**
½ **teaspoon salt**
2 **cups grated Parmesan or Romano cheese**

Boil noodles according to directions on package, or cook in a deep pot of boiling salted water until tender but still firm, about 7 minutes.

While noodles are cooking prepare sauce. Melt butter or margarine in a small saucepan. Add parsley, basil, garlic powder and pepper; blend in cream. Simmer till hot. DO NOT boil!

Drain noodles; return to pan. Sprinkle with salt. Combine cream mixture and noodles. Add grated cheese; toss lightly. Serve immediately. Makes 6 to 8 servings.

BARBECUE SAUCE

Our favorite sauce to accompany broiled or grilled chicken. Use the same sauce for barbecue chicken except — brush chicken frequently with sauce while it cooks.

¾ cup catsup
½ cup white vinegar
1 teaspoon sugar
¼ teaspoon salt
⅛ teaspoon pepper
    Generous sprinkling of cayenne pepper

Combine all ingredients in a small saucepan; mix thoroughly. Bring mixture to a boil; reduce heat and simmer, uncovered, for 20 to 30 minutes. Stir frequently. Serve with broiled chicken or use to baste chicken during broiling or grilling. Makes 1¼ cups or enough sauce for basting 2 or 3 broiler-fryers.

Variation:

Texas-Style Barbecue Sauce

Add ½ teaspoon chili powder and ½ teaspoon bottled hot pepper sauce to the above ingredients.

MUSHROOM SAUCE

The measure of a good cook claim the experts is in the quality of sauce — or gravy — served. How do you rate?

3 tablespoons butter or margarine
1 tablespoon finely chopped onion
3 tablespoons all-purpose flour
¾ cup milk
1 4-ounce can sliced mushrooms, undrained
1 tablespoon snipped fresh parsley
¼ teaspoon salt
    Dash pepper

In a saucepan melt butter or margarine. Add onion; cook till tender. Blend in flour. Cook over low heat, stirring constantly, till lightly browned. Stir in milk and undrained mushrooms. Cook and stir until mixture bubbles and thickens. Stir in parsley; season with salt and pepper. Makes 1½ cups.

Variation:

Brown Mushroom Sauce

Prepare recipe for Mushroom Sauce except — omit parsley and add ½ teaspoon gravy browning sauce with seasonings. Serve over grilled hamburgers.

❖ ❖

Keep temperatures low when cooking dishes in which milk is the main ingredient.

❖ ❖ ❖ ❖ ❖ ❖ ❖ ❖ ❖

In creamed sauces and soups, evaporated milk may be substituted for fresh milk.

❖ ❖

MEDIUM WHITE SAUCE

You'll find this basic white sauce is the beginning for a score of other dishes.

    4 tablespoons butter or margarine
    4 tablespoons all-purpose flour
    ½ teaspoon salt
    ⅛ teaspoon white pepper
    2 cups milk

In small saucepan melt butter or margarine over low heat. Add flour and seasonings, stirring constantly with a wooden spoon. Add milk; cook and stir continually till mixture is smooth and thick. Cook 2 minutes longer. Makes 2 cups.

TOMATO SAUCE

This is a good recipe to have handy when ripe tomatoes are plentiful; make the sauce, then freeze the surplus. Spice it up if you wish!

> **6 medium firm ripe tomatoes**
> **⅓ cup chopped celery**
> **½ teaspoon salt**
> **½ teaspoon sugar**
> **Dash pepper**
> **1 beef-flavored bouillon cube**
> **⅓ cup butter or margarine**
> **2 tablespoons finely chopped onion**
> **⅓ cup all-purpose flour**

Remove stem ends of tomatoes. Peel, if desired, and quarter — to make about 3 cups.

In medium saucepan combine tomatoes, celery, salt, sugar, pepper and bouillon cube. Cover and simmer for 20 minutes. Press mixture through a food mill or sieve; set purée aside.

Using same saucepan melt butter or margarine. Add onion; cook till tender. Blend in flour. Cook over low heat, stirring constantly, till lightly browned. Stir in tomato purée. Cook and stir until mixture bubbles and thickens. Serve with sliced beef. Makes 2½ cups.

Cooking Notes

Chapter 6

Vegetables are among the good things in life. They provide texture and flavor contrasts to any meal and contribute to your family's good health. They are versatile, economical and easy to prepare.

Tender-loving care is of paramount importance in vegetable cookery. To preserve the nutrients, pare fresh vegetables just prior to cooking and cook in a minimum amount of water. Cook only to the tender-crisp stage — overcooking destroys the nutrients as well as flavor, texture and color — and if draining is necessary, save the liquids for soups and chowders. Finally, serve immediately and enjoy!

Unlike cooks in earlier times, today we are blessed with a year-round supply of fresh, frozen and canned vegetables to brighten our meals. This sampler of delightful dishes, for both stove-top and oven preparation, includes a variety of vegetables to serve in interesting and delectable ways. The basic nutritive qualities have been retained and much taste-and-eye-appeal added. Even the most reticent vegetable palate should find them appealing.

While it is healthful to include raw fresh vegetables in the diet, cooking encourages greater use of them. But the way they are cooked makes a difference. Vegetables more than any other group of foods suffer greatly from improper cooking.

Vegetable cookery is intended to spark the imagination and turn mealtime into a memorable dining experience. Experiment to find seasonings to your liking and in the right amount. Remember, good seasoning enhances good cooking, but it is no substitute for poor cooking. Good health to you and yours!

Vegetables & Rice

ASPARAGUS QUICHE

Asparagus addicts will approve of this combination. Use canned or frozen asparagus when fresh is cost prohibitive or out-of-season.

12 to 15 whole fresh asparagus stalks (about 1 pound)
1 9-inch unbaked pie shell
6 strips bacon
3 eggs
1 cup light cream or half-and-half
½ teaspoon salt
⅛ teaspoon pepper
  Dash nutmeg
1 cup shredded Swiss cheese

Wash the asparagus; remove tough lower portions of the stalks. Cook asparagus, covered, in small amount of boiling salted water till just tender. Drain and reserve 6 asparagus stalks for garnish; chop remaining asparagus. Set aside.

Line unpricked pie shell with a piece of foil; cover foil with dried beans to prevent pastry from puffing up while baking. Bake in a 425-degree oven for 7 minutes; carefully remove foil with beans and continue baking for 3 minutes. Remove from oven and gently prick any air bubbles with a fork.

Meanwhile, in skillet cook bacon till crisp; drain and crumble. In bowl beat eggs lightly. Beat in cream, salt, pepper and nutmeg; stir in chopped asparagus.

Spread crumbled bacon over bottom of warm pie shell. Sprinkle cheese atop bacon. Pour egg mixture evenly over cheese. Arrange 6 asparagus stalks spoke-fashion over top of mixture. Bake in a 325-degree oven for 40 to 45 minutes or till knife inserted 1-inch from center comes out clean. Let stand 10 minutes. Makes 6 servings.

No fresh asparagus? Use one 10-ounce package frozen cut asparagus, cooked and drained or one 15-ounce can asparagus, well-drained.

STIR-FRIED GREEN BEANS

How do I love green beans? Let me count the ways . . . and add another. This method won the approval of one diner who thought, "I couldn't take another green bean, but these are delicious!"

    1 pound fresh green beans
    2 or 3 green onions including tops
    2 tablespoons cooking oil
    1 chicken-flavored bouillon cube
    ½ teaspoon salt
    ½ cup boiling water

Prepare and measure all ingredients before starting to cook. Snip ends off beans; cut beans on the bias in 2-inch lengths (makes about 3 cups). Bias-slice green onions into ½-inch lengths.

Heat oil in a heavy 10-inch skillet over medium-high heat. Add beans and onion; stir-fry for 3 minutes.

Combine bouillon cube, salt and boiling water, stirring to dissolve bouillon. Add to green bean mixture. Reduce heat to medium. Cover and cook until beans are tender-crisp, about 5 to 7 minutes. Makes 4 to 6 servings.

Note:
   If electric skillet is used, increase the amount of water to ¾ cup. Heat skillet to 375 degrees. When remaining ingredients are added, reduce heat to 220 degrees. Cover and cook with vent closed.

SWEET AND SOUR GREEN BEANS

Still another way to serve this ubiquitous vegetable . . . a sweet and sour mixture adds flavor; bacon interest to either fresh or frozen green beans!

    2 strips bacon, diced
    1 small onion, peeled and chopped
    1 tablespoon sugar
    ¾ teaspoon salt
    ⅛ teaspoon pepper
    2 tablespoons vinegar
    3 cups hot cooked French-style or cut-up green beans

In a small skillet cook bacon till crisp; remove from pan and drain. Add onion to skillet and cook till tender. Stir onion with bacon drippings, bacon, sugar, salt, pepper and vinegar into hot beans; mix well. Serve hot. Makes a nice companion to chicken or cheese dishes. Makes 4 servings.

BEET-ONION CASSEROLE

Even diners claiming to dislike beets find this dish palatable. It's very popular at our house when fresh beets are available, but canned beets may be substituted for year-round enjoyment!

       8 medium-sized beets
       1 large onion
       ¼ cup sugar
       ¾ teaspoon salt
       ¼ teaspoon paprika
       1 tablespoon lemon juice
       3 tablespoons butter or margarine
       ½ cup water

Peel raw beets; cut in very thin slices. Peel onion; slice thinly and separate into rings. In a buttered casserole, alternate layers of beets and onion rings. Season with sugar, salt, paprika and lemon juice. Dot with butter or margarine. Add ½ cup cold water. Cover casserole and bake in a 350-degree oven for 1¼ hours or till beets are tender. Makes 4 to 6 servings.

Marinate leftover vegetables in Italian dressing and use them in salads.

One pound of shredded cabbage makes about 3½ cups of raw cabbage or 2½ cups cooked cabbage.

MARINATED BRUSSELS SPROUTS

Delicious as a cold vegetable for barbecues and picnics or as a salad ingredient!

1 pound fresh brussels sprouts (2¼ cups)
½ cup Italian-Style Dressing (recipe on page 151)

Trim stems of sprouts and discard wilted leaves. Wash. Place in a medium saucepan and cook in a small amount (not more than 1 cup per pound of sprouts) of boiling salted water till tender-crisp, about 10 to 15 minutes. Drain well.

Pour dressing over hot sprouts; stir gently to coat with marinade. Cool slightly. Place sprouts in a glass bowl or jar and cover. Chill several hours — at least 4 — or overnight. Drain and serve. Makes 4 side-dish servings.

When fresh sprouts aren't available, use one 10-ounce package of frozen sprouts. Cook following directions on package.

BOHEMIAN CABBAGE

"A fan" shares a novel way to prepare the garden surplus!

5 to 6 cups finely shredded cabbage (1 small head)
¼ cup water
1 tablespoon minced onion
1 teaspoon salt
½ teaspoon caraway seed
¼ teaspoon pepper
½ cup dairy sour cream

In large skillet combine cabbage, water, onion, salt, caraway seed and pepper; mix lightly. Cover. Cook over low heat for 5 minutes or till tender-crisp. Stir in sour cream. Heat through. Makes 6 servings.

CONNIE'S BAKED RED CABBAGE

A beautiful dish for the holidays from a cook who continues a family custom of serving red cabbage frequently. Raisins may be substituted for grapes.

> 1 small head red cabbage (see note)
> ½ cup seedless grapes
> 2 cooking apples, pared and thinly sliced
> 1 small onion, finely chopped
> 2 tablespoons sugar
> ¾ teaspoon salt
> ⅓ cup claret or other red wine
> 1 tablespoon butter or margarine
> 1 tablespoon all-purpose flour

Remove outer wilted leaves from cabbage. Cut into quarters; core and shred. Cook, uncovered, in boiling salted water for 5 to 8 minutes or until just tender. Drain and reserve 1 cup of the liquid. Place a layer of cabbage in a 2-quart casserole or baking dish.

Combine grapes, apples, onion, sugar and salt. Spread half of this mixture over cabbage; add second layer of cabbage, then remaining grape mixture. Top with remainder of vegetable.

Mix together the reserved cabbage liquid and wine; pour over cabbage and dot with butter or margarine. Cover. Bake in a 375-degree oven for 1 hour. Shake flour over top; mix lightly with a fork. Return to 375-degree oven for 15 minutes. Makes 6 servings.

Note:

To preserve color of red cabbage, add 1 tablespoon vinegar or lemon juice to the cooking water.

To complete an oven meal, place a 10-ounce package of frozen vegetables in a 1-quart casserole. Add 2 tablespoons butter and ¼ teaspoon salt. (Add ¼ cup water to lima beans.) Cover and bake at 325 to 375 degrees for 40 to 60 minutes or till tender-crisp.

MORAVIAN CABBAGE

Sausages and cabbage are combined in this German-style dish, rated by one diner as "the very best cabbage ever eaten." You may have to hide it — Moravian Cabbage must have a 24-hour rest period!

1 3-pound cabbage
1 teaspoon caraway seed
⅓ cup butter or margarine
2 large onions, peeled and chopped
⅔ cup all-purpose flour
1 cup water or reserved cabbage liquid
1 cup cider vinegar
1 cup sugar
1 pound cooked sausage links, cut into 1-inch chunks

Wash and quarter cabbage; discard core and shred coarsely. Place shredded cabbage and caraway seed in a large saucepan with ½ cup water and 1 teaspoon salt. Cook, uncovered, for a few minutes; cover and cook, stirring occasionally, for 5 to 7 minutes or till cabbage is tender-crisp. Drain, reserving cooking liquid.

Melt butter or margarine in a large, heavy skillet. Add onions and cook till tender but not brown. Blend in flour; cook, stirring, for 2 or 3 minutes to brown flour.

Meanwhile, in a saucepan heat 1 cup water or cabbage liquid, vinegar and sugar till sugar is dissolved. Add " syrup" mixture to flour mixture in skillet, stirring constantly to avoid lumps. (A wire whip helps keep the mixture smooth.)

Add drained cabbage and sausage pieces; mix well. Refrigerate, covered, for at least 24 hours before serving. Makes 10 to 12 servings.

If "perfect rice" means fluffy grains of rice served as a meat accompaniment, then long-grain rice is a partial answer. Cook rice following package directions; DO NOT remove cover from the pan during this process. Remove pan from heat; uncover and separate grains with a fork. Serve immediately!

SCALLOPED CORN

An old-fashioned dish from a male food writer. "It's like mother used to make."

6 strips bacon
½ cup chopped onion
½ cup chopped green pepper
1 12-ounce can vacuum-packed whole-kernel corn
⅔ cup soft bread cubes (1 slice)
⅔ cup milk
1 egg, slightly beaten
½ teaspoon salt
¼ teaspoon pepper
¼ cup fine dry bread crumbs
1 tablespoon butter or margarine, melted

In a large skillet cook bacon till crisp; remove and drain on paper toweling. Crumble and set aside.

Pour off all but 1 tablespoon bacon drippings in skillet. Add onion and green pepper; cook till tender. Remove pan from heat. Stir in undrained corn, bread cubes, milk, egg, seasonings and bacon pieces.

Pour mixture into a buttered 1-quart casserole. Combine dry bread crumbs and melted butter or margarine; sprinkle atop casserole. Bake in a 350-degree oven for 30 minutes or till crumbs are browned and mixture is hot. Makes 4 to 6 servings.

CAULIFLOWER CUSTARD

A winner from a local recipe contest! Thaw, but don't cook the cauliflower unless absolutely necessary is the secret to presenting a perfect dish. When available, use fresh cauliflower but keep pre-cooking to a minimum.

1 10-ounce package frozen cauliflower, thawed
2 eggs
¾ cup milk
¾ cup shredded sharp Cheddar cheese
3 tablespoons butter or margarine, melted

2 tablespoons grated Parmesan cheese
1 tablespoon snipped fresh parsley
1 tablespoon finely minced onion
1 teaspoon salt
Dash pepper
¼ cup fine dry bread crumbs
1 tablespoon grated Parmesan cheese
1 tablespoon butter or margarine, melted

Drain cauliflower. Arrange in a buttered 1-quart casserole. In medium mixing bowl beat eggs lightly; beat in milk. Add Cheddar cheese, 3 tablespoons butter or margarine, 2 tablespoons Parmesan cheese, parsley, onion, salt and pepper; mix well. Pour over cauliflower.

Combine bread crumbs and 1 tablespoon Parmesan cheese; mix with 1 tablespoon melted butter or margarine. Sprinkle atop casserole.

Bake in a 350-degree oven for 30 to 40 minutes or till knife inserted near center comes out clean. Makes 4 to 6 servings.

EGGPLANT PARMIGIANA

An Italian couple, who often work as a team in their kitchen, introduced this ethnic dish to guests at a community supper. It received raves! When the zucchini plants bear profusely, substitute zucchini for the eggplant. It's super good!

2 eggs
¼ cup all-purpose flour
1 tablespoon grated Parmesan cheese
1 teaspoon dried parsley flakes
½ teaspoon salt
⅛ teaspoon pepper
1 medium eggplant, peeled and cut into ⅓-inch slices
½ cup cooking oil
2 cups (8-ounce pkg.) shredded mozzarella cheese
1 pint meatless spaghetti sauce
¼ cup grated Parmesan or Romano cheese

In medium bowl combine eggs, flour, 1 tablespoon grated Par-

mesan cheese, parsley flakes, salt and pepper; beat till smooth.
Dip eggplant slices in batter, shaking off excess. Fry, a few slices
at a time, in hot oil in a large skillet until lightly browned on both
sides. Drain on paper toweling. Arrange, overlapping slices, in a
13x9x2-inch baking dish.

Sprinkle mozzarella cheese evenly over slices. Cover with
spaghetti sauce. Sprinkle generously with Parmesan or Romano
cheese. Bake in a 350-degree oven for 20 minutes or until bubbly
and golden brown. Serve either as a main or side dish. Makes 6
servings.

Variation:

Zucchini Parmigiana

Follow recipe for Eggplant Parmigiana except — substitute 2
medium unpared zucchini for eggplant.

*To make fine dry bread crumbs, place slices of stale bread in a
shallow pan. Dry in a 300-degree oven for 30 minutes. Place
dried bread in a heavy plastic bag and crush into fine crumbs
using a rolling pin. Store in a cool, dry place.*

SAUTEED MUSHROOMS

*Perfect partners — sautéed mushrooms and a thick, juicy
steak! Or serve over toasted slices of French bread for a nice luncheon dish. Cook fresh mushrooms immediately after preparing
to prevent darkening; adding a little lemon juice during cooking
helps, however.*

2½ cups sliced fresh mushrooms (8 ounces)
4 tablespoons butter or margarine
½ cup finely chopped onion

¼ **cup snipped fresh parsley**
1 **tablespoon lemon juice**
½ **teaspoon salt**
   Dash pepper

Rinse mushrooms; pat dry and slice. Set aside. In a large skillet melt butter or margarine. Add onion and cook, stirring, for 2 minutes or till golden. Add mushrooms; cook 5 minutes. Stir in parsley, lemon juice, salt and pepper. Serve as a beef accompaniment. Makes 4 servings.

Note:
   One 8-ounce can mushrooms, drained may be substituted for fresh mushrooms.

CREAMED ONIONS

"Simple and relatively inexpensive," says the cook who totes this dish to Grange suppers, "and everyone seems to like it."

6 **medium onions (2 pounds)**
½ **teaspoon salt**
2 **tablespoons butter or margarine**
2 **tablespoons all-purpose flour**
1 **cup milk (see note)**
½ **teaspoon salt**
¼ **teaspoon pepper**
½ **cup shredded Cheddar cheese**

Peel onions; cut in ⅛-inch slices. Place in a saucepan with ½ teaspoon salt and a small amount of boiling water. Cook, covered, until tender. Drain. Place in a bowl and set aside.

In same saucepan melt butter or margarine over low heat. Blend in flour, stirring constantly. Gradually add milk, stirring, till mixture comes to a boil and thickens slightly. Add seasonings and cheese, stirring till cheese melts.

Return onions to pan; mix lightly with a fork. Heat for 5 minutes and serve. Makes 6 servings.

Note:
   If desired, substitute half of the milk with water drained from cooked onions.

HAM AND POTATOES AU GRATIN

A compatible trio — ham, potatoes and cheese — teams up in a flavorful dish. One of my favorites for using leftover ham!

    2 tablespoons butter or margarine
    1 small onion, peeled and chopped
    ¼ cup chopped green pepper
    1 tablespoon all-purpose flour
      Dash pepper
    1 cup milk
    1 cup shredded Cheddar or Swiss cheese
    ¼ cup mayonnaise or salad dressing
    3 medium potatoes, cooked and diced (about 3 cups)
    2 cups diced cooked ham
    ¼ cup fine dry bread crumbs
    1 tablespoon butter or margarine, melted
      Snipped fresh parsley

In saucepan melt 2 tablespoons butter or margarine; add onion and green pepper and cook till tender. Stir in flour and pepper. Add milk; bring to a boil, stirring constantly. Reduce heat and add shredded cheese and mayonnaise or salad dressing; stir till cheese melts.

Stir potatoes and ham into sauce; mix well. Season to taste with salt. Turn mixture into a shallow buttered baking dish.

Combine bread crumbs and melted butter or margarine; spread atop casserole. Sprinkle with snipped parsley. Bake in a 350-degree oven for 30 minutes or till hot and bubbly. Makes 4 to 6 servings.

PANNED POTATOES WITH CHEESE

Broil a steak, toss the salad and serve Panned Potatoes With Cheese and you will have an All-American meal. Expect a compliment or two!

    4 large russet potatoes
    4 tablespoons butter or margarine (½ stick)
    1 small onion, peeled and chopped

½ teaspoon salt
⅛ teaspoon pepper
1 cup (4-ounce pkg.) shredded sharp Cheddar cheese
½ of a 3-ounce can French-fried onion rings

Peel potatoes; cut into ¼-inch slices. In large skillet, over medium heat, melt butter or margarine; remove skillet from heat.

Arrange half of potatoes over bottom and slightly up sides of skillet; add onion and sprinkle generously with salt and pepper. Repeat potato layer and seasonings.

Cover and cook over medium-low heat for 10 minutes. With a wide spatula, carefully turn potatoes over, a portion at a time. Cover and cook 10 minutes longer or until potatoes are tender. Sprinkle with cheese and onion rings. Cook, uncovered, for 1 minute longer or till cheese is melted. Garnish with snipped parsley, if desired. Makes 4 servings.

POTATOES BYRON

A super company dish from an excellent cook and hostess!

6 large russet or baking potatoes
½ cup butter or margarine
½ cup chopped onion
½ cup light cream
½ teaspoon salt
⅛ teaspoon pepper
½ cup shredded Swiss cheese

Scrub potatoes and pat dry; prick with a fork. Bake in a 425-degree oven for 50 to 60 minutes or until tender.

Remove potatoes from oven and scoop out insides with a spoon. Place potato in a shallow casserole or baking dish and break up coarsely.

In small skillet melt butter or margarine; add onion and cook until golden. Pour mixture over potato. Add cream, salt and pepper; mix only enough to blend ingredients. Let stand 30 minutes.

Sprinkle shredded cheese atop casserole. Bake in a 350-degree oven for 25 minutes or till hot and cheese is melted. If more browning is desired, place under broiler for 1 to 2 minutes. Makes 6 to 8 servings.

RALPH'S POTATO SCALLOP

A potato scallop flavored with mushroom soup is the favorite of an agricultural expert and cooking enthusiast. It's a dandy with ham.

> **5 or 6 medium potatoes, peeled and thinly sliced**
> **1 large onion, peeled and thinly sliced**
> **1 teaspoon salt**
> **⅛ teaspoon pepper**
> **2 tablespoons butter or margarine**
> **1 10¾-ounce can condensed cream of mushroom soup**
> **¼ cup milk**
> **1 cup (4-ounce pkg.) shredded Cheddar cheese**

In buttered 2-quart casserole arrange a third of the potatoes and onion in layers. Season with salt and pepper; dot with butter or margarine.

In small bowl blend together soup and milk; pour a third of the mixture over first layer of vegetables in casserole. Sprinkle with a third of the cheese. Make a second layer in the same order: potatoes, onion, seasonings, butter or margarine, soup mixture and cheese. Repeat once more.

Bake in a 350-degree oven for 1½ hours or until potatoes are tender. Makes 6 servings.

SCALLOPED POTATOES

A Pantry Shelf original! Parboiling the vegetables not only shortens oven-cooking but eliminates the risk of curdling.

> **4 or 5 medium potatoes**
> **2 small onions**
> **4 tablespoons all-purpose flour**
> **1 teaspoon salt**

⅛ teaspoon pepper
1 cup milk
2 tablespoons butter or margarine
½ cup shredded Cheddar cheese

Peel and thinly slice potatoes and onions. In saucepan arrange vegetables in alternate layers. Cook in small amount of boiling salted water until potatoes are partially cooked but still firm. Drain only if absolutely necessary.

Layer half of the vegetables in a buttered 1½-quart casserole. Sprinkle 2 tablespoons of the flour and half of the salt and pepper over first layer. Repeat.

Pour milk over all. Dot with butter or margarine. Sprinkle cheese atop. Bake, uncovered, in a 350-degree oven for 30 minutes or until potatoes are tender. Makes 4 to 6 servings.

Brown rice, which retains most of the natural bran, requires a longer cooking period than "regular" rice. Brown rice has a shelf life of about 6 months. Refrigerate for longer storage.

GREEN RICE

A super-easy, high-protein dish to accompany baked ham. It also makes a great companion for Italian Sausages and Green Peppers.

¼ cup butter or margarine
1 small onion, peeled and chopped
2 eggs
2 cups milk
1 10-ounce package frozen chopped broccoli, thawed and drained
1½ cups shredded sharp Cheddar cheese
1½ cups cooked rice
1 teaspoon garlic salt

In small skillet melt butter or margarine; add onion and cook until tender. In large mixing bowl beat eggs until light. Stir in milk, broccoli, cheese, rice and onion mixture. Season with garlic salt.

Pour mixture into a buttered 2-quart casserole. Bake in a 325-degree oven for 1 hour or until knife inserted 1 inch from center comes out clean. Makes 6 servings.

FRIED RICE

An exotic dish from the native land of a local cook makes practical use of any cooked meat, poultry or seafood.

2 tablespoons butter or cooking oil
½ cup finely chopped onion
½ cup finely chopped green pepper
1 egg, slightly beaten
2 cups cooked long-grain rice
½ cup shredded or diced cooked shrimp, crabmeat,
**   ham, bacon, pork or poultry**
2 tablespoons soy sauce

Heat butter or oil in skillet. Add onion and green pepper; cook over low heat till tender. Add egg; cook and stir just till set. Stir in rice and meat. Heat, tossing lightly with a fork to keep rice light and fluffy. Add soy sauce; stir gently to mix. Cook 2 minutes longer. Makes 4 servings.

Long-grain rice tends to stand apart after cooking and is ideal for fried rice and curries. Medium-grain rice, which tends to become sticky after cooking, is tender and moist and suitable for puddings and molds.

To preserve nutrients, rice should not be rinsed before or after cooking!

PECAN PILAF

A recipe from a Southern cook to please a Yankee palate! For a change of flavor, try almonds or walnuts.

    3 tablespoons butter or margarine, divided
    ½ cup coarsely chopped pecans
    1 small onion, peeled and finely chopped
    1 cup uncooked long-grain rice
    2 cups chicken broth, heated
    ½ teaspoon salt
    Dash pepper
    1 tablespoon snipped fresh parsley

In large skillet melt 1 tablespoon butter or margarine. Add pecans and sauté for 2 or 3 minutes or till lightly browned. Remove pecans; cover and set aside.

In same skillet melt remaining butter or margarine. Add onion; cook till tender but not brown. Add rice and stir to thoroughly coat grains. Stir in chicken broth, salt and pepper. Simmer, covered, for 18 to 20 minutes or until rice is tender and all liquid is absorbed. Remove from heat. Stir in pecans and parsley. Makes 4 servings.

SPANISH RICE

A delicious idea from a Southwestern cook to use up your home-canned tomatoes.

    1 cup uncooked long-grain rice
    4 tablespoons butter or margarine (½ stick)
    1 small onion, peeled and finely chopped
    1 green pepper, cored, seeded and finely chopped
    1 stalk celery, chopped (¼ cup)
    1 16-ounce can tomatoes or 1 pint home-canned tomatoes
    1 teaspoon salt
    ⅛ teaspoon pepper

Prepare rice by following directions on package. Or, bring 2½

cups of water to a boil. Add 1 teaspoon salt and 1 tablespoon butter or margarine. Stir in rice; reduce heat and simmer, covered,
until rice is tender and water absorbed, about 20 minutes.

In skillet melt butter or margarine. Add onion, green pepper
and celery; sauté until onion is golden and vegetables are tender.
Add tomatoes, salt and pepper. Cook slowly for 15 minutes. Carefully stir in hot rice and simmer for 5 minutes. Serve hot. If desired, sprinkle grated cheese or crumbled crisp bacon over top.
Makes 4 to 6 servings.

*DO NOT wash packaged rice. Studies show that whether rice is
brown or white, long or medium grain, there are tremendous
losses in nutrients when rice is washed — either before or after
cooking.*

*To cook rice, combine 1 cup regular rice, 2 cups liquid (water,
broth or vegetable juices), 1 teaspoon salt and 1 tablespoon butter
or margarine in a large saucepan. Bring to a boil, stirring once
or twice. Reduce heat and simmer, covered, for 15 to 20 minutes
or till tender. Makes about 3 cups.*

BAKED ACORN SQUASH

*Baking vegetables along with an oven meal conserves energy.
Baked acorn squash is served right in the shell.*

    2 medium acorn squash
      Salt and pepper
    4 tablespoons butter or margarine

Wash and cut squash in half lengthwise; remove fiber and seeds.
Place cut side down in a shallow baking pan. Add ¼-inch hot
water.

Bake in a 350-degree oven for 30 to 40 minutes or until squash start to get tender. Drain off water, if any remains, and turn squash pulp side up. Season with salt and pepper. Dot each half with 1 tablespoon butter or margarine. Return to oven and bake 15 to 20 minutes longer or until tender. Makes 4 servings.

Variation:

Glazed Squash

Sprinkle 1 teaspoon brown sugar over each cooked squash. Place in oven long enough to melt sugar.

SUMMER SQUASH CASSEROLE

A Down East cook shares her recipe which combines the delicate flavor of summer squash with a savory herb stuffing topping. A zesty dish to adorn your buffet table!

> 2 **pounds yellow summer squash (see note)**
> ¼ **cup chopped onion**
> 1 **10¾-ounce can condensed cream of chicken soup**
> 1 **cup dairy sour cream**
> 1 **cup shredded raw carrot**
> 1 **8-ounce package herb-seasoned stuffing mix**
> ½ **cup butter or margarine, melted**

Scrub squash; cut off ends, but do not pare. Slice to make 6 cups. In saucepan, cook sliced squash and chopped onion in small amount of boiling salted water for 5 minutes; drain well.

Combine soup and sour cream. Stir in shredded carrot. Fold in drained squash and onion mixture.

Combine stuffing mix and butter or margarine. Spread half of stuffing mixture in bottom of 12x8x2-inch baking dish. Spoon vegetable mixture atop and sprinkle remaining stuffing over vegetables. Bake, uncovered, in a 350-degree oven for 25 to 30 minutes or until heated through. Makes 6 to 8 servings.

Note:
   Substitute 3 cups of sliced zucchini squash for 3 cups of the yellow summer squash.

BAKED STUFFED TOMATOES

A recipe not to be overlooked when vine-ripened tomatoes are at their peak in supply and flavor. Great companion to a meat-and-potato meal. Or, incorporate bits and pieces of cheese, cooked meat or fish into the filling for a nice luncheon dish.

6 medium tomatoes
½ cup crisp-cooked, crumbled bacon
¼ cup finely chopped celery
1 small onion, peeled and finely chopped
1 cup soft bread crumbs
½ teaspoon salt
½ cup grated Parmesan cheese, divided
2 tablespoons butter or margarine

Wash, but do not peel tomatoes. Cut thin slice from stem end and scoop out pulp. Drain shells.

In medium bowl, chop pulp; add bacon, celery, onion, bread crumbs, salt and ¼ cup of the Parmesan cheese. Mix well.

Place tomato shells in a buttered baking dish. Fill centers with bacon mixture. Sprinkle remaining cheese atop tomatoes; dot each with 1 teaspoon butter or margarine.

Bake in a 375-degree oven for 20 to 25 minutes or till heated through and crumbs are lightly browned. Makes 6 servings.

RUTH'S SCALLOPED TOMATOES

Makes one wonder how any dish so simple to fix could taste this good! Dress up your home-canned tomatoes with a bit of seasoning, chopped onion, green pepper and celery; then proceed with the recipe.

1 16-ounce can sliced stewed tomatoes
1 cup soft bread crumbs (1½ slices)
1 cup (4-ounce pkg.) shredded sharp Cheddar cheese

In a buttered 1-quart casserole combine tomatoes and bread crumbs; mix well. Sprinkle cheese evenly over top. Bake in a 350-degree oven for 25 minutes or till hot and bubbly and cheese is melted. Makes 4 servings.

SUE'S TURNIP SUPREME

"Fill the steins to dear old Maine" and three cheers to the correspondent who shared her recipe in exchange for a bit of trivia from this alumna of the University of Maine. This old-time dish with an updated twist is a wonderful accompaniment to roast pork! Bake it along with the pork in a 325-degree oven for 2 hours.

    1 medium (1½ pounds) yellow turnip
    3 or 4 medium tart apples
    ¼ cup butter or margarine, melted
    1 cup apple juice or Burgundy wine
    1 tablespoon all-purpose flour
    2 teaspoons instant beef bouillon granules
    ¼ teaspoon dried basil, crushed
    ¼ teaspoon dried marjoram, crushed
    ⅛ teaspoon pepper

Peel and thinly slice turnip to make about 3 cups. Wash and core apples; cut into ¼-inch slices to make 3 cups. In a buttered 2-quart casserole alternate layers of turnip and apple.

Combine remaining ingredients in a blender container. Cover and blend till smooth. (Or, beat with a rotary beater until mixture is smooth.) Pour over turnip and apple slices.

Bake, covered, in a 350-degree oven for 1½ hours or till turnip is tender. Serve hot. Makes 6 servings.

To make soft crumbs, pull or break off pieces of a firm-textured bread with the fingers.

To make dry crumbs, allow stale bread to dry at room temperature or toast lightly, then crush.

ITALIAN ZUCCHINI PIE

"A pizza in a pie shell!" This recipe is an adaptation of a national contest winner which won a Southern cook a huge sum of money.

> 1 9-inch unbaked pie shell
> 4 tablespoons butter or margarine
> 4 medium zucchini, unpared and thinly sliced (4 cups)
> 1 large onion, peeled and chopped (1 cup)
> 1 clove garlic, peeled and minced
> ½ cup snipped fresh parsley
> ½ teaspoon salt
> ¼ teaspoon pepper
> ¼ teaspoon dried basil, crushed
> ¼ teaspoon dried oregano, crushed
> 2 eggs
> 2 cups (8-ounce pkg.) shredded mozzarella cheese

Line unpricked pie shell with a piece of foil and weight it down with dry beans. Bake in a 425-degree oven for 7 minutes; carefully remove foil and beans. Return shell to oven to continue baking for 3 minutes.

Meanwhile, melt butter or margarine in a large skillet; add zucchini, onion and garlic. Cook and stir for 10 minutes. Stir in parsley, salt, pepper, basil and oregano.

In large mixing bowl beat eggs till light; stir in shredded cheese. Add zucchini mixture; mix well. Place in pastry shell, spreading evenly to edges.

Bake in a 350-degree oven for 25 minutes or till center is set. Let stand 10 minutes. Serve warm. Make 6 servings.

All types of summer squash, including yellow and zucchini, are harvested when the entire squash is tender and edible. Harvest the yellow type when about 4 to 6 inches long, zucchini, at 6 to 8 inches. Wash, but do not pare; cut off ends and slice.

ZUCCHINI SOUFFLÉ

A food expert with a Maine connection shares this recipe. Truly a marvelous way to fix this prolific vegetable, and it goes together in ten minutes!

3 to 4 small zucchini (1 to 1½-inches thick)
1 egg
¼ cup milk
3 tablespoons butter or margarine, melted
¾ cup shredded Monterey Jack cheese, divided
½ teaspoon salt
⅛ teaspoon pepper

Scrub zucchini; trim off ends. Cut unpared squash into ¼-inch slices. (There should be 3 to 4 cups.) Place in a saucepan with a small amount of boiling salted water. Cook, covered, for 3 minutes. Drain well.

In small bowl, beat egg lightly; stir in milk, butter or margarine, half of the cheese and seasonings.

Layer the zucchini in a buttered 1-quart casserole, pouring cheese mixture between layers. Sprinkle remaining cheese atop. Set casserole in a pan of hot water (1-inch deep).

Bake in a 400-degree oven for 40 minutes or till set. Makes 4 to 6 servings.

ZUCCHINI-TOMATO-ONION CASSEROLE

A delightful side dish to complete an oven meal.

2 cups thinly sliced zucchini (2 small)
1 large, firm ripe tomato, thinly sliced
1 medium onion, peeled and thinly sliced into rings and halved
3 tablespoons grated Parmesan cheese

In a small buttered casserole layer half of the zucchini, tomato and onion. Sprinkle with half of the cheese. Repeat. Bake, uncovered, in a 350-degree oven for 40 minutes. Cover casserole and bake for 20 minutes longer. Serve hot. Makes 4 servings.

CHINESE VEGETABLES

An Oriental style of preparing four familiar vegetables. Marvelous for perking up winter meals!

2 tablespoons water
1 tablespoon soy sauce
1 tablespoon catsup
2 tablespoons cooking oil
4 medium carrots, bias-sliced
4 stalks celery, bias-sliced
1 large green pepper, seeded and sliced
1 large onion, peeled and sliced

In small bowl combine water, soy sauce and catsup. Set aside. In large skillet heat cooking oil; add vegetables and stir-fry over medium heat for 3 minutes. Add soy sauce mixture to skillet; stir into vegetables.

Cover and cook over low heat until vegetables are just tender-crisp, about 10 minutes. Makes 4 to 6 servings.

Overcooking vegetables causes unnecessary loss of valuable nutrients.

Cooking Notes

Chapter 7

Salads have earned a place of honor on the contemporary cook's menu. They lend a special touch to any meal and are testimony to the cook's good taste and ingenuity.

Nourishing, versatile and delicious, salads can be a simple slaw for everyday enjoyment or an elegant mold for the memorable moments in our lives. They are a cook's creation, a dieter's dream and a diner's delight. Some are light and refreshing side-dishes; others, hearty main-dish fare.

Epicures maintain it is the dressing that makes the salad. Be daring! Experimenting with new flavors makes salad-eating adventurous; and creating your own dressings adds dimension to your cooking skills.

During my growing up years, salads were considered company fare; yet, I have pleasant recollections of a few favorites: a banana-pineapple creation for the Christmas season, a potato-tuna salad for picnics and light suppers, and a cabbage-pineapple or carrot-raisin combination to accompany baked beans.

Assembled in this collection is a range of salad recipes, such as Danish Cucumber Salad, Blueberry Salad Mold and Cranberry Orange Relish. Whether the choice is tossed or molded, marinated or main-dish, there's a flavorful combination to tempt every palate and a colorful arrangement to complement every occasion. Surely, you'll want to tuck away a Frozen Fruit Salad for unexpected guests and prepare a molded Mustard Ring to accompany your holiday ham. With a bit of imagination and artistic flair, your arrangements not only will beautify your table, but please the eye as well as the taste buds. Pleasant and pleasurable dining!

Salads & Dressings

Continued

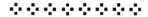

ANTIPASTO

In Italian cookery, antipasto is the appetizer, so it is only natural that this recipe is from a good Italian cook. Sweet cherry peppers are not to be confused with the hot variety. You'll find both sweet and hot peppers in the pickle section at your supermarket.

    1 **quart sweet cherry peppers, drained, seeded and cut into strips**
    1 **20-ounce can chick peas, drained**
    1 **4-ounce can mushroom stems and pieces, drained**
    1 **2-ounce jar stuffed olives, drained**
    1 **cup thinly sliced celery**
      French Dressing (recipe on page 150)

Arrange ingredients attractively on a large platter or place a small amount of each ingredient on lettuce leaves for individual servings. Drizzle with French Dressing. Makes 4 to 6 servings.

ARTICHOKE-RICE SALAD

A contemporary recipe from a hostess who uses it frequently for casual meals at the family summer residence. As a side dish, it's a perfect companion to barbecued chicken; or, add cooked chicken and Presto! a main-dish salad for a ladies luncheon.

1 7-ounce package chicken-flavored rice
1 6-ounce jar marinated artichoke hearts
3 green onions with tops, sliced
½ cup chopped green pepper
½ cup sliced green olives
½ teaspoon curry powder
½ cup mayonnaise or salad dressing

Prepare rice mixture as directed on package except — omit butter. Cool.

Drain artichokes, reserving marinade. Chop artichokes; add to rice mixture with green onions, green pepper, olives and curry powder.

Slowly combine mayonnaise or salad dressing with artichoke marinade. Stir into rice mixture; mix well. Cover and chill for 24 hours. Keeps up to a week under refrigeration. Makes 6 servings.

Variation:

Main-Dish Chicken-Rice Salad

Combine 2 whole chicken breasts, halved, with 1 cup water; add 1 slice onion, ½ medium carrot and ½ stalk celery with leaves. Season with salt and pepper. Cover saucepan; simmer about 1 hour or until chicken is tender. Cool. Separate meat from bones. Discard skin and bones. Cut meat into 1-inch cubes. Stir into rice mixture. Chill.

White pepper is milder in flavor than black pepper. Use white pepper in dishes with a pale color or a delicate flavor.

CHEF'S SALAD

A whole-meal salad to please the palate and offer good eating on a hot summer day. It's wonderful with warm Dill Pickle Rye Bread, cut in thick slabs and dripping with butter!

1 small head lettuce or combination of salad greens
4 radishes, thinly sliced
1 medium cucumber, unpared and thinly sliced
1 green pepper, seeded and cut into strips
1 onion, sliced and separated into rings
4 ounces cooked ham or beef tongue, cut into thin strips
4 ounces cooked chicken or turkey, cut into thin strips
4 ounces Swiss cheese, cut into thin strips
2 ripe tomatoes, cut into wedges
4 hard-cooked eggs, peeled and sliced
Black olives

Wash and drain lettuce or greens. Chill. Tear into bite-size pieces and line 4 individual salad bowls with greens. Add radishes, cucumbers, green pepper and onion rings. Lay meat and cheese strips across vegetables. Garnish each salad with tomato wedges, egg slices and black olives. Serve with favorite dressing. Makes 4 servings.

CHINESE NOODLE SALAD

An unusual luncheon entrée from a cook in the Midwest, who thought it would appeal to New Englanders. The recipe she says, "won first place in a local contest." For a complete meal, serve Chinese Noodle Salad with tiny whole wheat rolls and lots of ripe tomatoes and crispy cucumbers.

1 16-ounce can bean sprouts, drained
2 cups small cooked shrimp (see note)
1 8-ounce can water chestnuts, drained and shredded
¼ cup minced green onion
¼ cup minced celery
Soy Dressing (recipe follows)
1 3-ounce can (2¼ cups) chow mein noodles

In a bowl combine bean sprouts, shrimp, water chestnuts, green onions and celery. Add Soy Dressing; mix well. Cover and chill. Just before serving, toss with chow mein noodles. Serve on crisp lettuce leaves. Makes 3 to 4 servings.

Soy Dressing

¾ **cup mayonnaise or salad dressing**
1 **tablespoon lemon juice**
1 **tablespoon soy sauce**
¼ **teaspoon ground ginger**

Combine mayonnaise or salad dressing, lemon juice, soy sauce and ginger in a small bowl; blend till smooth.

Note:
One 16-ounce can red salmon, drained and skin and bones discarded, may be substituted for the shrimp.

MOCK LOBSTER SALAD

For those times when your palate says yes; your purse says no! Certainly not a dish to fool the most discriminating diner, but good, nonetheless.

2 **pounds haddock, fillets or dressed**
1 **medium onion, peeled and sliced**
2 **cups water**
½ **teaspoon salt**
2 **cups diced celery**
½ **cup dairy sour cream**
½ **cup chili sauce**
¼ **cup mayonnaise**
1 **tablespoon prepared horseradish**
1 **tablespoon lemon juice**
Salt and pepper

Place haddock and onion in a large saucepan; add water and salt; simmer for about 5 minutes or till fish flakes easily when tested with a fork. Drain, reserving liquid for a future chowder. Cool.

If necessary, remove skin and check fish carefully for bones. Flake fish into large pieces. In a large bowl combine fish and celery

In small bowl combine sour cream, chili sauce, mayonnaise, horseradish and lemon juice. Blend with fish; season to taste with salt and pepper. Refrigerate. Stir well before serving on lettuce leaves. Sprinkle lightly with paprika, if desired. Makes 8 servings.

MACARONI AND CHEESE SALAD

This hearty make-ahead salad, combining pasta with early garden vegetables and Cheddar cheese, makes a great dish for your barbecue table.

    4 cups cooked elbow macaroni (8-ounce pkg.)
    1 cup (4-ounce pkg.) shredded Cheddar cheese
    1 cup thinly sliced celery
    ½ cup sliced green onions
    ¼ cup sliced radishes
    2 tablespoons snipped fresh parsley
    1 cup mayonnaise
    2 tablespoons vinegar
    1 teaspoon salt
    ½ teaspoon celery seed

In a large mixing bowl combine all ingredients; mix well. Taste salad to check seasoning; add salt, if necessary. Cover and chill thoroughly, at least 3 hours. Serve in a lettuce-lined bowl and garnish with pepper rings, carrot curls or tomato wedges. Makes 6 servings.

HOT GERMAN POTATO SALAD

A Pennsylvania Dutch specialty! It's great either hot or cold — but don't count on having any leftover salad.

    6 medium potatoes
    8 strips bacon
    1 medium onion, peeled and chopped

2 tablespoons all-purpose flour
1½ tablespoons sugar
1½ teaspoons salt
½ teaspoon celery seed
  Dash pepper
¾ cup water or potato liquid
⅓ cup vinegar

Cook potatoes in jackets till tender; drain, reserving liquid. Peel and slice or dice; keep warm.

In a skillet cook bacon till crisp. Remove bacon from skillet; drain and crumble. Pour off all but 2 tablespoons of bacon drippings. Cook onion in bacon drippings until tender but not brown.

Blend in flour, sugar, salt, celery seed and pepper. Cook over low heat to blend. Remove from heat to stir in water or reserved potato liquid and vinegar. Return to heat and bring to a boil, stirring constantly. Boil for 1 minute.

Gently stir in warm potatoes and crumbled bits of bacon. Heat through. Remove from heat, cover; let set until serving time. Makes 6 servings.

SOUR CREAM POTATO SALAD

The favorite potato salad of a seasoned cook! It's a creamy version with superb flavor!

7 medium potatoes
⅓ cup clear French or Italian dressing
¾ cup diced celery
⅓ cup sliced green onions with tops
4 hard-cooked eggs
1 cup mayonnaise
½ cup dairy sour cream
1½ teaspoons prepared horseradish mustard
  Salt and celery seed
⅓ cup diced pared cucumber

Cook potatoes in jackets; cool slightly. Peel and slice. (There should be 6 cups.) While potatoes are still warm, pour dressing over them. Chill for 2 hours. Add celery and onion. Chop egg whites; add to potato mixture.

Sieve egg yolks, saving a small amount to garnish top. Combine remaining egg yolk with mayonnaise, sour cream and horseradish mustard. Fold into potato mixture. Season to taste with salt and celery seed. Cover and chill for 2 hours.

Just before serving fold in diced cucumber. Sprinkle reserved egg yolk over top of salad. Makes 8 servings.

CUCUMBERS IN SOUR CREAM

Sour cream adds a tangy touch. It's a nice change from a vinegar dressing.

    3 medium cucumbers, pared and thinly sliced
       (3 cups)
    1 medium onion, peeled and very thinly sliced
    1 tablespoon salt
    ⅔ cup dairy sour cream
    1 tablespoon vinegar
    1 teaspoon celery seed

Layer cucumbers and onion in a bowl; cover with cold water. Sprinkle with salt; let stand for 20 to 30 minutes at room temperature. Drain well.

Blend together sour cream, vinegar and celery seed. Add to cucumber mixture; toss gently. Cover and chill. Serve in small dessert dishes. Makes 4 servings.

DANISH CUCUMBER SALAD

International fare from a native of Copenhagen! This delightful salad, also known as Agurkesalat, gives cucumbers the crunch of pickles and the flavor of fresh. It will keep in the refrigerator for several days.

    2 large firm cucumbers
    1 tablespoon salt
    2 tablespoons sugar
    2 tablespoons boiling water
    ¼ cup cider or white vinegar

⅛ **teaspoon pepper**

Pare cucumbers; cut in paper-thin slices. Place cucumbers in a shallow dish; sprinkle with salt. Place 2 or 3 plates on top to press out water. Leave at room temperature 2 hours. Drain.

In measuring cup melt sugar in boiling water. Add vinegar and pepper; pour over cucumbers. Marinate for 1 hour at room temperature. Chill and serve. Makes 4 servings.

To snip fresh parsley, wash and thoroughly dry sprigs of parsley. Place in a tall, wide-mouth jar or glass. Snip parsley with kitchen shears.

MARINATED BEAN SALAD

In the category of family favorites, this recipe has a definite place. It goes to every picnic, buffet or barbecue — year-round.

1 16-ounce can cut green beans, drained
1 16-ounce can cut wax beans, drained
1 16-ounce can lima beans, drained
1 16-ounce can red kidney beans, drained and rinsed
1 cup diced green pepper
1 medium onion, peeled and chopped
½ cup sugar
½ cup vinegar
½ cup salad oil
1 teaspoon salt
½ teaspoon dry mustard
½ teaspoon dried tarragon, crushed
½ teaspoon dried basil, crushed
2 tablespoons snipped fresh parsley

In large mixing bowl combine all drained beans, green pepper and onion.

In a jar with a tight-fitting lid combine sugar, vinegar, salad oil, salt, dry mustard, tarragon, basil and parsley. Shake vigorously to mix together. Pour dressing over vegetables; stir gently to coat. Cover. Marinate in refrigerator for several hours or overnight, stirring several times. Before serving, stir to coat vegetables and drain. Makes 10 to 12 servings.

MARINATED CARROTS

A comment from one diner, "At last a cooked carrot that I really like!"

1½ cups sliced cooked carrots or 1 16-ounce can carrots, drained
½ cup diced green pepper
½ cup cider vinegar
¼ cup salad oil
1 tablespoon sugar
1 tablespoon snipped fresh parsley
¼ teaspoon salt
Dash pepper

In a medium bowl combine cooked carrots and green pepper. Combine vinegar, salad oil, sugar, parsley, salt and pepper in a jar with a tight-fitting lid. Cover and shake vigorously. Pour mixture over carrots and green pepper; mix well.

Cover bowl and refrigerate until thoroughly chilled, at least 3 hours. Stir occasionally. Drain before serving as a salad ingredient or relish. Makes 2½ cups.

To make croûtons, remove crusts from stale pieces of bread; brush both sides lightly with melted butter or margarine. Cut into ½-inch cubes; spread in a shallow pan. Dry cubes in a 300-degree oven for 30 minutes or till crisp, turning several times. Store in a tightly covered container in the refrigerator.

CHEESE-MARINATED ONIONS

Super! Use either as a salad ingredient or as an accompaniment to barbecued meat

    4 medium onions
    ¾ cup (3 ounces) blue cheese, crumbled
    ½ cup salad oil
    2 tablespoons lemon juice
    1 teaspoon salt
      Dash pepper
      Dash paprika

Peel and thinly slice onions. Separate into rings (makes about 1 quart) and place in a deep bowl.

Combine blue cheese, salad oil, lemon juice, salt, pepper and paprika in a jar with a tight-fitting lid. Cover and shake vigorously to blend ingredients.

Pour over onion rings; mix well. Cover bowl and chill thoroughly, at least 4 hours, stirring occasionally. Serve as a salad ingredient or meat condiment. Makes 3 cups.

MARINATED TOMATOES

A summertime delight! Make this when garden tomatoes are plentiful and save the dressing. You'll be asked for an encore — soon!

    6 large firm ripe tomatoes
      Salt and pepper
    3 green onions with tops, sliced or ½ cup chopped
      onion
    2 tablespoons finely chopped fresh basil (see note)
    ¾ cup salad oil
    ¼ cup wine or cider vinegar
    1 clove garlic, peeled and minced
    1 teaspoon salt
    ½ teaspoon sugar
    ¼ teaspoon pepper
    1 teaspoon Worcestershire sauce

In a serving dish arrange tomato slices attractively in layers; sprinkle each layer with salt, pepper, onion and basil.

In a jar with a tight-fitting lid combine salad oil, vinegar, garlic, salt, sugar, pepper and Worcestershire sauce. Cover and shake well. (Or, combine marinade ingredients in a glass bowl and beat with a rotary beater.)

Pour mixture over tomato slices. Cover. Chill thoroughly before serving. Makes 6 servings.

Note:

2 teaspoons dried basil, crushed may be substituted for fresh basil.

MARY'S MARINATED VEGETABLE SALAD

A wonderful salad to serve when lettuce and other greens are expensive and of poor quality. The fresh vegetables give a marvelous contrast to the soft texture of the canned ingredients. For fewer servings, use 8-ounce cans of green beans and peas; halve remaining ingredients.

1 16-ounce can French-style green beans, drained
1 16-ounce can sweet green peas, drained
1 medium onion, thinly sliced and separated into rings
1 medium carrot, peeled and diced
1 cup diced celery
½ cup diced green pepper
1 2-ounce jar pimiento, chopped
¾ cup vinegar
½ cup salad oil
½ cup sugar
½ teaspoon salt

In mixing bowl combine green beans, peas, onion rings, carrot, celery, green pepper and pimiento.

In a jar with a tight-fitting lid combine vinegar, salad oil, sugar and salt; cover and shake to dissolve sugar and salt. Pour marinade over vegetables; stir gently to coat. Cover and refrigerate for 24 hours, stirring several times. Drain off dressing before serving. Garnish with carrot curls, if desired. Makes 6 servings.

SAUERKRAUT SALAD

Prepare this tangy salad today; serve it tomorrow! To please timid palates, you may want to rinse and then drain the sauerkraut.

1 2-pound package or 2 16-ounce cans sauerkraut,
  drained
1 cup chopped celery
1 cup chopped green pepper
1 cup chopped onion
1 cup shredded carrot
1 2-ounce jar pimiento, drained and chopped
½ cup sugar
½ cup vinegar
¼ cup salad oil

In mixing bowl combine sauerkraut, celery, green pepper, onion, carrot and pimiento.

In a jar with a tight-fitting lid combine sugar, vinegar and oil; cover and shake well. Pour over sauerkraut mixture; toss. Cover and chill for at least 8 hours. Stir occasionally. If desired, drain off dressing before serving. Makes 6 to 8 servings.

24-HOUR CABBAGE SALAD

Terrific! A wonderful accompaniment to most foods.

2½ to 3 pound cabbage
1 large onion, peeled and chopped
1 cup vinegar
¾ cup salad oil
¾ cup sugar
1 teaspoon salt

Remove outer wilted leaves from cabbage; cut into quarters and remove center core. Wash and drain. Chop or shred enough to make about 10 cups. Place cabbage and onion in a large bowl.

In small saucepan combine vinegar, salad oil, sugar and salt. Bring mixture to a boil and boil gently for 1 minute. Pour hot "syrup" over cabbage mixture; mix well. DO NOT MOVE for 1½ hours.

Stir again. Cover and refrigerate for 24 hours. Drain off dressing before serving. Makes 8 to 10 servings.

SPINACH SALAD

A recipe from a Keystone State home economist with Maine roots! You'll have extra dressing, but it will be ready for your next salad.

1 10-ounce package fresh spinach
½ medium head lettuce
4 hard-cooked eggs
½ pound bacon (10 strips)
Dressing (recipe follows)

Wash spinach, discarding tough stems; dry well. Wash lettuce and pat dry. Tear greens into large bite-size pieces. Chill. Peel and chop eggs. Store, covered, in the refrigerator. Cut bacon into ¼-inch pieces. Fry crisp and drain.

When ready to serve, combine salad greens, chopped eggs and bacon bits in a large wooden bowl; toss lightly. Sprinkle Dressing over salad and toss to evenly coat greens. Makes 8 to 10 servings.

Dressing

⅓ cup sugar
⅓ cup vinegar
1 cup salad oil
1 teaspoon celery salt
1 teaspoon garlic salt
1 teaspoon salt

Combine sugar, vinegar, salad oil and seasonings in blender container. Cover and blend till smooth.

(Or, combine all ingredients in a jar with a tight-fitting lid. Cover and shake vigorously to blend.)

Store in the refrigerator. Shake well before using. Makes 1½ cups.

WILTED SPINACH SALAD

A recipe from the heart of Amish Country! As a side-dish or salad, it's a delicious way to serve this perennial plant.

1 10-ounce package fresh spinach
4 green onions with tops, sliced or 1 small onion,
    peeled and chopped
    Pepper
5 or 6 strips bacon, diced
2 tablespoons vinegar
1 tablespoon lemon juice
1 teaspoon sugar
½ teaspoon salt
1 hard-cooked egg, peeled and coarsely chopped

Wash spinach, discarding stems. Pat dry and tear into large bite-size pieces to make about 6 cups.

Place spinach in a large bowl; add onion. Sprinkle with freshly ground pepper. Cover and refrigerate till thoroughly chilled.

At serving time, cook bacon in a deep skillet till crisp. Slowly stir in vinegar, lemon juice, sugar and salt. Add spinach and onion mixture; toss till leaves are coated and slightly wilted but not cooked, 1 to 2 minutes. Sprinkle with chopped egg. Serve immediately. Makes 4 servings.

Variation:

Wilted Dandelion Salad

Prepare recipe following directions for Wilted Spinach Salad except — substitute dandelion greens for spinach.

To crisp salad greens, trim and rinse greens in several waters; drain well. Wrap loosely in a clean kitchen towel or paper toweling and refrigerate in a plastic bag for at least 1 hour. Tear greens into bite-size pieces.

BLUEBERRY SALAD MOLD

Blueberries and fluffy cream cheese layered in gelatin make this picture-pretty . . . and good to eat!

1 3-ounce package black raspberry-flavored gelatin
1 cup boiling water
1 cup orange juice
1 cup fresh or frozen blueberries
1 8-ounce package cream cheese, softened
½ cup chopped nuts

In medium bowl combine gelatin and boiling water; stir till gelatin dissolves. Mix in orange juice. Chill in refrigerator until slightly thickened.

Remove half of slightly thickened gelatin to another bowl; let stand at room temperature. To the remaining gelatin, fold in blueberries. Pour into a wet 4-cup ring mold. Chill until set, but not firm.

Meanwhile, whip reserved gelatin until light and fluffy. Add cream cheese; beat until smooth. Stir in nuts.

Spread cream cheese mixture over blueberry layer. Chill till firm, at least 3 hours. Unmold. Serve on crisp lettuce with a dollop of mayonnaise, if desired. Makes 6 servings.

COTTAGE CRANBERRY SALAD

This "yummy cranberry salad" isn't just for holidays! It's so quick and easy you'll want to serve it anytime with poultry or pork.

1 3-ounce package cherry- or raspberry-flavored gelatin
1 cup boiling water
3 tablespoons orange juice
1 16-ounce can whole cranberry sauce (1¾ cups)
1½ cups small-curd cottage cheese
¼ cup whipping cream, whipped
½ cup chopped nuts

In medium bowl dissolve gelatin in boiling water. Add orange juice and cranberry sauce; stir till sauce melts. Pour mixture into a wet, shallow 1½-quart baking dish. Chill until set but not firm.

In medium bowl beat cottage cheese with electric beater till smooth. (Or, put through a sieve.) Fold in whipped cream and nuts. Spoon mixture evenly over cranberry layer. Chill till firm, at least 2 hours. Serve on crisp lettuce with a dollop of mayonnaise, if desired. Makes 6 to 8 servings.

MANDARIN ORANGE MOLD

A team of gelatin, orange sherbet and whipped cream makes an impressive mold for either a light, refreshing salad or a cool dessert.

   1 6-ounce package lemon-flavored gelatin
   1 cup boiling water
   1 pint orange sherbet
   1 11-ounce can mandarin orange segments in light
     syrup
   ½ cup whipping cream, whipped

In a large bowl dissolve gelatin in boiling water; mix well. Gradually blend in orange sherbet, stirring till melted and smooth.

Stir in undrained orange segments. Fold in whipped cream; blend thoroughly. Pour into a wet 5-cup mold. Chill till firm, at least 3 hours. Unmold. Makes 5 cups or 8 to 10 servings.

To chill a gelatin mold "till set, but not firm" means it appears set but is sticky to the touch.

To chill a gelatin mold "till firm" means that the gelatin does not move when tilted in the mold.

MUSTARD RING

From a good family cook comes this tangy mold to accompany your holiday ham.

¾ cup sugar
1 envelope (1 tablespoon) unflavored gelatin
1½ tablespoons dry mustard
½ teaspoon turmeric
¼ teaspoon salt
4 eggs, beaten
1 cup water
½ cup cider vinegar
1 cup whipping cream

In small bowl thoroughly mix sugar and gelatin; blend in mustard, turmeric and salt.

In top of double boiler combine beaten eggs, water and vinegar. Add sugar mixture. Cook, stirring constantly, over hot water till slightly thickened. Chill till thick.

In small mixer bowl beat chilled cream until soft peaks form. Fold into gelatin mixture. Pour into a wet 6-cup ring mold. Chill till firm. Unmold. Makes 4½ cups or 8 to 10 servings.

PINEAPPLE-CARROT SALAD

"My favorite," volunteers the cook sharing this simple, but attractive molded salad.

1 3-ounce package lemon-flavored gelatin
1 cup boiling water
1 tablespoon packed brown sugar
1 8-ounce can crushed pineapple in juice
1 cup coarsely grated carrot (2 medium)

In medium bowl dissolve gelatin in boiling water. Add brown sugar; stir to dissolve. Stir in undrained pineapple. Add carrots and pour into wet 3- or 4-cup mold. Chill until firm, about 3 hours. Unmold. Garnish, if desired. Makes 4 to 6 servings.

ROSINE'S BEET SALAD

A colorful salad to serve either as a relish to accompany meat or as an appetizer.

5 medium fresh beets (see note)
1 3-ounce package lemon-flavored gelatin
¼ teaspoon salt
3 tablespoons vinegar
1 tablespoon prepared horseradish
2 teaspoons grated onion
¾ cup diced celery

Wash beets. Cook, covered, in boiling salted water for 35 to 40 minutes or till tender. Drain, reserving liquid. Peel and dice beets to make 1½ cups; set aside.

Add water to reserved beet liquid to make 1¾ cups; bring to a boil. Add gelatin and salt, stirring until gelatin dissolves. Add vinegar, horseradish and onion. Chill until mixture is slightly thickened, about 1½ to 2 hours.

Fold in diced beets and celery. Place in a wet 4-cup mold. Chill till firm. Unmold. Serve on crisp lettuce leaves with a dollop of mayonnaise. Makes 8 servings.

Note:
One 16-ounce can whole or sliced beets may be substituted for fresh beets. Drain, reserving liquid; add water to make 1¾ cups liquid. Dice beets.

SUMMER GREEN SALAD

This light and refreshing salad adds a festive touch to your Easter dinner.

1 3-ounce package lime-flavored gelatin
1½ cups boiling water
½ cup miniature or diced marshmallows
1 8-ounce package cream cheese, softened
⅓ cup mayonnaise
⅔ cup whipped cream
1 8-ounce can crushed pineapple, undrained

In medium bowl dissolve gelatin in boiling water. Stir marshmallows into mixture; allow to soften and mix well. Add cream cheese; beat until blended. Chill until slightly thickened.

Blend mayonnaise, whipped cream and crushed pineapple into gelatin. Spoon into a wet 4-cup ring mold or individual molds. Chill until firm. Unmold. Serve with a dollop of sour cream, if desired. Makes about 4 cups, or 6 to 8 servings.

SWEET APPLE RING SALAD

A country cook shares this tangy salad consisting of apples, grapes and pineapple.

1¾ cups cider or apple juice
1 3-ounce package pineapple- or lemon-flavored
  gelatin
½ teaspoon salt
1 8-ounce can crushed pineapple or pineapple tidbits
1½ cups diced unpared tart apple (2 small)
1 cup seedless grapes
¾ cup miniature or diced marshmallows

Bring cider or apple juice to a boil. Add gelatin and salt, stirring till dissolved. Add undrained pineapple. Chill until mixture is slightly thickened, about 1½ to 2 hours.

Add diced apple, grapes and marshmallows. Pour mixture into a wet 5-cup ring mold. Chill till firm. Unmold onto crisp lettuce. Makes 8 servings.

CRANBERRY ORANGE RELISH

To accompany your holiday turkey!

4 cups (1 pound) fresh or frozen cranberries
2 medium seedless oranges
1 cup sugar

Pick over and wash cranberries. Wash and peel oranges, discarding white inner part of peel. Put cranberries, orange peel and orange pulp through food grinder using fine blade; reserve juices and add to pulp.

In a bowl combine prepared cranberries and oranges with sugar; mix well. Let stand several hours before serving to develop flavors. Store in an airtight container in refrigerator. Makes 4 cups.

ELEGANT CRANBERRIES

Patience, please! Cooked in this manner, fresh cranberries remain whole and are considered unusually glamorous.

4 cups firm fresh cranberries
1 cup sugar
1 cup water
½ teaspoon salt
¼ teaspoon soda

Carefully pick over cranberries, discarding any soft berries; rinse. In a large saucepan combine sugar, water, salt and soda. Bring to a boil; add cranberries and return to a gentle boil. Reduce heat. Cover and simmer without removing cover for 15 minutes.

Remove pan from heat. DO NOT lift cover until cranberries have cooled to room temperature, at least 2 hours. Makes 3½ cups.

Store fresh berries, cherries and grapes in the refrigerator. DO NOT wash them until ready to use and DO NOT remove caps or stems until after washing!

To prevent bananas, peaches, apples and pears from darkening after being cut, dip in orange, lemon or grapefruit juice.

FROZEN FRUIT SALAD

A traditional Thanksgiving salad which adorns our family table. Any remaining salad may be returned to the freezer.

1 8-ounce package cream cheese, softened
½ cup mayonnaise or salad dressing
¼ teaspoon salt
1 8-ounce can crushed pineapple, drained
½ cup drained maraschino cherries, quartered
½ cup chopped nuts
3 firm bananas, cubed
1 cup whipping cream
2 tablespoons maraschino cherry juice (optional)

In large mixing bowl combine cream cheese, mayonnaise or salad dressing and salt; beat until smooth and creamy. Stir in drained pineapple, maraschino cherries, nuts and bananas.

In small mixer bowl beat chilled cream until soft peaks form. Fold whipped cream into fruit mixture. Tint with maraschino cherry juice, if desired.

Pour into a wet 9x5x3-inch loaf pan. Cover with foil or plastic. Freeze till firm, about 6 hours. To serve, let salad stand at room temperature for 10 minutes. Unmold onto serving tray. Cut into slices. Makes 10 to 12 servings.

MELON BOWL

Musts for celebrating the Fourth of July: a parade, fireworks and a melon bowl!

1 whole watermelon
Assorted fruits such as:
   Melon balls
   Strawberries
   Blueberries
   Sliced bananas
   Mandarin orange sections
   Seedless grapes
   Pineapple chunks

Cut watermelon lengthwise, removing top third. Scoop out seeds and pulp, leaving a thin rim of pink flesh for lining the bowl. Reserve watermelon fruit to add to other fruits in bowl. Using a sharp knife, cut points for a zigzag effect on top of bowl.

Fill bowl with ripe, seasonal fruits and berries or with a combination of fresh juice, if desired. Chill thoroughly before serving. Garnish with sprigs of fresh mint.

To unmold a gelatin salad, dip mold just to the rim in warm water for 10 seconds. Lift from water and run knife tip around top of gelatin. Place a chilled, moistened plate over mold and shake gently to loosen gelatin. Invert mold and plate together; carefully remove mold.

AUNT PHYL'S SALAD DRESSING

Like many recipes this one reached my kitchen in a roundabout way. The column cook sharing it said her husband requested the recipe after sampling our uncle's "brown bagged" shrimp salad. Try it with any seafood or chicken.

½ cup sugar
2½ tablespoons all-purpose flour
2 teaspoons dry mustard
1 teaspoon salt
2 eggs
1 cup milk
⅔ cup vinegar
1 pint (2 cups) dairy sour cream

In top of double boiler combine sugar, flour, dry mustard and salt; blend till smooth. Add eggs; mix well. Stir in milk, then vinegar.

Cook over simmering water until mixture comes to a boil and thickens; stir frequently. Remove from heat. Cool. Blend in sour cream. Store in a tightly-covered jar in the refrigerator. Makes 1 quart.

CUCUMBER DRESSING

My favorite when the garden cucumbers are waiting to be picked.

2 cups mayonnaise or salad dressing
1 medium cucumber, pared and quartered
1 small onion, peeled and halved
1 clove garlic, peeled
2 tablespoons lemon juice
1 teaspoon salt
Dash Worcestershire sauce

Combine all ingredients in blender container. Cover and process until smooth. Store tightly covered in refrigerator. Mix again just before serving. Serve over tossed salad or chilled vegetables. Makes 3 cups.

FRENCH DRESSING

An easy-to-make dressing for your antipasto or salad greens. Since the yield is ample — 1 quart — I generally reduce the recipe by half. Keep this dressing in mind when you have a ½ can of tomato soup on hand.

1 10¾-ounce can condensed tomato soup
1½ cups salad oil
¾ cup vinegar
½ cup sugar
2 teaspoons dry mustard
1 teaspoon salt
½ teaspoon pepper
2 teaspoons Worcestershire sauce
2 cloves garlic, peeled

In a 1-quart screw-top jar combine tomato soup, salad oil, vinegar, sugar, dry mustard, salt, pepper, Worcestershire sauce and garlic. Cover and shake well. Refrigerate for 24 hours to blend flavors. Remove garlic. Shake again just before serving. Pour over individual servings of antipasto or salad greens. Makes 1 quart.

FRUIT SALAD DRESSING

To accompany fruit salads — either fresh or molded.

½ cup whipped cream
½ cup mayonnaise or salad dressing
1 tablespoon confectioners' sugar
½ teaspoon grated lemon or orange peel

In small bowl fold whipped cream into mayonnaise or salad dressing. Add confectioners' sugar and lemon or orange peel; blend carefully. Chill. Serve with fruit salads. Makes 1 cup.

For making salad dressings, use a good quality vegetable oil which has been treated — "winterized" — to prevent clouding or solidifying at ordinary refrigerator temperatures.

ITALIAN-STYLE DRESSING

An interesting blend of seasonings to serve over salad greens or to marinate vegetables.

¼ cup vinegar
1 cup salad oil
1 tablespoon snipped fresh parsley
1 teaspoon salt
1 teaspoon sugar
1 teaspoon dry mustard
½ teaspoon dried oregano, crushed
½ teaspoon paprika
¼ teaspoon pepper
1 clove garlic, peeled and minced or pressed

Pour vinegar into a glass mixing bowl; gradually add oil beating vigorously with a wire whip. Add remaining ingredients and beat well to blend thoroughly.

(Or, combine all ingredients in a jar with a tight-fitting lid. Cover. Shake vigorously to blend.)
Cover and let stand at least 2 hours to blend flavors. Store in the refrigerator. Shake well before using. Makes 1½ cups.

LOW-CALORIE HERBAL DRESSING

A from-scratch dressing for the weight-conscious without sacrificing good flavor. The recipe is from a cook with an eye on calorie-control.

¾ cup vegetable cocktail or tomato juice
¼ cup cider vinegar
¼ cup salad oil
1 tablespoon prepared mustard
1 tablespoon lemon juice
1 tablespoon snipped fresh parsley
1 tablespoon chopped chives
½ teaspoon dried basil, crushed
⅛ teaspoon cayenne pepper
1 clove garlic, peeled and minced or pressed

In a jar with a tight-fitting lid combine all ingredients. Cover and shake vigorously. Store in the refrigerator. Shake again just before serving. Serve with tossed salads. Makes 1⅓ cups.

Variation:

Blue Cheese Dressing

Follow recipe for Low-Calorie Herbal Dressing except — add ¼ cup crumbled blue cheese to the ingredients.

To substitute fresh herbs for dried herbs, use 1 tablespoon fresh for 1 teaspoon dried.

PERSIAN DRESSING

Every neighborhood has a handful of cooks who are noted for their culinary expertise; ours is no exception. Persian Dressing is from one of them. The recipe makes 1 quart but is easily halved.

    2 cups salad oil
    ⅔ cup sugar
    ⅔ cup catsup
    ½ cup vinegar
    2 tablespoons prepared horseradish
    1 teaspoon salt
    1 small onion, peeled and quartered

In blender container combine salad oil, sugar, catsup, vinegar, horseradish, salt and onion. Cover and blend till smooth. Chill. Mix again just before serving. Makes 1 quart.

Keep mayonnaise and salad dressings made with eggs under refrigeration once the jar has been opened.

RUSSIAN DRESSING

The dressing preferred by many salad lovers for hearts of lettuce.

    ¾ cup mayonnaise or salad dressing
    ¼ cup chili sauce
    2 tablespoons sweet pickle relish, well drained
    2 tablespoons lemon juice
    2 tablespoons minced green onion

In a small bowl combine mayonnaise, chili sauce, pickle relish and lemon juice; mix well. Sprinkle green onion atop. Cover and chill thoroughly. Serve with tossed salads. Makes 1 cup.

VINAIGRETTE DRESSING

Just a simple oil and vinegar dressing with a classy name. So easy and so good you may never buy another bottled dressing.

¼ **cup vinegar**
¾ **cup salad oil**
2 **tablespoons lemon juice**
2 **tablespoons Dijon-style mustard**
1 **teaspoon salt**
¼ **teaspoon pepper**
¼ **teaspoon sugar**

Pour vinegar into a mixing bowl; gradually add oil, beating vigorously with a wire whip. Add remaining ingredients and beat till smooth.

(Or, combine all ingredients in a jar with a tight-fitting lid. Cover and shake vigorously to blend.)

Chill. Shake well before using. Serve over tossed salad or chilled vegetables. Makes 1¼ cups.

Cooking Notes

Chapter 8

Baking is not a lost art! Despite the popularity of packaged mixes and brown-and-serve breads, today's cook has discovered that one of the pleasures of cooking comes from making bread . . . both for personal satisfaction and bringing joy to others.

This warm and homey activity gives the cook a sense of creativity and contentment. The rewards of bread-making come later . . . when the family discovers that homemade bread provides them with some healthy, hearty eating and with the assurance that this endeavor improves the nutritional quality of their diet.

In earlier days families of pioneer background ate hot bread at every meal. It was the staff of life. Although its role is of less significance in my own family's diet, our daily bread is quite likely to be a homemade product. Mouth-watering family favorites, fresh from the oven, add a warm and loving touch to any meal.

The term "bread" refers to both quick and yeast breads. The difference between the two, however, is the leavening agent. Quick breads, which are relatively simple to make and perfect for spur-of-the-moment baking sprees, are leavened with baking powder, soda, eggs and steam.

In this chapter you will find a collection of back-to-the-basics for both quick and yeast breads: Ginger Buns, Lemon Loaf and Anadama Bread to name a few. Lovers of homemade breads will appreciate the good flavors and interesting textures. To all of them — ENJOY!

Quick Breads
& Yeast Breads

Continued

BAKING POWDER BISCUITS

Reminiscent of earlier days — the daily bread that nurtured this cook and nine siblings!

2 cups all-purpose flour
3 teaspoons baking powder
1 teaspoon salt
⅓ cup shortening
⅔ cup milk

Sift together flour, baking powder and salt into a large mixing bowl. Using a pastry blender cut in shortening till mixture is consistency of coarse cornmeal. Add enough of the milk to make a soft, but not sticky dough.

Turn out onto a lightly floured surface. Knead very lightly. Roll or pat out to a ¾-inch thickness; cut into rounds with a 2-inch round cutter. Place, 1 inch apart, on a lightly greased baking sheet. Dab tops with a small amount of butter (⅛ teaspoon), if desired.

Bake in a 450-degree oven for 12 to 15 minutes or till golden brown. Serve hot. Makes 14 biscuits.

POPOVERS

One of the most dramatic — and easiest — breads you'll ever bake. Guests ooh-and-aah!

2 eggs
1 cup milk
2 tablespoons butter or margarine, melted
1 cup all-purpose flour
½ teaspoon salt
2 tablespoons cooking oil

In medium bowl beat eggs with a rotary beater till frothy; beat in milk and melted butter or margarine. Add flour and salt; beat just till mixture is smooth. DO NOT OVERBEAT!

Put 1 teaspoon oil in each of 6 custard cups; tilt cups to spread sides evenly with oil. Fill ½ full with batter. Place cups on a shallow baking sheet.

Bake in a 425-degree oven for 30 to 35 minutes or till very brown and firm. DO NOT open oven door until 30 minutes have passed. Cut 2 small slits in top of each popover to release steam. Return to oven for 5 minutes. Use a sharp knife to loosen around edges of popovers. Serve immediately with plenty of butter and jam. Makes 6 large popovers.

Variation:

Yorkshire Pudding

Prepare recipe for Popovers except — place 2 tablespoons hot pan drippings from beef rib roast in a 10x6x1½-inch baking dish. Pour batter into pan and bake at 425 degrees for 35 to 45 minutes. Serve with roast beef.

APPLE CRUNCH MUFFINS

A muffin with a crunchy topping and a country kitchen taste.

1 egg
½ cup milk
¼ cup cooking oil
1½ cups all-purpose flour
½ cup sugar
2 teaspoons baking powder
½ teaspoon salt
½ teaspoon cinnamon
1 cup grated unpared tart apple
⅓ cup packed brown sugar
⅓ cup chopped nuts
½ teaspoon cinnamon

In small bowl beat egg lightly. Beat in milk and cooking oil. Set aside.

In large mixing bowl sift together flour, sugar, baking powder, salt and cinnamon. Stir grated apple into dry ingredients. Make a well in center of mixture; add egg mixture. Stir just to combine the two mixtures.

Spoon batter into greased muffin cups, filling each ⅔ full. Combine brown sugar, nuts and cinnamon. Sprinkle evenly over tops of muffins. Bake in a 400-degree oven for 20 to 25 minutes or till golden. Makes 12 muffins.

Self-rising flour, which contains leavening and salt, may be substituted for all-purpose flour in quick bread recipes. However, eliminate any baking powder, soda and salt called for in the recipe. DO NOT use in yeast bakings.

APPLESAUCE OATMEAL MUFFINS

Applesauce, rolled oats, raisins and nuts pack this muffin with flavor and nutrition.

½ cup butter or margarine, softened (1 stick)
¾ cup packed brown sugar
1 egg
¾ cup unsweetened applesauce
1 cup all-purpose flour
1 teaspoon baking powder
½ teaspoon cinnamon
¼ teaspoon soda
¼ teaspoon salt
1 cup quick-cooking rolled oats
½ cup seedless raisins
½ cup chopped nuts

In medium bowl cream butter or margarine with brown sugar till light and fluffy. Add egg; beat well. Stir in applesauce. Set aside.

In large mixing bowl sift together flour, baking powder, cinnamon, soda and salt; stir in rolled oats, raisins and nuts. Make a well in center of dry ingredients; add applesauce mixture. Stir just to blend.

Spoon batter in greased muffin cups, filling ⅔ full. Bake in a 375-degree oven for 20 to 25 minutes or till nicely browned. Turn out of pan to cool. Sift confectioners' sugar over tops, if desired. Serve warm. Makes 12 to 15 medium muffins.

Store baking powder, soda and cream of tartar in tightly covered containers in a cool, dry place.

❖ ❖ ❖ ❖ ❖ ❖ ❖ ❖

To test baking powder for potency, place 1 teaspoon baking powder in ½ cup hot water. Unless it bubbles enthusiastically, the baking powder should be replaced.

BLUEBERRY STREUSEL PUFFS

*A former Yankee sent this one for the folks back home to enjoy —
and we do! You, too, will sing praises for this Down East delight!*

  ¼ cup butter or margarine, softened
  ½ cup sugar
  1 egg
  1 teaspoon vanilla
1½ cups all-purpose flour
  2 teaspoons baking powder
  ½ teaspoon salt
  ½ cup milk
  1 cup fresh or frozen blueberries
  2 tablespoons butter or margarine
  2 tablespoons packed brown sugar
  ¼ teaspoon cinnamon
  ¼ cup chopped nuts

In large mixing bowl cream ¼ cup butter or margarine with
sugar until fluffy; beat in egg and vanilla.

Sift together flour, baking powder and salt; add flour mixture
and milk alternately to creamed mixture. Fold in blueberries.
Place batter in 12 well-greased muffin cups.

Make streusel by melting 2 tablespoons butter or margarine in
small saucepan; remove from heat. Stir in brown sugar, cinnamon
and nuts. Sprinkle mixture over batter. Bake in a 400-degree oven
for 25 minutes or till golden brown. Remove puffs from pan to
cooling rack. Makes 1 dozen puffs, 2½-inches in diameter.

CORN BREAD MUFFINS OR STICKS

*An old reliable tested over and over . . . and a MUST with pea
soup! Back on the farm, it's spread in a pan and called "Johnny
Cake."*

  2 eggs
  1 cup buttermilk
  ½ cup cooking oil
  1 cup all-purpose flour

 2 tablespoons sugar
 1 teaspoon baking powder
 1 teaspoon salt
 ½ teaspoon soda
 ¾ cup yellow cornmeal

In small bowl beat eggs lightly; stir in buttermilk and cooking oil. Set aside.

In large mixing bowl sift together flour, sugar, baking powder, salt and soda; stir in cornmeal. Make a well in center of dry ingredients; add egg mixture. Beat till fairly smooth.

Pour batter into greased muffin cups or hot well-greased corn stick pans, filling ⅔ full. Bake in a 400-degree oven for 20 to 25 minutes for muffins or 12 to 15 minutes for corn sticks. Remove from pans immediately. Serve hot with plenty of butter. Makes 1 dozen muffins or 14 corn sticks.

Variation:

Cornbread

Prepare recipe for Corn Bread Muffins except — spread the batter in a greased 9-inch square baking pan. Bake at 400 degrees for about 25 minutes or till golden brown.

CRANBERRY MUFFINS

It's the BEST of several recipes and BEST right out of the oven. A treat during the cranberry season!

 1½ cups coarsely chopped cranberries
 ¼ cup sugar
 1 teaspoon grated orange peel
 1 egg
 ½ cup milk
 ¼ cup cooking oil
 1½ cups all-purpose flour
 ¼ cup sugar
 2 teaspoons baking powder
 ½ teaspoon salt

In medium bowl combine cranberries, ¼ cup sugar and orange peel. Set aside.

In mixing bowl beat egg lightly. Beat in milk and cooking oil. Sift together flour, ¼ cup sugar, baking powder and salt. Add to egg mixture, stirring just to moisten dry ingredients. Fold in cranberry mixture. Spoon batter evenly into greased muffin cups, filling each ²/₃ full.

Bake in a 400-degree oven for 20 to 25 minutes or until muffins are golden. Remove from pan to wire rack. Serve hot with plenty of butter. Makes 1 dozen.

FIVE FRUIT MUFFINS

A novel idea from a Midwestern food editor . . . an all-season muffin filled with fruits. No fruit cocktail? Use 1½ cups drained leftover fruits and ½ to ⅔ cup of their syrup.

1 16-ounce can fruit cocktail
2 eggs
¼ cup butter or margarine, melted
1 tablespoon grated lemon peel
1¾ cups all-purpose flour
⅓ cup sugar
2 teaspoons baking powder
½ teaspoon salt
½ teaspoon nutmeg
¼ cup chopped nuts

Drain fruit cocktail, reserving syrup. Measure syrup and add water, if necessary, to make ⅔ cup liquid. Set aside.

In small bowl beat eggs lightly. Stir in reserved fruit liquid, melted butter or margarine and lemon peel.

In large mixing bowl sift together flour, sugar, baking powder, salt and nutmeg. Make a well in center of dry ingredients; add egg mixture. Stir only until dry ingredients are moistened. Fold in drained fruit and nuts. Fill greased muffin cups ⅔ full. Sprinkle tops with granulated sugar, if desired.

Bake in a 400-degree oven for 20 to 25 minutes or till golden. Allow muffins to remain in pans for 1 minute before removing to wire rack. Serve warm. Makes 1 dozen.

GINGER BUNS

Super! An old-fashioned recipe from a Grange friend.

1 egg
⅓ cup cooking oil
½ cup molasses
¼ cup sugar
1½ cups all-purpose flour
1 teaspoon soda
1 teaspoon salt
½ teaspoon cinnamon
½ teaspoon cloves
½ teaspoon ginger
½ cup boiling water

In mixing bowl beat egg. Add cooking oil, molasses and sugar; mix well.

Sift together flour, soda, salt, cinnamon, cloves and ginger. Add dry ingredients to egg mixture; mix thoroughly. Stir in boiling water. Spoon batter into greased muffin cups, filling each about ⅔ full. Bake in a 350-degree oven for 20 to 25 minutes or till nicely browned. Makes 1 dozen buns.

GRAHAM CRACKER MUFFINS

This recipe for a delectable, yet unusual muffin is printed in the memory of a late friend, lovingly referred to as my "muffin man."

1 egg
¾ cup milk
2 tablespoons butter or margarine, melted
1 cup all-purpose flour
⅓ cup sugar
3 teaspoons baking powder
½ teaspoon salt
¾ cup fine graham cracker crumbs

In small bowl beat egg lightly; beat in milk and melted butter or margarine. Set aside.

In large mixing bowl sift together flour, sugar, baking powder and salt. Stir in graham cracker crumbs. Make a well in center of dry ingredients; add liquid mixture. Stir lightly to combine mixtures.

Spoon batter into greased muffin cups, filling ⅔ full. Bake in a 375-degree oven for 20 to 25 minutes or till golden brown. Remove from pan; serve warm. Makes 1 dozen.

Diet margarine has less fat than regular margarine. DO NOT use as a substitute in baking.

❖ ❖ ❖ ❖ ❖ ❖ ❖ ❖ ❖

To avoid misshapen muffins, DO NOT overfill muffin cups. Fill only ⅔ full.

NORWEGIAN PRUNE MUFFINS

Says the cook sharing this recipe, "Whenever I want to impress my guests, I serve this muffin." Served with a dollop of whipped cream, Norwegian Prune Muffins makes a delightful dessert!

        ¼ cup butter or margarine, softened
        ½ cup packed brown sugar
        1 egg
        1½ cups all-purpose flour
        2 teaspoons baking powder
        ¼ teaspoon salt
        ⅛ teaspoon nutmeg
        ¾ cup milk
        ¾ cup chopped cooked prunes

In large mixing bowl cream butter or margarine and brown sugar till light. Add egg and beat well.

Sift together flour, baking powder, salt and nutmeg. Add flour mixture and milk alternately to creamed mixture. Beat well after each addition. Fold in prunes.

Fill greased muffin cups ⅔ full. Sprinkle tops with granulated sugar, if desired. Bake in a 400-degree oven for 20 to 25 minutes or till light brown. Remove muffins from pans to wire rack. Serve warm. Makes 12 large muffins.

QUANTITY REFRIGERATOR MUFFINS

A recipe developed so you can have fresh muffins everyday. The flavor is nostagically pleasing whether plain or dressed up with chopped dates, nuts or raisins.

> 2 cups whole bran cereal
> 4 large shredded wheat biscuits, crushed
> ½ cup boiling water
> 1 cup shortening
> 2 cups sugar
> 4 eggs
> 5 cups all-purpose flour
> 5 teaspoons soda
> 2 teaspoons salt
> ½ teaspoon baking powder
> 1 quart buttermilk

Combine cereals and boiling water. Set aside. In large mixing bowl cream shortening and sugar; beat in eggs. Stir in cereal mixture.

Sift together flour, soda, salt and baking powder. Add flour mixture and buttermilk alternately to creamed mixture; mix well.

To store: Place batter in a glass gallon jar. Cover and refrigerate up to a month. Bake as needed. If desired, add fruits and nuts before baking.

To bake: Fill greased muffin cups ⅔ full. Bake in a 400-degree oven for 20 to 25 minutes or till golden brown.

Loosen muffins with a metal spatula and then tip each muffin to one side in pan to cool slightly. Makes 4 to 5 dozen muffins.

SCOTCH OATMEAL MUFFINS

Buttermilk and rolled oats make a wholesome team and a delicately flavored muffin.

1 cup buttermilk
1 cup quick-cooking rolled oats
1 egg, beaten
⅓ cup packed brown sugar
⅓ cup cooking oil
1 cup all-purpose flour
1 teaspoon baking powder
½ teaspoon soda
½ teaspoon salt

In large mixing bowl combine buttermilk and rolled oats. Let soak for 15 minutes. Stir in beaten egg, brown sugar and cooking oil; mix well.

Sift together flour, baking powder, soda and salt; add to the rolled oats mixture. Stir only till blended.

Spoon batter into greased muffin cups, filling each ⅔ full. Bake in a 400-degree oven for 20 to 25 minutes or till golden brown. Serve hot. Makes 12 muffins.

STRAWBERRY-RHUBARB MUFFINS

Strawberry-and-rhubarb, a favorite combination for pies and sauce, also makes a delicious muffin. The recipe is from a food expert, friend and beloved instructor.

1 egg
¾ cup milk
⅓ cup cooking oil
1½ cups all-purpose flour
½ cup sugar
2½ teaspoons baking powder
½ teaspoon salt
¾ cup minced fresh rhubarb
½ cup sliced fresh strawberries (see note)

In small bowl beat egg lightly. Beat in milk and cooking oil. Set aside.

In large mixing bowl sift together flour, sugar, baking powder and salt. Make a well in center of dry ingredients; add egg mixture. Stir just till moistened. Fold minced rhubarb and strawberries into batter.

Fill greased muffin cups ⅔ full. Sprinkle tops with additional sugar. Bake in a 400-degree oven for 20 to 25 minutes or till golden. Allow muffins to remain in pan for 1 to 2 minutes before removing to wire rack. Serve warm. Makes 1 dozen.

Note:
 Frozen strawberries may be substituted for fresh berries; drain well before adding to batter.

VERY BERRY-ANA BUNS

My children's favorite! Originally this recipe was created to make use of a handful of black raspberries grown in the "Back Forty" and a fully ripened banana in the fruit bowl. Black raspberries remain a seasonal choice, but frozen blueberries are substituted for year-round enjoyment. We like 'em baked in miniature muffin cups and right out of the oven!

 2 fully ripe medium bananas, cut-up
 1 egg
 ½ cup sugar
 ⅓ cup cooking oil
 1½ cups all-purpose flour
 2 teaspoons baking powder
 ½ teaspoon salt
 ¼ teaspoon soda
 1 cup fresh or frozen blueberries

In large mixing bowl mash bananas with a fork or masher. Add egg and beat well. Blend in sugar and cooking oil.

Sift together flour, baking powder, salt and soda. Add to banana mixture; stir just till moistened. Fold in blueberries.

Fill greased muffin cups ⅔ full. Bake in a 400-degree oven for 20 to 25 minutes or until golden brown. Remove from pan. Serve warm. Makes 12 to 15 muffins.

ANNIE'S BRAN-ANA BREAD

A small loaf that's big on goodness! The bran lends texture; bananas, natural sweetness.

>   3 fully ripe medium bananas, cut-up
>   1 egg
>   ¼ cup cooking oil
>   1 cup whole bran cereal
>   1½ cups all-purpose flour
>   ½ cup sugar
>   2½ teaspoons baking powder
>   ½ teaspoon soda
>   ½ teaspoon salt

In large mixing bowl mash bananas with fork or masher (should be about 1½ cups); add egg and beat well. Stir in cooking oil and bran.

Sift together flour, sugar, baking powder, soda and salt; add to banana mixture. Stir just till blended. Turn into greased 8x4x3-inch loaf pan. Bake in a 350-degree oven for 50 to 60 minutes or till wooden pick inserted near center comes out clean. Let cool in pan for 10 minutes. Turn out and cool on wire rack. Makes 1 loaf.

BISHOP'S COLONIAL BREAD

It's chocked full of nuts, cherries and dates — a wonderful tea bread from a wonderful baker!

>   1½ cups sifted all-purpose flour
>   1½ teaspoons baking powder
>   ¼ teaspoon salt
>   ⅔ cup semi-sweet chocolate morsels
>   1 cup finely snipped pitted dates
>   1 cup chopped nuts
>   1 cup chopped candied red cherries
>   3 eggs
>   1 cup sugar

In bowl sift together flour, baking powder and salt. Add chocolate morsels, dates, nuts and cherries, stirring to coat evenly.

In large mixer bowl, beat eggs till thick and lemon-colored. Add sugar; beat well. Fold in flour mixture, stirring only to moisten. Turn batter into greased 9x5x3-inch loaf pan.

Bake in a 325-degree oven for 60 to 65 minutes, or till tester comes out free of batter. Cool on wire rack for 10 minutes; remove from pan and cool completely. Wrap and store one day before slicing. Makes 16 slices.

To blend smoothly with other ingredients, use only fully-ripened banana.

DO NOT thaw frozen blueberries before adding to cake or bread batter as wet berries stain the batter.

BLUEBERRY BANANA LOAF

It's mouth-watering right out of the oven, but makes neater slices when allowed to set. Try it — soon!

⅓ **cup butter or margarine, softened**
⅔ **cup sugar**
2 **eggs**
1¾ **cups all-purpose flour**
2 **teaspoons baking powder**
½ **teaspoon salt**
¼ **teaspoon soda**
1 **cup mashed ripened banana (2 medium)**
1 **cup fresh or frozen blueberries**

In large mixing bowl cream butter or margarine and sugar until light and fluffy. Add eggs, one at a time, beating well after each addition.

Measure flour; set aside 2 tablespoons to coat berries. Sift together remaining flour, baking powder, salt and soda. Add flour mixture alternately with mashed banana to creamed mixture. Beat till smooth after each addition.

Use reserved 2 tablespoons flour to coat blueberries; carefully fold into batter. Turn into well-greased 9x5x3-inch loaf pan. Bake in a 350-degree oven for 50 minutes or till tester comes out free of batter. Remove from oven to wire rack. Allow to cool for 5 minutes; remove from pan. Cool. Makes 1 loaf.

GOLDEN THREAD LOAF

A Southern delight! Shredded gratings of raw sweet potato are scattered throughout the loaf to give the appearance of golden threads. Golden raisins are my choice for this quick bread; they enhance its good looks and taste.

1½ cups shredded raw sweet potato (see note)
½ cup chopped nuts
¼ cup golden raisins
1 tablespoon lemon juice
2 eggs
¼ cup cooking oil
¾ cup orange juice
1¾ cups all-purpose flour
1 cup sugar
1½ teaspoons baking powder
1 teaspoon salt
½ teaspoon soda
¼ teaspoon nutmeg

In medium bowl combine shredded sweet potato, nuts and raisins; sprinkle with lemon juice. Set aside.

In large mixing bowl beat eggs till light. Stir in cooking oil and orange juice.

Sift together flour, sugar, baking powder, salt, soda and nutmeg; add to egg mixture, stirring to moisten dry ingredients. Fold in sweet potato mixture. Turn batter into 2 greased and floured loaf pans, filling ⅔ full. Sprinkle top lightly with cinnamon-sugar, if desired.

Bake in a 350-degree oven for 35 to 40 minutes or until wooden pick inserted in center comes out clean. Cool in pan for 5 minutes. Turn out onto wire rack to cool completely. Freezes well. Makes 2 medium loaves.

Note:
>   1½ cups shredded raw carrot may be substituted for sweet potato.

GOVERNOR MILLIKEN'S WHOLE WHEAT BREAD

"An honest-to-goodness original" created for a politican who was very fond of dark bread. There is neither egg nor shortening in this bread.

>   **1 cup whole wheat flour**
>   **½ cup all-purpose flour**
>   **¼ cup sugar**
>   **1 teaspoon baking powder**
>   **1 teaspoon soda**
>   **½ teaspoon salt**
>   **⅓ cup raisins**
>   **1 cup buttermilk**
>   **¼ cup molasses**

In large mixing bowl sift together flours, sugar, baking powder, soda and salt; mix in any course bran remaining in sifter. Add raisins and toss to coat with flour mixture.

In small bowl combine buttermilk and molasses; add to sifted dry ingredients, stirring just to dampen flour mixture. Turn into well-greased 8x4x3-inch loaf pan.

Bake in a 375-degree oven for 35 to 40 minutes or till no batter remains on wooden pick inserted in center of loaf. Turn out onto wire rack to cool. Makes 1 loaf.

Variation:

Date-Honey Bread

Prepare as above except — substitute ⅓ cup snipped pitted dates and ¼ cup honey for raisins and molasses.

HARRIET'S CARROT BREAD

Colorful and flavorful! You may have to put it under lock and key if you want it to develop its full flavor.

> 2 eggs
> 1 cup sugar
> ¾ cup cooking oil
> 1 teaspoon vanilla
> 1½ cups all-purpose flour
> 1 teaspoon baking powder
> 1 teaspoon salt
> 1 teaspoon cinnamon
> ¾ teaspoon soda
> 1 cup shredded raw carrot
> ½ cup chopped nuts

In large mixing bowl beat eggs till light. Stir in sugar, cooking oil and vanilla; mix well.

Sift together flour, baking powder, salt, cinnamon and soda. Add to egg mixture; beat till smooth. Fold in carrot and nuts. Turn batter into greased and floured 9x5x3-inch loaf pan.

Bake in a 350-degree oven for 50 to 60 minutes or till wooden pick inserted in center of loaf comes out clean. Cool in pan for 5 minutes. Turn out onto wire rack. Makes 1 loaf.

KITTY'S APPLE BREAD

A delicious loaf made moist with any cooking apple. Let it develop its full flavor before slicing.

> ½ cup shortening
> 1 cup sugar
> 2 eggs
> 1½ tablespoons buttermilk or soured milk
> ½ teaspoon vanilla
> 2 cups all-purpose flour
> 1 teaspoon baking powder
> 1 teaspoon soda
> ¼ teaspoon salt
> 1 large shredded unpared tart apple (about 1 cup)

In a large bowl cream shortening and sugar till light. Add eggs, one at a time, beating well after each addition. Stir in buttermilk or soured milk and vanilla.

Sift together flour, baking powder, soda and salt. Add dry ingredients to creamed mixture, stirring just till smooth. Fold in shredded apple.

Turn into a greased and floured 9x5x3-inch loaf pan. Bake in a 350-degree oven for 50 to 60 minutes or till tester inserted in center comes out free of batter. Cool in pan for 5 minutes. Turn out and cool on wire rack. Flavor improves after 24 hours. Makes 1 loaf.

Variation:

Apple-Nut Bread

Prepare recipe for Kitty's Apple Bread except — add ½ cup coarsely chopped nuts with the shredded apple.

LEMON LOAF

A rich, moist and delicately flavored tea bread. A lemon-sugar mixture which is spooned onto the hot crust and allowed to set makes an eye-appealing glaze.

  6 tablespoons shortening
  1 cup sugar
    Grated peel of 1 lemon
  2 well-beaten eggs
  1½ cups all-purpose flour
  1 teaspoon baking powder
  ½ teaspoon salt
  ½ cup milk
    Juice of 1 lemon
  ½ cup sugar

In mixing bowl cream shortening with 1 cup sugar until light and fluffy. Blend in lemon peel and eggs.

Sift together flour, baking powder and salt. Add flour mixture and milk alternately to creamed mixture, beating just till smooth after each addition.

Turn into a lightly greased 8x4x3-inch loaf pan. Bake in a 350-degree oven for 45 to 50 minutes or till wooden pick inserted in center comes out free of batter. Remove from oven to wire rack. Let cool in pan for 5 minutes.

Combine lemon juice with remaining sugar; mix till sugar is dissolved. Prick top of loaf with a fork, then slowly pour lemon mixture over hot loaf. Let bread remain in pan until glaze is absorbed. Remove to wire rack and cool completely. Wrap in aluminum foil and store for 24 hours before slicing. Makes 1 loaf.

To avoid tunnels and coarseness in quick breads, DO NOT overmix!

❖ ❖ ❖ ❖ ❖ ❖ ❖ ❖ ❖

The crack down the center of a loaf is characteristic of quick breads.

ORANGE-CRANBERRY BREAD

This handsome loaf makes an excellent holiday gift from your kitchen. It's pleasing to most Yankee palates and at its best a day or two after baking.

> ¾ cup orange juice
> 1 tablespoon grated orange peel
> 1 beaten egg
> ¼ cup cooking oil
> 2 cups all-purpose flour
> 1 cup sugar
> 1½ teaspoons baking powder
> 1 teaspoon salt
> ½ teaspoon soda
> 2 cups coarsely chopped fresh or frozen cranberries
> ½ cup chopped nuts

In bowl combine orange juice, orange peel, egg and cooking oil. In large mixing bowl sift together flour, sugar, baking powder, salt and soda. Add orange mixture; stir just till moistened. Carefully fold in cranberries and nuts. Turn into greased 9x5x3-inch loaf pan, spreading corners and sides slightly higher than center.

Bake in a 350-degree oven for 1 hour, or till crust is golden brown and inserted wooden pick comes out clean. Remove from pan; cool on wire rack. Wrap and store overnight. Makes 1 loaf.

SPICY PUMPKIN BREAD

You can count on its spicy, fragrant aroma to fill your kitchen and its irresistible flavor to whet your appetite. Spread with cream cheese for a delectable tea sandwich.

    4 eggs
    2 cups sugar
    1¼ cups cooking oil
    1 16-ounce can solid pack pumpkin (or 2 cups cooked
        pumpkin)
    3 cups all-purpose flour
    2 teaspoons baking powder
    2 teaspoons soda
    1 teaspoon salt
    1 teaspoon cinnamon
    1 teaspoon nutmeg
    1 teaspoon ground cloves
    1 cup seedless raisins
    ½ cup chopped nuts

In large mixing bowl beat eggs until light and fluffy. Add sugar, cooking oil and pumpkin; mix well.

Sift together flour, baking powder, soda, salt, cinnamon, nutmeg and cloves; add to pumpkin mixture, a little at a time, and stir until thoroughly blended. Fold in raisins and nuts. Pour batter into 2 greased and floured 9x5x3-inch loaf pans, dividing batter evenly between the two.

Bake in a 350-degree oven for 1 hour and 5 minutes or till tester comes out free of batter. Cool in pans for 5 minutes. Turn out onto racks to cool. Wrap and store. Makes 2 loaves.

WILLIE'S WILD BLUEBERRY BREAD

An all-time any-time bread that's a MUST at every Down East family gathering.

½ cup butter or margarine, softened
1½ cups sugar
2 eggs
2¼ cups all-purpose flour
½ teaspoon soda
½ teaspoon salt
½ cup buttermilk or soured milk
2½ cups fresh or frozen blueberries
¼ cup flour

In large mixing bowl cream butter or margarine and sugar till light and fluffy. Add eggs, one at a time, beating well after each addition.

Sift together 2¼ cups flour, soda and salt; stir into creamed mixture alternately with buttermilk or soured milk. Beat just till thoroughly blended.

Toss berries gently with remaining ¼ cup flour. Fold carefully into batter. (Batter is thick!) Spread batter in a greased and floured 13x9x2-inch baking pan. Sprinkle top lightly with sugar for a crust. Bake in a 350-degree oven for 35 to 40 minutes or until wooden pick inserted in center comes out clean. Remove from oven to cooling rack. Serve warm. Makes 16 servings.

ZUCCHINI BREAD

Terrific! It's moist, not too sweet and the "best zucchini bread I've ever tasted!"

3 cups all-purpose flour
1½ cups sugar
1 teaspoon baking powder
1 teaspoon salt
1 teaspoon cinnamon
¾ teaspoon soda
2 cups shredded unpared zucchini
1 cup seedless raisins

¾ **cup coarsely chopped nuts**
3 eggs
1 cup cooking oil

In large bowl sift together flour, sugar, baking powder, salt, cinnamon and soda. Stir in zucchini, raisins and nuts.

In small bowl beat eggs and cooking oil till light. Pour over flour mixture; stir until moistened. Turn batter into 2 greased and floured medium loaf pans.

Bake in a 350-degree oven for 55 to 60 minutes or until tester inserted in center comes out clean. Cool in pan for 5 minutes. Turn out onto wire rack. Cool completely. Makes 2 medium loaves.

To sour milk, combine 1 tablespoon vinegar or lemon juice and enough fresh milk to make 1 cup. Let stand for 5 minutes; stir and use.

BUFFY'S CINNAMON FLIP FLOP

A recipe from Pennsylvania Dutch Country. Serve warm with coffee — any time of day!

1 tablespoon butter or margarine
1 cup sugar
2 cups sifted all-purpose flour
2 teaspoons baking powder
¼ teaspoon salt
1 cup milk
½ cup packed brown sugar
½ cup butter or margarine (1 stick)
1 teaspoon cinnamon
½ teaspoon nutmeg

In large mixing bowl cream 1 tablespoon butter or margarine and sugar. (No egg in recipe!)

Sift together flour, baking powder and salt; add alternately with milk to creamed mixture. Beat until smooth. Pour batter into a greased and floured 8-inch square baking pan. Dredge lightly with flour. Then sprinkle brown sugar evenly over top. Cut small pieces from the stick of butter and poke down into batter. Sprinkle top with cinnamon and nutmeg. Bake in a 400-degree oven for 25 minutes, or till wooden pick inserted in center of cake comes out free of batter. Serve warm. Makes 9 servings.

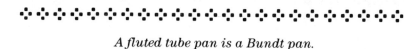

A fluted tube pan is a Bundt pan.

CRANBERRY COFFEECAKE

Handsome for a holiday brunch! Present it on a footed cake plate.

½ cup butter or margarine (1 stick)
1 cup sugar
2 eggs
1 teaspoon almond extract
2 cups all-purpose flour
1 teaspoon baking powder
1 teaspoon soda
½ teaspoon salt
1 cup dairy sour cream
1 16-ounce can whole cranberry sauce
½ cup chopped nuts
¾ cup sifted confectioners' sugar
2 tablespoons warm water
½ teaspoon almond extract

In mixing bowl cream butter or margarine and sugar till light and fluffy. Beat in eggs, one at a time; add 1 teaspoon almond extract.

Sift together flour, baking powder, soda and salt. Add flour mixture and sour cream alternately to creamed mixture. Beat just till smooth.

Spread half of batter in a greased and floured 9-inch tube pan. Cover with half of the cranberry sauce. Add remaining batter, then cranberry sauce. Sprinkle nuts atop.

Bake in a 350-degree oven for 55 minutes or till tester inserted near center comes out free of batter. Remove pan from oven to cooling rack. Cook 5 minutes before removing from pan. Cool completely.

In small bowl combine confectioners' sugar, water and almond flavoring, stirring till smooth. Using a spoon, drizzle icing over cake, letting it run down sides of cake. Makes 1 coffeecake.

To make your own cinnamon-sugar mixture, use 3 parts sugar to 1 part cinnamon; blend thoroughly.

MURK'S COFFEECAKE

Bake this for your next coffee klatch and bring on the coffee. All you will need is a pretty plate, a lace doily and — friends!

½ cup butter or margarine, softened
¾ cup sugar
2 eggs
1 cup dairy sour cream
1 teaspoon vanilla
2 cups all-purpose flour
1 teaspoon baking powder
1 teaspoon soda
½ teaspoon salt
½ cup chopped nuts
¼ cup seedless raisins
½ cup packed brown sugar
1 teaspoon cinnamon

In a large mixing bowl cream butter or margarine and sugar till light. Add eggs, one at a time, beating well after each addition. Blend in sour cream and vanilla.

Sift together flour, baking powder, soda and salt; add to creamed mixture. Stir in nuts and raisins. Turn batter into a greased and floured 10-inch tube or Bundt pan.

In a small bowl combine brown sugar and cinnamon; mix well. Sprinkle mixture over batter and cut through batter with a knife.

Bake in a 350-degree oven for 45 to 50 minutes or till wooden pick inserted in center comes out free of batter. Cool in pan for 10 minutes. Loosen edges with a knife and remove from pan to cool completely on a wire rack. Makes 1 coffeecake.

SOUR CREAM RHUBARB COFFEECAKE

A taste of springtime in a very light and moist coffeecake. My family loves it!

1 cup packed brown sugar
½ cup shortening or margarine, softened
1 egg
2 cups all-purpose flour
1 teaspoon soda
½ teaspoon salt
1 cup dairy sour cream
2 cups rhubarb, cut into ½-inch lengths
½ cup chopped nuts
½ cup granulated sugar
1 teaspoon cinnamon
1 tablespoon butter or margarine, melted

In large mixing bowl cream brown sugar and shortening or margarine. Beat in egg. Sift together flour, soda and salt. Add flour mixture and sour cream alternately to creamed mixture. Fold in rhubarb. Spread batter in a greased and floured 13x9x2-inch baking pan.

Combine nuts, granulated sugar and cinnamon; stir in butter or margarine. Sprinkle evenly over batter. Bake in a 350-degree oven for 40 to 45 minutes or till wooden pick inserted in center of cake comes out clean. Cool in pan on wire rack. Serve warm or cold. Makes 1 coffeecake.

APPLESAUCE DOUGHNUTS

Cider and doughnut holes — a taste of autumn!

2 tablespoons butter or margarine
⅔ cup packed brown sugar
1 egg
½ cup tart applesauce
2 cups all-purpose flour
½ teaspoon soda
¼ teaspoon salt
¼ teaspoon cinnamon
¼ teaspoon nutmeg
    Cooking oil or shortening for deep-fat frying
3 tablespoons sugar mixed with 1 teaspoon cinnamon

In a large mixing bowl cream butter or margarine with brown sugar till light and fluffy. Add egg; beat well. Stir in applesauce.

Sift together flour, soda, salt, cinnamon and nutmeg. Gradually add to applesauce mixture; stir just to blend after each addition. Cover and chill dough.

Roll out on a lightly floured surface to ⅜-inch thickness. Cut with floured 2½-inch doughnut cutter. Fry, a few doughnuts at a time, in deep fat heated to 360 degrees for 3 minutes or till browned on both sides, turning once. Drain on paper toweling. Roll in cinnamon-sugar mixture while warm. Makes 1 dozen doughnuts or 4 dozen doughnut holes.

Store honey in a warm, dry place to retard granulation.

Occasionally, honey granulates even when stored on the pantry shelf. Should this happen, place the jar in a bowl of warm water and allow to stand until all crystals are dissolved.

BLUEBERRY PANCAKES

Blueberries and pancakes: steady companions at the breakfast table! Rather than add the berries to the batter, we prefer to scatter 'em atop after the batter has been poured on the griddle.

　1¼ cups all-purpose flour
　1 tablespoon sugar
　1 teaspoon baking powder
　½ teaspoon soda
　½ teaspoon salt
　1 egg
　1¼ cups buttermilk or soured milk
　2 tablespoons cooking oil
　1 cup fresh or frozen blueberries

Sift flour, sugar, baking powder, soda and salt into a large mixing bowl.

In smaller bowl combine egg, buttermilk or soured milk and cooking oil; beat well. Gradually add to dry ingredients, stirring till blended but still slightly lumpy.

Pour or ladle batter in pools on hot, lightly greased griddle or skillet. Scatter a heaping tablespoon of blueberries over each pancake. Turn as soon as pancakes puff and are full of bubbles, but before bubbles break. Turn and brown other side. Serve hot with melted butter and hot maple syrup. Makes 10 to 12 4-inch pancakes.

Note:
　　DO NOT STACK PANCAKES! To keep hot, place pancakes between folds of towel in a 200-degree oven.

The thickness of the batter determines the thickness of the pancake. For thinner pancakes, add a little more liquid; a little flour for thicker pancakes.

❖ ❖

AN INTRODUCTION TO YEAST BREAD-MAKING TO MAKE YOU A MASTER OF THE ART

Basically, bread-making involves a series of steps: mixing, kneading, rising, shaping and baking. Each step has a purpose and each is essential — although not difficult. If you count the actual minutes it takes to mix, knead and shape, neither is bread-making all that time consuming.

Simply stated, bread requires five basic ingredients: flour, liquid, sugar, salt and yeast. It is the quantity and quality of these ingredients which gives character to each loaf of bread, although the baker influences the final results.

Flour, of course, forms the basic structure of the dough since it contains gluten (protein). When the flour is stirred and kneaded with a liquid, the gluten stretches to form the elastic framework that holds the gas bubbles formed by the yeast. This makes the structure of the loaf.

All-purpose enriched flour — a blend of hard and soft wheats — is the type of flour most generally available; consequently, it is the type of flour most often used not only for bread-making, but for pastries and cookies as well.

All-purpose flour can be bleached or unbleached. The labels tell you which brand is bleached and which is unbleached. Most experts agree, however, that unbleached, all-purpose flour is superior for making breads.

Incidentally, self-rising flour that contains leavening and salt is not recommended for yeast breads!

Whole wheat, or graham flour — the names are synonymous — contains bran and germ of the wheat; but since it contains less gluten than white flour, whole wheat produces a bread dough of closer texture and less volume than white dough.

Generally, whole grain breads include all-purpose flour with the whole wheat. (Rice and soy flour contain no gluten so must be combined with all-purpose flour.)

Since the type and quality of flour varies greatly, a recipe cannot state the precise amount of flour to use. The exact amount is determined by "feel." Remember, however, that the amount stated in a recipe includes enough for kneading. Save at least ¾ cup for this step. Too much flour makes a dry product!

Liquids may be water, potato water or milk. Water produces a bread with a crusty surface (such as French and Italian) while milk gives a soft crust and a creamy texture. Milk also adds nutrients.

Sugar or honey supplies food for the yeast to manufacture gas; **salt**, on the other hand, controls fermentation as well as adding flavor.

Perhaps the ingredient requiring the most attention is the **yeast**, only because it is a live plant and very sensitive. Too much heat kills the yeast; too little stunts its growth. Whenever yeast is reconstituted in a warm liquid, the temperature should not exceed 120 degrees. (105 to 115 degrees is ideal!) A thermometer may prove beneficial for the beginner.

Remember, if the temperature of the liquid is too hot the bread will be coarse and dry and barely rise.

After mixing, the dough requires a minimum of 5 to 8 minutes of kneading for proper structure. In case you wonder why there is a need to knead, let me point out that kneading is one of the most important steps in bread-making. This two-step motion of "push and pull" and "fold and press" is necessary to strengthen and develop the dough. It is far better to over-knead than under-knead.

Most recipes state, "Knead until the dough is smooth and elastic," and give the approximate number of minutes required to reach this stage. Others may read, "knead until light" or "knead until the dough no longer sticks to the fingers."

I am adding a personal description: Knead until the dough squeaks. For, when the dough has formed little blisters or bubbles under the surface, it begins to squeak; and when the dough reaches this stage, you have the makings of a culinary experience.

Set the dough to rise, covered with a clean cloth, in a draft-free place with temperature around 80 to 85 degrees. Allowing the dough to rise in an overheated spot gives the bread a sour or yeasty flavor.

(For those of us with central heating and a temperature no higher than 68 degrees, the ideal place may be an unheated oven with a large pan of hot water underneath the bowl. Of course, refrigerator breads are an exception to this tip.)

One more hint: Although the number of risings will not adversely affect the bread's texture, allowing the dough to rise more than double in size results in a coarse product filled with holes. If shaping into loaves at a precise moment is inconvenient, it is better to punch down the dough and allow it to have an additional rising.

After the dough is shaped, fill bread pan about two-thirds full and allow dough to rise until slightly above the top of the pan. The dough continues to rise at the beginning of the baking stage; and if it has more than doubled in size, it may collapse and result in a flat, heavy bread.

Practice makes perfect! Don't worry if your first "success" is less than perfect. Once you have experienced the aroma of fresh bread permeating the kitchen you will have discovered the ultimate satisfaction which comes from this aspect of cooking. The fruits of your labor will not only delight your family, but contribute to their well-being.

ANADAMA BREAD

The bread that nurtured our children and, in the opinion of one, "is a part of our blood." Although there are several versions of how this old-time bread was named, the legend I like tells of the lazy fisherman's wife who served her spouse cornmeal mush and molasses every day of their long married life. Finally, out of desperation, the old Yankee threw yeast and white flour into his porridge and shouted, "ANNA, damn her!" While you may not believe this tale, neither will you believe that a bread can be so good — not until you taste it, that is!

2¼ cups hot water
1 teaspoon salt
½ cup yellow cornmeal
½ cup molasses
3 tablespoons butter or margarine
1 package active dry yeast
¼ cup warm water (105 to 115 degrees)
5½ cups all-purpose flour

In small saucepan bring water and salt to a boil. Slowly sprinkle in cornmeal, stirring constantly to avoid lumping. Return mixture to a boil and cook until thickened. Remove from heat. Turn mixture into large mixing bowl. Add molasses and butter or margarine, stirring till butter melts. Cool to lukewarm.

Dissolve yeast in ¼ cup warm water. Combine with cornmeal mixture. Add 2 cups of the flour and beat until smooth. Add, 1 cup at a time, as much of the remaining flour as needed to make a moderately soft dough.

Turn out onto lightly floured surface. Knead until dough is smooth and elastic, about 5 to 8 minutes. Place in a well-greased bowl, turning to grease top of dough. Cover with a loose clean dish towel. Allow to rise in a draft-free warm place until double, about 1½ hours.

Turn out onto floured surface. Divide dough in half. Knead down and shape each half into a loaf. Place each in a well-greased 8x4x3-inch loaf pan. Cover and let rise till double, about 40 minutes.

Bake in a 375-degree oven for 40 to 45 minutes or until loaves sound hollow when lightly tapped on top with a finger. Remove from oven. Brush tops with melted butter or margarine. Turn out onto wire racks to cool. Makes 2 medium loaves.

BUTTERMILK BREAD

Bring joy to others with old-fashioned goodness in a loaf! Originally developed to make use of soured milk, this bread also makes use of off-flavored evaporated milk, cream or yogurt. It's a good choice for beginning bread-makers.

4½ to 5 cups all-purpose flour
½ cup wheat germ
¼ cup sugar
2 teaspoons salt
¼ teaspoon soda
1 package active dry yeast
2 cups buttermilk
3 tablespoons margarine
1 egg

In large bowl combine 1½ cups of the flour, wheat germ, sugar, salt, soda and dry yeast.

In saucepan heat buttermilk and margarine until very warm (120 to 130 degrees). Margarine does not need to melt. Add warm liquid and egg to flour mixture. Blend at low speed of electric mixer until moistened. Beat 2 minutes at medium speed, scraping bowl occasionally.

By hand, stir in enough of the remaining flour to make a soft dough. Cover; let rise in a warm place (85 degrees), free from draft, until doubled in size (about 1 hour).

Stir dough down. Turn out onto floured surface and knead for 5 minutes. Divide dough in half. Shape each half into a smooth ball. Cover and let rest for 10 minutes.

Shape each ball into a loaf and place in a greased 8x4x3-inch loaf pan. Cover; let rise in a draft-free warm place until double in size, about 30 to 45 minutes.

Bake in a 375-degree oven for 35 to 45 minutes or until loaves sound hollow when lightly tapped. Remove from oven and brush tops with melted or softened butter or margarine. Turn out onto wire rack. Turn right side up and cool completely. Makes 2 loaves.

DILL PICKLE RYE BREAD

A bread that is uniquely different and a great way to utilize pickle juice. It's a summertime sensation at our house with a main-dish salad!

  3 cups all-purpose flour
  2 cups rye flour
  2 packages active dry yeast
  ½ cup boiling water
  2 teaspoons dill seed
  ½ cup water
  ½ cup dill pickle liquid
  ½ cup buttermilk
  2 tablespoons sugar
  2 tablespoons cooking oil
  2 teaspoons salt
  2 teaspoons caraway seed

In large bowl combine all-purpose and rye flours; stir. In second large mixing bowl combine 2 cups of the flour mixture and dry yeast.

In small bowl pour boiling water over dill seed. Soak for 10 minutes; DO NOT drain.

In saucepan combine ½ cup water, dill pickle liquid, buttermilk, sugar, cooking oil and salt; heat until warm (120 to 130 degrees). Stir in dill seed-water mixture and caraway seed. Pour over flour-yeast mixture; beat mixture at high speed of electric mixer for 3 minutes. Stir in enough of the remaining flour to make a soft dough.

Turn out onto lightly floured surface and knead until smooth, about 5 to 8 minutes. Cover dough with bowl and let rest for 40 minutes.

Divide dough in half; shape into balls. Place each ball in a greased 1-quart round casserole. With a sharp knife cut 3 slits in top of each loaf. Brush tops with cooking oil. Cover and let rise in a warm place until double in size, about 40 minutes.

Bake in a 350-degree oven for 45 to 50 minutes or till loaves sound hollow when lightly tapped. (To prevent excessive browning loosely cover tops of bread for the last 10 minutes of baking with pieces of aluminum foil.)

Remove bread from pans to cooling racks. Brush tops with butter or margarine. Makes 2 round loaves.

DOROTHY'S RAISIN BREAD

A Christmas morning tradition at a friend's house! The bread is made and frozen long before the holiday rush. After Santa's arrival, the frozen — or partially frozen — loaf is foil-wrapped and reheated in a slow oven. It is then frosted and decorated with candied cherry slices and chopped nuts.

> 1 cup milk
> 1 package active dry yeast
> 3½ cups all-purpose flour
> ⅓ cup butter or margarine
> ½ cup sugar
> 1 egg
> 1½ teaspoons salt
> ¼ teaspoon nutmeg
> 1 teaspoon almond extract
> 1½ cups seedless raisins

Heat milk until film forms, but DO NOT boil. Cool to lukewarm. Combine milk with yeast in a large bowl; stir to dissolve yeast. Stir 1½ cups of the flour into yeast mixture. Cover and let stand until double.

Cream butter or margarine and sugar in small bowl. Beat in egg, salt, nutmeg and almond extract. Stir into yeast mixture.

Mix raisins with ½ cup of the flour; add to dough. Gradually stir in remaining flour to make a soft dough. If dough is too sticky, add more flour. Cover bowl; let dough rise in a warm place until double, about 1½ hours.

Punch down and shape into round loaf. Place on a greased baking sheet or in a greased 2-quart casserole. Brush top with cooking oil or butter. Cover loosely and let rise until doubled (about 45 minutes).

Bake in a 350-degree oven for 45 to 50 minutes or until loaf sounds hollow when top is lightly tapped with a finger. If crust browns too quickly, cover loosely with foil for last 15 minutes of baking time. Remove from pan to wire rack. Drizzle with confectioners' sugar icing, if desired. Makes 1 round loaf.

Dry yeast and cake yeast can be used interchangeably!

GARLIC PARMESAN BREAD

Serve this pull-apart bread at your next Italian meal. It's marvelous and your guests will be impressed!

    1 package active dry yeast
    ¼ cup warm water (115 to 120 degrees)
    2 cups milk
    1 cup grated Parmesan cheese
    2 tablespoons sugar
    2 tablespoons shortening
    2 teaspoons salt
    ⅛ teaspoon cayenne pepper
    5½ cups all-purpose flour
    3 tablespoons melted butter
    2 teaspoons garlic salt

In bowl dissolve yeast in warm water. Scald milk. In large mixer bowl combine Parmesan cheese, sugar, shortening, salt and cayenne pepper. Add hot milk; stir till sugar dissolves and shortening melts. Cool to lukewarm.

Stir in 2 cups of the flour and beat well at low speed of electric mixer. By hand, stir in softened yeast and add enough of the remaining flour to make a moderately stiff dough. Turn out onto lightly floured surface and knead until smooth and satiny, 5 to 8 minutes. Shape into a ball. Place in lightly greased bowl, turning to grease surface of ball. Cover; let rise in a warm place till double (about 1¼ hours).

Punch dough down; turn out onto lightly floured surface. Divide into 2 portions and form each into a ball. Cover and let rest for 10 minutes. Roll out half of dough to 10x16-inch rectangle. Brush with half of melted butter and sprinkle with 1 teaspoon garlic salt.

Cut into 4x10-inch rectangles. Stack rectangles on top of one another, buttered side up. Cut into 5 stacks, 2 inches wide and 4 inches long. Place stacks in rows in greased 9x5x3-inch loaf pan, placing the long cut side down (resembles a sliced loaf of bread). Repeat with second half of dough.

Cover; let rise in draft-free warm place until double, about 1 hour. Bake in a 375-degree oven for 35 to 45 minutes or until loaves sound hollow when lightly tapped and are a deep golden brown. Remove from oven; brush tops lightly with butter. Remove from pans and cool slightly on wire rack before serving. To serve, pull slices of bread from loaf. Makes 2 loaves.

TRAPPERS BREAD

An old Canadian recipe from a childhood chum! This bread with a slightly sweet taste is one that her family enjoys for sandwiches on their ski holidays. We think it is marvelous toasted, too!

> ¾ **cup seedless raisins**
> ¾ **cup currants**
> 1⅓ **cups hot water**
> ½ **cup packed brown sugar**
> 1½ **teaspoons salt**
> ½ **cup margarine (1 stick)**

⅓ cup molasses
1 tablespoon sugar
½ cup warm water (110 to 115 degrees)
1 package active dry yeast
6 cups all-purpose flour

In small bowl combine raisins and currants. Cover with boiling water; allow to plump, then drain.

In large mixing bowl combine hot water, brown sugar, salt, margarine and molasses. Stir until margarine melts; cool to luke-warm. Add raisins and currants.

Dissolve sugar in warm water. Add dry yeast; let stand for 10 minutes. Combine with molasses mixture.

Mix in 3 cups of the flour; beat until smooth. Add enough of the remaining flour to make a moderately soft dough. Turn out onto a lightly floured surface. Knead until smooth and satiny, about 5 to 8 minutes. Place in a greased bowl, turning to grease top of dough. Cover. Let rise in a warm place until double in size, about 2 hours.

Punch dough down. Turn out onto floured surface. Divide in half. Shape each half into a loaf; place in a greased 9x5x3-inch loaf pan. Let rise, covered, for 45 minutes or till double in size.

Bake in a 375-degree oven for 45 to 50 minutes or till loaves sound hollow when lightly tapped on top. Check after 35 to 40 minutes; cover loosely with foil if tops are too brown. Remove from oven. Brush tops with melted butter. Turn out onto wire rack to cool. Makes 2 loaves.

To "proof" yeast to be sure it is alive and working, dissolve yeast and 1 teaspoon sugar in warm water (105 to 115 degrees). Wait 10 minutes. If the yeast ferments — becomes very bubbly — you know it is working!

Water — 110 to 115 degrees — feels comfortably warm when tested on the inside of your wrist. Water — 120 to 130 degrees — feels considerably hotter, but not hot enough to burn the skin.

MOLASSES YEAST ROLLS

Sharing a spot in this popular recipe, which came from a school cafeteria baker, are two naturals — rolled oats and molasses. In earlier times rolled oats were added to s-t-r-e-t-c-h the white flour. Contemporary bakers prize this old-time grain not only because it makes the bread taste good, but because it contributes to our good health. A suggestion from this baker: shape the dough into two loaves and bake in a 375-degree oven. It makes a wonderful toast!

1½ cups boiling water
1 cup quick-cooking or old-fashioned rolled oats
½ cup molasses
⅓ cup shortening
1 tablespoon salt
2 packages active dry yeast
½ cup warm water (110 to 115 degrees)
2 eggs, slightly beaten
6 to 6½ cups all-purpose flour

In large mixing bowl pour boiling water over rolled oats, molasses, shortening and salt. Cool to lukewarm.

Dissolve yeast in warm water. Add yeast, eggs and 3 cups of the flour to oats mixture. Beat until smooth. Stir in enough of the remaining flour to form a soft dough.

Turn out onto lightly floured surface. Knead until smooth and elastic, about 5 minutes. Place in a greased bowl, turning to grease top. Cover bowl and let dough rise in a warm place until double in size, about 1 hour.

Punch down dough. Shape into rolls and place in a shallow greased baking pan. Cover loosely; let rise in a warm place till double in size, 30 to 40 minutes. Bake in a 350-degree oven for 20 to 25 minutes or till a deep golden brown. Brush tops with melted butter. Turn out onto rack to cool slightly. Makes 3 dozen rolls.

For yeast rolls with soft sides, place balls of dough with sides touching in a shallow greased baking pan.

BASIC SWEET DOUGH

Bring joy into the lives of your loved ones . . . sweet breads are a treat for any occasion!

1¼ cups milk
½ cup butter or margarine (1 stick)
½ cup sugar
1 teaspoon salt
2 packages active dry yeast
4½ to 5 cups all-purpose flour
2 eggs

In saucepan heat milk, butter or margarine, sugar and salt till milk is warm (110 to 115 degrees). Pour into a large mixing bowl.

Sprinkle in dry yeast; stir till dissolved. Beat in 2 cups of the flour. Add eggs; beat with an electric mixer till smooth, about 3 minutes, scraping down sides of bowl often.

By hand, stir in enough of the remaining flour to make a soft, almost sticky dough. (Too much flour makes a dry product.) Turn dough out onto lightly floured surface. Knead till smooth and elastic, about 5 minutes.

Place in a greased bowl, turning greased side up. Cover loosely and let rise in a warm, draft-free place until double in size, about 1 hour. Punch down. Use to prepare the following variations:

Variations:

Cinnamon Rolls

A family-favorite with a bit of sentiment added: At seventeen I left the warm homespun childhood kitchen to pursue a higher education in the culinary arts. My away-from-home residence was a cooperative girl's dormitory with about sixty students. Almost immediately I was relegated to the pantry — my assignment was bread-maker.

Muffins and scones became the daily bread, while a variety of fancy yeast rolls graced the dining table every Wednesday and Sunday. Needless to say, by the time school recessed for the holidays, I had gained considerable expertise as a baker. My proficiency in the family kitchen sparked an appreciative remark by an adolescent brother, "Gracie makes the BEST mashed potato and — CINNAMON ROLLS!"

½ recipe Basic Sweet Dough (recipe on page 195)
2 tablespoons butter or margarine, softened
3 tablespoons sugar
1½ teaspoons cinnamon
¼ cup seedless raisins
2 tablespoons chopped nuts
Melted butter

Roll dough out to form a 12x8-inch rectangle. Spread with butter or margarine. Combine sugar, cinnamon, raisins and nuts; sprinkle over dough.

Starting with a long end, roll up tightly, jelly-roll fashion. Stretch and shape till even. Cut into 12 1-inch slices.

Place cut side up in a greased 12x8x2-inch baking pan. Brush with melted butter. Cover and let rise till double in size, about 30 minutes.

Bake in a 375-degree oven for 25 to 30 minutes or till nicely browned. Remove from pan to cooling rack. Drizzle tops while warm with confectioners' sugar icing, if desired. Makes 1 dozen rolls.

Swedish Tea Ring

Like gathering the family, this is a holiday tradition at our house!

Prepare Cinnamon Rolls as above recipe directs except — DO NOT SLICE. Place shaped roll seam side down on a lightly greased baking sheet.

Shape into a ring, pinching ends of dough together to seal. Snip, going halfway through dough, at 1-inch intervals. Push each section on its side. Place a greased 6-ounce custard cup in center of ring to help retain shape during rising. Cover lightly and let rise till double in size, about 30 minutes.

Bake in a 375-degree oven for 25 to 30 minutes or till golden brown. Remove from baking sheet to cooling rack. While warm drizzle with confectioners' sugar icing. Decorate with slices of candied cherries and chopped nuts. Makes 1 ring.

CINNAMON TWISTS

Little kneading and one rising is all that's required for this festive bread which is guaranteed to vanish fast!

1 cup dairy sour cream
3 tablespoons sugar
1 teaspoon salt
⅛ teaspoon soda
1 package active dry yeast
1 egg, beaten
2 tablespoons cooking oil
3 cups all-purpose flour, approx.
2 tablespoons butter or margarine, softened
⅓ cup packed brown sugar
1 teaspoon cinnamon

In large saucepan heat sour cream until lukewarm. Remove from heat; stir in sugar, salt and soda. Sprinkle in dry yeast; stir till dissolved. Add egg and cooking oil. Stir in enough of the flour to make a moderately soft dough.

Turn dough out onto lightly floured surface. Knead until smooth, about 3 minutes. Roll dough into a 24x6-inch rectangle. Spread softened butter or margarine over top of dough. Combine brown sugar and cinnamon; sprinkle mixture over half of dough (width).

Fold uncovered half of dough over sugar-covered half, making a 24x3-inch rectangle. Cut into 24 strips, 1 inch wide and 3 inches long.

Take each strip and twist in opposite directions. Place 2 inches apart on greased baking sheet. Firmly press both ends against sheet so they do not unwind during baking. Cover and let rise in a warm spot until light, about 1 hour.

Bake in a 375-degree oven for 12 to 15 minutes or till golden brown. Remove from pan to cooling rack and drizzle confectioners' sugar icing over tops. Serve warm. Makes 24 twists.

Unbleached all-purpose flour may be used for bleached flour.

HOT CROSS BUNS

A traditional Easter favorite and what a treat! The buns are best served warm — either fresh or reheated, although it is better to frost them just before serving!

1 cup milk
2 tablespoons butter or margarine
1 package active dry yeast
¼ cup warm water (110 to 115 degrees)
4 cups all-purpose flour, divided
⅓ cup sugar
1 teaspoon salt
½ teaspoon cinnamon
1 cup seedless raisins
¼ cup finely shredded citron (optional)
2 eggs, well-beaten
Melted butter

Scald milk; stir in 2 tablespoons butter or margarine and cool to lukewarm. Dissolve yeast in ¼ cup warm water.

In large mixing bowl sift together 2 cups of the flour, sugar, salt and cinnamon. Stir raisins and citron into flour mixture. Add eggs, cooled milk and yeast; blend well. Add remaining flour (or a little more or less) to make a soft dough. Turn dough out onto a lightly floured board and knead until smooth and elastic (5 to 8 minutes). Place in a greased bowl, turning to grease top. Cover bowl; let rise in a warm place until double in size (about 1½ hours).

Punch down dough. Pinch off pieces of dough and form smooth, rounded balls (1½ inches in diameter). Dip each ball into melted butter and place on a greased baking sheet, spacing 2 inches apart. Gently snip a ½-inch deep cross in center of each bun with greased scissors. Let buns rise in a warm place until double in size (about 30 minutes). Bake in a 375-degree oven for 15 to 18 minutes, or till lightly browned. Cool on wire racks about 5 minutes. Then, with the tip of a spoon, drizzle icing on cross. Serve warm. Makes 2½ dozen buns.

To make icing: Combine 1 cup sifted confectioners' sugar, 1 tablespoon melted butter and ½ teaspoon vanilla; mix until smooth. If necessary, thin with a spoonful or two of milk.

NANCY'S BUTTER KUCHEN

A German sweet bread! This one-bowl, no-knead kuchen was developed by a young homemaker to please the man in her life, who exclaimed, "It's just like Mother's!" To make one pan of kuchen, use just 1 teaspoon of yeast and a third of the amounts of remaining ingredients.

> 2 cups milk
> 1 package active dry yeast
> ½ cup butter or margarine, softened (1 stick)
> 2 tablespoons sugar
> ½ teaspoon salt
> 3 eggs
> 5 to 6 cups all-purpose flour
> ¾ cup cold firm butter (1½ sticks)
> ¾ cup sugar

In a large saucepan heat milk till warm (105 to 115 degrees). Remove from heat. Sprinkle in dry yeast; stir till dissolved.

Add softened butter or margarine, 2 tablespoons sugar, salt, eggs and 2 cups of the flour. Beat with electric mixer till smooth, scraping down sides of pan often.

By hand, stir in enough of the remaining flour to form a soft, sticky dough. Place in a greased bowl, turning to grease top of dough. Cover with a clean dish towel. Let rise in a warm, draft-free place until double in size, about 1 hour.

Butter hands; punch down dough. Divide into thirds; spread each third in a greased 15x10x1-inch jelly roll pan. (The dough has to be stretched to fit bottom of pan.)

Cut butter into small cubes; press 4 tablespoons into each pan of dough. Sprinkle each with ¼ cup sugar. Cover loosely and let rise till double in size, about 30 minutes. Bake in a 350-degree oven for 20 minutes or till golden brown. Serve hot. Makes 3 pans kuchen.

Chapter 9

Dessert is the happy ending to mealtime; for many diners, no meal is complete without it!

More than one reputable cook holds the opinion that a dessert is of utmost importance — it is the climax of a meal. When diners recall a meal, they are most likely to remember the ending — the dessert — first, and the beginning — the appetizer — last.

In earlier days, with the exception of desserts, most recipes were committed to memory. Practically every family has an old notebook filled with the family heirlooms: cakes, cookies and puddings. However, these "recipes" of yesteryear appear vague. Descriptive rather than standard measurements — "butter the size of an egg" or a "coffee cup heaping full" — are common; while methods for combining ingredients and specifics like oven temperature, baking times and pan sizes are practically nonexistent. It was assumed every female was a born cook!

This section boasts a bevy of beauties — desserts suitable for every mood and any occasion. Old-Fashioned Strawberry Shortcake can redeem the plainest meal while Jody's Cheesecake might be the choice when you throw all caution to the winds. Included are many of the old-time nostalgics as well as a few contemporary recipes that make use of convenience foods for short-cut preparation.

Next time someone asks, "What's for dessert?" present a homespun special or a fancy favorite and light a smile on the face of a loved one. Be prepared to serve a repeat . . . and soon!

Desserts

Continued

BAKED APPLE PUDDING

Oftentimes, recipes state "grated or chopped apple" with no mention of paring. Then the question arises, "Should I pare the apples?" My suggestion is do as you please, but a thought to keep in mind: apple peelings add fiber to the diet!

    ⅓ cup butter or margarine, softened
    1 cup sugar
    1 egg
    1 cup all-purpose flour
    1 teaspoon soda
    ¼ teaspoon salt
    ¼ teaspoon cinnamon
    ¼ teaspoon nutmeg
    1 teaspoon vanilla
    2 cups grated unpared tart apple
    ½ cup chopped nuts
      Whipped cream

In mixing bowl cream butter or margarine and sugar till light and fluffy. Stir in egg; beat well.

Sift together flour, soda, salt, cinnamon and nutmeg. Gradually add sifted dry ingredients to creamed mixture, beating well to combine mixtures. Stir in vanilla, apples and nuts. Turn batter into a greased 8-inch square baking pan.

Bake in a 350-degree oven for 30 to 35 minutes or until tester inserted in center comes out clean. Remove pan from oven to wire rack. Cut into squares. Serve warm or cold with a dollop of whipped cream. Makes 8 servings.

BAKED INDIAN PUDDING

The traditional Thanksgiving dessert and childhood memory of a neighborhood cook!

¼ **cup yellow cornmeal**
1 **teaspoon salt**
1 **cup cold water**
2 **cups scalded milk**
1 **egg**
¼ **cup sugar**
½ **cup molasses**
1 **tablespoon butter**
1 **teaspoon cinnamon**
½ **teaspoon ginger**
1 **cup cold milk**
Hard Sauce (recipe on page 232)

In saucepan mix together cornmeal, salt and water. Stir in scalded milk and bring to a boil. Cook, stirring, for 10 minutes or till thick. Remove from heat.

In small bowl lightly beat the egg; blend in sugar, molasses, butter and spices. Slowly pour egg mixture into cornmeal mixture, stirring constantly. Turn into a buttered 1½-quart casserole.

Bake in a 300-degree oven for 30 minutes. Remove from oven and stir in 1 cup cold milk. Bake at 250 degrees for 2 hours. Let stand 30 minutes after baking for a slightly firmer pudding. Serve warm with a slice of Hard Sauce or a scoop of vanilla ice cream. Makes 6 servings.

Note:

Indian Pudding is soft and looks slightly curdled.

BLUEBARB PUDDING

Blueberries and rhubarb make a wonderful combination. Try it!

½ cup sugar
1 teaspoon quick-cooking tapioca
2 cups fresh or frozen blueberries
1½ cups unpeeled rhubarb cut in 1-inch lengths
⅔ cup all-purpose flour
⅔ cup quick-cooking or old-fashioned rolled oats
½ cup sugar
¼ cup butter or margarine, melted
Ice cream or whipped cream

In large mixing bowl combine ½ cup sugar and tapioca; stir in blueberries and rhubarb, tossing lightly to coat with mixture. Place in a buttered 1½-quart casserole or baking dish.

In same bowl mix together flour, rolled oats and remaining ½ cup sugar. Blend in melted butter or margarine until mixture resembles coarse crumbs. Spread evenly over fruit mixture.

Bake in a 350-degree oven for 45 minutes or until rhubarb is tender and topping is crisp. Serve warm with ice cream or whipped cream. Makes 4 to 6 servings.

In recipes specifying quick-cooking or old-fashioned rolled oats, it is a cook's choice. Since they differ only in thinness of flakes, the varieties are interchangeable. In quick oats, cutting is done before rolling, but food value remains unchanged.

Although instant oats are used in special, quick recipes, DO NOT use them in recipes calling for quick-cooking or old-fashioned rolled oats.

CHERRY PUDDING

A home-spun dessert from a cook with Dixie roots! It's a good one for celebrating Washington's birthday.

1 16-ounce can water-packed tart pitted cherries
½ cup sugar
2 teaspoons cornstarch
½ teaspoon almond extract
2 tablespoons butter or margarine, softened
½ cup sugar
1 egg
1 cup all-purpose flour
1 teaspoon baking powder
¼ teaspoon salt
½ cup milk
 Whipped cream or vanilla ice cream

Drain cherries, reserving liquid. Add water to make 1½ cups liquid. Combine sugar and cornstarch in a saucepan; add liquid. Cook, stirring constantly, till thick and clear. Stir in almond extract and cherries. Keep hot.

In a medium mixing bowl cream butter or margarine and ½ cup sugar till light and fluffy. Add egg; beat well. Sift together flour, baking powder and salt; add to creamed mixture alternately with milk. Beat just till smooth. Turn into a buttered 1½-quart baking dish.

Spoon hot cherry sauce over batter. Bake in a 350-degree oven for 35 to 40 minutes or till dough puffs up and browns. Serve warm with whipped cream or ice cream. Makes 8 servings.

For best results, thoroughly chill cream, bowl and beaters before whipping the cream.

Avoid using a plastic bowl when beating egg whites (or whipping cream) as oils retained in plastic prevent whites from forming peaks.

DATE-NUT TAPIOCA PUDDING

The favorite pudding of a proficient cooking buff . . . and the recipe is from his mother's handwritten cookbook!

2½ cups cold water
¼ cup quick-cooking tapioca
½ cup packed brown sugar
⅛ teaspoon salt
1 cup snipped pitted dates
1 cup Grape-Nuts
1 teaspoon vanilla
Whipped cream

Combine cold water, tapioca, brown sugar and salt in top of double boiler. Place over hot water; cook, stirring occasionally, for 15 minutes or till transparent.

Remove pudding from heat. Stir in dates, Grape-Nuts and vanilla. Serve warm or cold with whipped cream. Makes 6 servings.

DOWN EAST BLUEBERRY PUDDING

Keep this dessert in mind for topping off an authentic Down East meal. Delectable!

2 cups fresh or frozen blueberries
1 tablespoon lemon juice
¼ cup butter or margarine, softened
½ cup sugar
1 egg
1 cup all-purpose flour
1 teaspoon baking powder
¼ teaspoon salt
½ cup milk
¾ cup sugar
1 tablespoon cornstarch
⅛ teaspoon salt
1 cup hot water
Vanilla ice cream or whipped cream

Spread blueberries in a buttered 8-inch square baking pan. Drizzle lemon juice over berries.

In mixing bowl cream butter or margarine and ½ cup sugar till light and fluffy. Add egg; beat well.

Sift together flour, baking powder and ¼ teaspoon salt. Add to creamed mixture alternately with milk; beat just until smooth. Spread batter over berries.

Mix together ¾ cup sugar, cornstarch and ⅛ teaspoon salt. Sprinkle evenly over batter. Gently pour hot water over top. Bake in a 375-degree oven for 55 to 60 minutes, or till nicely browned on top. Serve warm with vanilla ice cream or whipped cream. Makes 8 servings.

Store cereals in their packages in a cool, dry place!

MOCK INDIAN PUDDING

This super-simple dessert recipe from a column friend combines shredded wheat biscuits, eggs, milk and molasses.

2 large shredded wheat biscuits
2 eggs
½ cup molasses
1 tablespoon butter or margarine
½ teaspoon cinnamon
½ teaspoon salt
2 cups milk, scalded
   Ice cream or whipped cream

Crumble shredded wheat into a buttered 1-quart casserole. In medium bowl beat eggs until foamy. Add molasses, butter or margarine, cinnamon and salt, mixing only until combined. Scald milk.

Gradually add hot milk to egg mixture, stirring constantly with a fork until butter is melted. Pour milk mixture over biscuits.

Bake in a 325-degree oven for 50 to 55 minutes or till knife inserted near center comes out clean. Serve warm with ice cream or whipped cream. Makes 4 servings.

OLD-FASHIONED RICE PUDDING

Creamy and nutritious . . . full of old-fashioned goodness. Stirring is essential in order to disperse the rice.

   ⅓ cup medium-grain rice
   ¼ cup sugar
   ¼ teaspoon salt
   1 quart milk
   1 teaspoon vanilla
   ⅓ cup seedless raisins
   Cinnamon

In a 1½-quart casserole combine rice, sugar, salt and milk. Bake, uncovered, in a 300-degree oven for 2 hours, stirring every 20 minutes. Remove from oven and stir in vanilla and raisins; sprinkle generously with ground cinnamon. Bake, unstirred, 30 minutes longer. Serve warm or cold. Makes 6 servings.

RHUBARB PUDDING CAKE

Makes a big hit with the rhubarb buffs! The cake rises to the top while it's in the oven. Be sure there is extra sauce to pass.

   4 cups unpeeled rhubarb cut in ½-inch lengths
   ¾ cup sugar
   ¾ cup water
   ¼ cup butter or margarine, softened
   ½ cup sugar
   1 egg
   ½ teaspoon vanilla
   1 cup all-purpose flour
   2 teaspoons baking powder
   ¼ teaspoon salt
   ½ cup milk

In medium saucepan combine rhubarb, ¾ cup sugar and water; bring to a boil. Reduce heat; cover and simmer for 5 minutes or till rhubarb is tender. Keep hot.

In medium mixing bowl cream butter or margarine and sugar

till light and fluffy. Beat in egg and vanilla.

Sift together flour, baking powder and salt; add dry ingredients to creamed mixture alternately with milk. Beat until smooth.

Turn batter into a buttered 9-inch square baking pan. Spoon hot rhubarb sauce over batter. Bake in a 350-degree oven for 40 minutes or till cake pulls away from sides of pan and tester inserted in center comes out free of batter. Serve with additional rhubarb sauce and sweetened whipped cream, if desired. Makes 9 servings.

THANKSGIVING PLUM PUDDING

A good old-days steamed pudding from the ancestral kitchen of my maternal grandmother. Serve with Lemon Sauce.

1¾ cups sifted all-purpose flour
1 teaspoon cinnamon
1 teaspoon cloves
½ teaspoon ginger
½ teaspoon salt
1 cup finely snipped pitted dates
1 cup seedless raisins
½ cup chopped nuts
1 egg
1 tablespoon butter, melted
⅔ cup boiling water
1 cup molasses
1 teaspoon soda
Lemon Pudding Sauce (recipe follows)

Sift flour, cinnamon, cloves, ginger and salt into a medium bowl. Stir in dates, raisins and nuts. Set aside.

In a large mixing bowl beat egg till light and fluffy. Stir in butter; gradually add water, stirring rapidly, so as not to coagulate egg mixture. Mix together, then blend in molasses and soda.

Add flour mixture to egg mixture; blend thoroughly. Turn into a well-greased 1½-quart mold with a tight-fitting cover. Or, divide mixture between 2 well-greased 28-ounce size cans or 3 well-greased 20-ounce size cans, filling ½ to ⅔ full. Cover the cans with aluminum foil and tie tightly with a string.

Place covered mold or cans on a trivet in a deep kettle; pour in enough boiling water to reach halfway up mold. Cover kettle. Keep water boiling over low heat to steam pudding for 1¾ hours or till wooden pick inserted in center of pudding comes out clean. Add more water to kettle, if necessary, to keep up steam; lift lid and quickly add the water. (Lift cover away from you to avoid being scalded.)

Remove mold from kettle; remove cover and loosen around edges with a spatula. Unmold on serving platter; cut into slices and serve hot with Lemon Pudding Sauce. Makes 10 to 12 servings.

To dry out top of pudding: place pudding, uncovered, in a 350-degree oven for 5 minutes.

Lemon Pudding Sauce

½ cup sugar
2 tablespoons cornstarch
⅛ teaspoon salt
2 cups hot water
1 tablespoon butter
1 teaspoon lemon extract
1 teaspoon vanilla
 Dash nutmeg

In a medium saucepan combine sugar, cornstarch and salt; gradually add hot water. Cook and stir over medium heat till clear and slightly thickened. Simmer 1 to 2 minutes.

Remove from heat. Add butter, lemon extract and vanilla. A dash of nutmeg enhances the flavor. Serve hot or cold. Makes 2 cups.

APPLE CRACKLE

This quick and easy dessert is served in wedges like pie — only easier to make. It gets its name from the crackled surface.

   2 eggs
   ¾ cup sugar
   ½ cup all-purpose flour
   1½ teaspoons baking powder
   ½ teaspoon salt
   1 cup diced unpared tart apple
   ½ cup chopped nuts
   1 teaspoon vanilla
   Ice cream or whipped cream

In mixing bowl beat eggs till light. Add sugar; beat well. Sift together flour, baking powder and salt. Blend into egg mixture. Stir in apple, nuts and vanilla. Pour into buttered 9-inch pie pan. Bake in a 350-degree oven for 35 to 40 minutes or till lightly brown. Cut into wedges. Serve topped with ice cream or whipped cream. Makes 6 to 8 servings.

APPLE CRUMBLE

Bring out the apples! This combination apple crisp-bar is from a family-oriented cook.

   6 large tart cooking apples
   1 cup all-purpose flour
   1 cup sugar
   1 teaspoon baking powder
   ½ teaspoon salt
   1 egg
   ½ cup coarsely broken nuts
   ⅓ cup butter or margarine, melted
   Cinnamon
   Ice Cream or whipped cream

Pare, core and cut apples into ¼-inch slices to make 6 cups. Place in a buttered 9-inch square baking dish.

In medium bowl combine flour, sugar, baking powder, salt and egg; toss with a fork until mixture is crumbly. Sprinkle evenly over apple slices. Scatter coarsely broken nuts over top; drizzle with melted butter or margarine. Sprinkle cinnamon over mixture.

Bake in a 350-degree oven for 40 to 45 minutes or until apples are tender and topping is lightly browned. Cool slightly and cut into squares. Serve warm with ice cream or whipped cream. Makes 9 servings.

APPLE DELIGHTS

A recipe popular in a Maine household "when the children were home." They are a delight to make and an even greater delight to eat!

6 medium baking apples
2 cups all-purpose flour
1½ teaspoons baking powder
½ teaspoon salt
¼ cup butter or margarine
1 cup milk
1 egg
½ cup sugar
1 teaspoon cinnamon
2 tablespoons butter or margarine
Vanilla Sauce (recipe on page 233)

Pare apples; remove center core and cut in half crosswise.

In a medium mixing bowl combine flour, baking powder and salt; cut in ¼ cup butter or margarine till mixture is coarse. Combine milk and egg. Add to dry ingredients; mix well.

Drop a rounded tablespoonful of batter in each of 12 well-greased large muffin or 6-ounce custard cups. Place an apple section over batter. Combine sugar and cinnamon; fill each cavity with 2 teaspoonfuls of mixture. Dot with ½ teaspoon butter.

Bake in a 375-degree oven for 40 to 45 minutes or until apples are tender and tops are nicely browned. Serve warm with Vanilla Sauce. Makes 12 servings.

BAKED APPLES

Brings out sentiment in at least two cooks: the one sharing the recipe because it was her minister's wife who "introduced me to Chinese Chop Suey and Baked Apples" and this one because it was the first recipe to appear in my weekly cooking column.

  6 medium baking apples
  ½ cup seedless raisins
  ⅓ cup sugar
  2 tablespoons all-purpose flour
  ½ teaspoon cinnamon
  3 tablespoons butter or margarine
  ¼ cup chopped nuts
  ½ cup orange juice
  ½ cup water
    Light cream

Wash apples and core without cutting through blossom end. Arrange in a buttered baking dish. Fill centers with raisins.

In a small bowl combine sugar, flour, cinnamon and butter or margarine. Using a fork, mix till crumbly; stir in nuts. Sprinkle mixture over apples.

Combine orange juice and water; pour over and around apples. Basting every 15 minutes, bake in a 350-degree oven for 50 minutes or till tender. Serve warm with light cream. Makes 6 servings.

Apples like cool temperatures — preferably below 40 degrees — and high humidity.

DO NOT store apples and carrots together — the carrots will develop a bitter taste.

DIVINE APPLE SQUARES

This dessert features a tart apple filling inside a tender crust with a confectioners' sugar icing glaze. It's nice for a tea.

2 cups all-purpose flour
2 tablespoons sugar
1 teaspoon salt
½ teaspoon baking powder
⅔ cup shortening
⅓ cup milk
1 teaspoon lemon juice
1 egg yolk
2 cups cornflakes, coarsely crushed
5 cups pared, thinly sliced apples
⅔ cup sugar
1 teaspoon cinnamon
   Dash nutmeg
1 egg white
1 cup sifted confectioners' sugar
2 tablespoons lemon juice

In a large mixing bowl sift together flour, 2 tablespoons sugar, salt and baking powder. With a pastry blender cut in shortening till mixture resembles coarse crumbs. Combine milk, 1 teaspoon lemon juice and egg yolk; mix lightly with a fork. Add to dry ingredients, mixing just enough for dough to shape into a ball.

Divide dough into 2 balls, making one slightly larger. On a lightly floured surface roll larger ball into a 14x10-inch rectangle; transfer to a 13x9x2-inch baking pan, extending crust ½-inch up sides of pan.

Sprinkle with cornflake crumbs; spread evenly with apple slices. Mix together ⅔ cup sugar, cinnamon and nutmeg; sprinkle over apples.

Roll remaining dough for top crust. Place over apples and pinch together edges of top and bottom crusts. Prick holes in top crust to release steam.

Beat egg white with a fork till frothy; brush evenly over top crust. Bake in a 400-degree oven for 45 to 50 minutes or until golden brown and apples are tender. Remove pan from oven to cooling rack.

Mix together confectioners' sugar and 2 tablespoons lemon

juice. Drizzle over hot crust. Cool and cut into squares. Makes 15
servings or 3 dozen tea servings.

FRENCH APPLE COBBLER

My favorite apple dessert for summertime! The secret for making a memorable dessert: use a TART apple. The first of the season pie and sauce apples — LODI — is this cook's choice!

½ **cup sugar**
2 **tablespoons all-purpose flour**
½ **teaspoon cinnamon**
¼ **teaspoon salt**
6 **cups pared, thinly sliced tart apples**
½ **cup water**
1 **teaspoon vanilla**
1 **tablespoon butter or margarine**
2 **tablespoons butter or margarine, softened**
½ **cup sugar**
1 **egg**
½ **cup all-purpose flour**
½ **teaspoon baking powder**
¼ **teaspoon salt**
   Light or whipped cream

In large bowl combine ½ cup sugar, 2 tablespoons flour, cinnamon and ¼ teaspoon salt; stir to blend. Add apples; toss to coat with sugar mixture. Turn into a buttered 9-inch square baking pan. Mix together water and vanilla; pour over apples. Dot with butter or margarine.

In medium bowl cream 2 tablespoons butter or margarine with ½ cup sugar; add egg and beat well. Sift together ½ cup flour, baking powder and ¼ teaspoon salt; add to creamed mixture. Beat till smooth. Drop batter in 9 portions on apples, spacing evenly. Batter spreads during baking.

Bake in a 375-degree oven for 35 to 40 minutes or until apples are tender and crust is golden brown. Serve warm with light or whipped cream. Makes 6 to 8 servings.

CRANBERRY CRUNCH

Stock your freezer while cranberries are in-season and enjoy them in a multitude of dishes year-round.

½ cup sugar
1 tablespoon cornstarch
¼ teaspoon salt
1 teaspoon vanilla
½ cup water
2 cups fresh or frozen cranberries
½ cup seedless raisins
1 cup quick-cooking or old-fashioned rolled oats
½ cup all-purpose flour
½ cup packed brown sugar
⅓ cup butter or margarine
Vanilla ice cream

In medium saucepan combine sugar, cornstarch, salt, vanilla and water. Stir in cranberries and raisins. Bring mixture to a boil over medium heat; reduce heat and simmer till thick and clear and berries begin to pop, about 5 minutes. Set aside.

In medium bowl combine rolled oats, flour and brown sugar; cut in butter or margarine till mixture is crumbly. Press half of mixture in bottom of a buttered 9-inch square baking pan. Spread with filling. Sprinkle remaining rolled oat mixture atop.

Bake in a 350-degree oven for 35 to 40 minutes or till top is golden brown. Serve warm or cold with a scoop of vanilla ice cream. Makes 8 servings.

RHUBARB CRUMBLE

Avid rhubarb fans will approve of this one! An easy dessert for a family supper.

½ cup butter or margarine, softened
1 cup all-purpose flour
1 cup packed brown sugar
1 teaspoon cinnamon

¾ **cup quick-cooking or old-fashioned rolled oats**
4 **cups unpeeled rhubarb cut in ½-inch lengths**
¾ **cup sugar**
2 **tablespoons cornstarch**
1 **cup water**
1 **teaspoon vanilla**
  Whipped cream

In large mixing bowl combine butter or margarine, flour, brown sugar and cinnamon; mix till consistency of coarse crumbs. Stir in rolled oats. Place half of mixture in a buttered 9-inch square baking pan. Spread rhubarb atop.

In small saucepan combine sugar, cornstarch, water and vanilla. Cook, stirring constantly, till mixture comes to a boil and thickens. Pour hot sauce evenly over rhubarb in pan.

Sprinkle remaining crumb mixture over all. Bake in a 350-degree oven for 50 to 55 minutes or till bubbly and lightly browned on top. Cut in squares and serve warm or cold with a dollop of whipped cream. Makes 9 servings.

OLD-FASHIONED STRAWBERRY SHORTCAKE

Brings back a childhood memory: picking wild berries along the riverbank and Mama's strawberry shortcake. For this seasonal splurge, the strawberries must be fresh and vine-ripened, the topping, real cream — whipped, sweetened and flavored with pure vanilla; and, hopefully, the soul will be satisfied until next strawberry season!

1 **quart fresh strawberries**
4 **to 6 tablespoons sugar**
2 **cups all-purpose flour**
2 **tablespoons sugar**
3 **teaspoons baking powder**
½ **teaspoon salt**
6 **tablespoons butter or margarine**
⅔ **cup milk**
  Whipped cream

Wash and hull strawberries; slice into thirds or quarters. Sprinkle with sugar to desired sweetness; set aside.

Into a large mixing bowl sift together flour, 2 tablespoons sugar, baking powder and salt. Using a pastry blender cut in butter or margarine till mixture resembles coarse crumbs. Add milk, all at once, and stir with a fork until a stiff dough forms.

Turn dough out onto a lightly floured surface. Pat or roll the dough to a ½-inch thickness. Cut into six 3-inch rounds. Place on ungreased baking sheet. Bake in a 450-degree oven for 12 to 15 minutes or till lightly browned.

Split shortcakes horizontally while warm; butter insides. To serve, place bottom half of individual shortcakes in deep dessert dishes. Spoon half of berries over bottoms. Cover with top halves. Spread remaining berries over top layer. Serve with sweetened whipped cream. Makes 6 large shortcakes.

To freeze a frozen dessert, freeze until firm; wrap in heavy aluminum foil, seal and return to freezer.

❖ ❖

COFFEE MARSHMALLOW MOLD

A cool and refreshing dessert to serve on a hot summer day!

1 10-ounce package marshmallows
1 cup hot coffee
1 cup whipping cream

In large saucepan combine marshmallows and hot coffee. Stir over low heat until marshmallows melt. Remove from heat and cool.

In small mixer bowl beat the chilled cream until soft peaks form. Fold whipped cream into coffee mixture. Pour into a shallow 11x7x1½-inch pan. Cover with foil or plastic and freeze until partially set, about 1 hour.

Remove from freezer. Stir mixture till smooth. Spoon into a wet 4-cup mold or loaf pan. Cover and freeze till firm, about 4 hours.

To unmold, dip frozen mold in lukewarm water to depth of contents for a few seconds. Invert onto a chilled serving plate; remove mold. Cut into 5 or 6 slices. Serve with a dollop of whipped cream and chopped nuts, if desired. Makes 5 or 6 servings.

Products containing large amounts of eggs should be kept under refrigeration and only for a limited time.

CREAM PUFFS

Mama's specialty! Unmatched by any cook, her cream puffs were light and airy with a creamy custard sauce and a delicate chocolate icing. Delicious memories of days past!

½ cup butter or margarine (1 stick)
1 cup boiling water
1 cup all-purpose flour
¼ teaspoon salt
4 eggs
Cream Filling (recipe follows)

Combine butter or margarine and water in a medium saucepan; place over low heat till butter melts.

Add flour and salt, stirring vigorously with a wooden spoon until mixture forms a ball and leaves side of pan. Remove from heat. Cool 5 minutes.

Add eggs, one at a time, beating till smooth after each addition; continue to beat till smooth and glossy.

Drop by tablespoonfuls onto a greased baking sheet, spacing 3 inches apart and rounding each spoonful up as high as possible. Bake in a 400-degree oven for 30 minutes or until puffed up and beads of moisture no longer appear on surface. DO NOT open oven door until 30 minutes have passed.

Remove from pan to cool on wire rack away from drafts. Cool. Cut a small slice from top of each puff; remove soft dough from inside. Fill with a double recipe of Cream Filling; replace tops. Frost with chocolate icing, if desired. Refrigerate. Makes 12 puffs.

Cream Filling

1 cup milk
½ cup sugar
2½ tablespoons all-purpose flour
¼ teaspoon salt
2 eggs, slightly beaten
1 teaspoon vanilla
1 tablespoon butter

In medium saucepan heat milk until tiny bubbles appear around the edge. Blend together sugar, flour and salt; add to hot milk. Cook and stir over medium heat till mixture comes to a boil. Cook, stirring constantly, 2 minutes longer.

Gradually pour a small amount of hot mixture into beaten eggs, stirring constantly; return to saucepan. Cook and stir for 3 minutes or till mixture comes just to a boil. Remove from heat. Stir in vanilla and butter. Cool. Makes 1½ cups.

Variation:

Ice Cream Puffs

Omit Cream Filling and fill puffs with ice cream. Pour hot Fudge Sauce (recipe on page 232) atop each puff.

When separating eggs, the whites must be carefully separated from the yolks as fat inhibits foaming action. It takes but a speck of yolk to prevent the whites from whipping up.

EASY PUFF PASTRIES

It's flattering remarks and requests for the recipe whenever these dainty treats appear on a dessert tray. They disappear in minutes!

    1 cup butter or margarine, firm but not hard (2 sticks)
    1½ cups all-purpose flour
    ½ cup dairy sour cream
      Strawberry or raspberry jam
    1 cup sifted confectioners' sugar
    1 tablespoon light cream or milk
    ¼ teaspoon vanilla
      Dash salt

Cut butter or margarine into flour with a pastry blender till completely mixed. Stir in sour cream with a fork until thoroughly blended. Form into a ball and chill for at least 8 hours or till ready to use. (Unbaked pastry will keep for several days in the refrigerator.)

Roll out on lightly floured surface till ¼-inch thick. Cut into desired shapes. Place on ungreased cookie sheet. Bake in a 375-degree oven for 12 minutes or till lightly browned and crisp. Remove from cookie sheet to wire rack. Cool completely. Sandwich the pastries in pairs with ½ teaspoon jam.

In bowl mix sifted sugar, light cream or milk, vanilla and salt till smooth. Drizzle glaze over tops of pastries. If desired, decorate tops with bits of candied cherries or nuts. Makes 2 to 2½ dozen tea-size puffs.

Whole eggs separate best when taken right out of the refrigerator.

For maximum volume, let egg whites stand at room temperature for 30 minutes before beating!

FRUIT DELIGHT

This much-requested recipe was picked up at a neighborhood Christmas get-together. It's colorful for the holidays and easily halved for fewer servings.

> **6 egg whites**
> **¾ teaspoon cream of tartar**
> **2 cups sugar**
> **2 cups finely crushed saltine crackers**
> **2 teaspoons vanilla**
> **¾ cup chopped nuts**
> **1 8-ounce container frozen non-dairy whipped topping, thawed**
> **1 21-ounce can cherry pie filling**

Bring egg whites to room temperature. In large mixing bowl beat egg whites and cream of tartar till frothy. Gradually add sugar, a small amount at a time, beating till very stiff peaks form and sugar is dissolved. Fold in saltine crumbs, vanilla and nuts.

Spread meringue in a buttered 13x9x2-inch baking pan. Bake in a 325-degree oven for 25 to 30 minutes or till delicately browned and crusty. Cool overnight.

With a spatula, press crust flat in pan. Cover crust evenly with whipped topping. Chill for 1 hour. Carefully spread pie filling evenly over topping. Refrigerate. Makes 12 to 15 servings.

Beat until egg whites stand in peaks before adding sugar. If sugar is added too early, a marshmallow-like consistency results!

Store leftover egg white, tightly covered, in the refrigerator for 2 or 3 days. Or, label with number of whites in container and freeze up to 6 or 8 months. Use as soon as they are thawed.

CHOCOLATE CHEESECAKE

Chocoholics will love this combination — chocolate and cream cheese with a yummy coco-nut topping.

1¼ cups fine chocolate wafer crumbs
2 tablespoons sugar
3 tablespoons butter or margarine, melted
2 8-ounce packages cream cheese, softened, plus
1 3-ounce package cream cheese, softened
1 cup sugar
¼ cup unsweetened cocoa
3 eggs
1½ teaspoons vanilla
   Coco-Nut Topping (recipe follows)

In medium bowl combine crumbs and 2 tablespoons sugar. Add melted butter or margarine; mix till blended. Press mixture evenly on bottom and 1-inch up the sides of a buttered 9-inch spring-form pan. Bake in a 350-degree oven for 10 minutes. Cool.

Meanwhile, in large mixer bowl beat cream cheese till light. Gradually add 1 cup sugar and cocoa; beat until fluffy. Add eggs, one at a time, beating well after each addition. Blend in vanilla. Pour mixture over crust.

Bake in a 300-degree oven for 55 to 60 minutes or until center is just set. Cool to room temperature, away from drafts, on a wire rack. Spread with Coco-Nut Topping. Use a metal spatula to loosen crust from side of pan. Cover with foil and refrigerate for at least 3 hours. Loosen and remove side of pan. Makes 12 servings.

Coco-Nut Topping

2 tablespoons butter or margarine
⅓ cup light cream or evaporated milk
2 tablespoons packed brown sugar
1 egg (or 2 egg yolks)
½ teaspoon vanilla
½ cup shredded coconut
½ cup chopped nuts

In small saucepan combine butter or margarine, cream or evaporated milk, brown sugar and egg; cook over low heat, stirring constantly, until mixture thickens. Remove from heat; stir in vanilla, coconut and nuts. Cool.

JODY'S CHEESECAKE

The BEST of several recipes results in a super-tasting beauty for very special occasions. The oatmeal crust takes this one out of the ordinary class!

1½ cups quick-cooking rolled oats
½ cup chopped nuts
¼ cup packed brown sugar
⅓ cup butter or margarine, melted
3 8-ounce packages cream cheese, softened
¾ cup sugar
3 tablespoons lemon juice
1 tablespoon grated lemon peel
4 eggs
1 teaspoon vanilla
1 cup dairy sour cream
2 teaspoons sugar
1 teaspoon vanilla

In medium bowl combine rolled oats, nuts and brown sugar. Add melted butter or margarine; blend until mixture is crumbly. Pack mixture evenly on bottom and 1-inch up sides of a buttered 9-inch springform pan. Bake in a 350-degree oven for 15 minutes or till golden brown. Cool.

Meanwhile, place cream cheese in a large mixing bowl; beat till fluffy. Gradually blend in sugar, lemon juice and peel. Add eggs, one at a time, beating well after each addition. Blend in 1 teaspoon vanilla. Pour mixture over crumb crust.

Bake at 325-degrees for 60 to 65 minutes or till center is firm. Remove from oven and cool on wire rack, away from drafts, for 15 minutes.

Combine sour cream, 2 teaspoons sugar and 1 teaspoon vanilla; mix well. Gently spread atop cheesecake. Return to oven and bake at 450 degrees for 5 minutes to set topping.

Allow to cool. Use a metal spatula to loosen crust from side of pan. DO NOT remove side of pan. Cover with foil and refrigerate for 24 hours. Loosen and remove side of pan. If desired, garnish with canned cherry pie filling, fresh strawberries or melted red currant jelly. Makes 12 servings.

Store baking chocolate in a cool dry place. When stored at a high temperature, the chocolate surface becomes gray — which is known as "bloom."

ECLAIR CAKE

A new look for an old childhood favorite! This one requires no baking . . . it's made with graham crackers, instant pudding and whipped topping. Easy and delicious!

    1 1-pound package graham crackers
    2 packages (4 serving-size) instant vanilla pudding and
      pie filling
   3½ cups chilled milk
    2 cups frozen non-dairy whipped topping, thawed
    2 1-ounce squares unsweetened chocolate
    3 tablespoons butter or margarine
   1½ cups sifted confectioners' sugar
    3 tablespoons milk
    2 teaspoons light corn syrup
    1 teaspoon vanilla

Butter bottom of a 13x9x2-inch baking pan. Line with a layer of graham crackers. In a large bowl combine pudding mix and milk. Beat at medium speed of mixer for 2 minutes or until thoroughly blended. Fold in whipped topping. Spread half of mixture over graham crackers in pan. Cover with second layer of crackers. Repeat with remaining pudding mixture and cover with crackers. Cover and chill in refrigerator for 2 hours.

Meanwhile, in small saucepan melt chocolate and butter or margarine over hot water. Remove from heat; cool. Stir in confectioners' sugar, milk, corn syrup and vanilla. Beat till smooth. Spread evenly atop Eclair Cake. Chill for 24 hours. Makes 12 to 15 servings.

LUCY'S CHOCOLATE DESSERT

A recipe from the Southern Gateway to New England is our choice for St. Patrick's Day! It's simple to prepare, made in advance and a perfect finale to a hearty meal.

**2 cups fine chocolate creme-filled cookie crumbs
(about 24 cookies)
¼ cup butter or margarine, melted
1 pint whipping cream
1 7-ounce jar marshmallow creme
¼ cup green creme de menthe**

In medium bowl combine chocolate crumbs with melted butter or margarine until well mixed. Press half of mixture evenly into an ungreased 13x9x2-inch pan.

In chilled bowl beat whipping cream until stiff. Fold in marshmallow creme and creme de menthe. Pour evenly over crumbs in pan. Cover with remaining crumb mixture. Freeze until firm, about 4 hours. Makes 12 servings.

PETITE PECAN TARTS

My sister Lorraine's claim to fame. You'll love these nut-filled tarts. For a change, try the cream cheese pastries; they're good, too!

**1¼ cups butter or margarine (2½ sticks)
1 8-ounce package cream cheese, softened
2½ cups all-purpose flour
⅛ teaspoon salt
3 eggs**

1½ cups packed brown sugar
3 tablespoons butter, melted
½ teaspoon vanilla
⅛ teaspoon salt
1 cup chopped pecans

In bowl cream butter or margarine until fluffy. Add softened cream cheese and blend until smooth. Gradually add flour and salt; mix well. Gather dough into a ball. Cover and refrigerate at least 1 hour or till ready to use. (Pastry will keep up to 2 weeks in refrigerator.)

Form into small balls the size of walnuts. Place in tiny, ungreased muffin cups. Press against sides and bottom with your fingers, making sure crust is not too thick.

In mixing bowl beat eggs till light. Add brown sugar, melted butter, vanilla and salt; mix thoroughly. Stir in pecans. Spoon 1 teaspoon mixture into each crust. Bake in a 350-degree oven for 15 to 20 minutes or until golden brown. Cool 10 minutes. Remove from pans to wire racks. Top with whipped cream, if desired. Makes 4 to 5 dozen tarts.

Variation:

Cream Cheese Pastries

Make and chill dough as for Petite Pecan Tarts except — roll dough out, a portion at a time, on a lightly floured surface to no more than a ³⁄₁₆-inch thickness. Cut out with fancy cookie cutters, making pairs of each shape.

Place bottom half on ungreased cookie sheet; brush lightly with milk, then spread with ½ teaspoon of strawberry, raspberry or apricot preserves. Cover with top half and seal by pressing down around edge. Brush top lightly with more milk and sprinkle with colored sugar.

Bake in a 350-degree oven for 10 to 12 minutes or till golden. Remove from pan to wire rack. Makes about 3 dozen pastries.

❖ ❖

Bring butter or margarine to room temperature before creaming.

❖ ❖

SHIRLEY'S LEMON SQUARE GEMS

A contemporary recipe made simple with convenience foods.
Serve this tri-layered dessert on a warm summer day!

1 cup all-purpose flour
½ cup butter or margarine, softened
¾ cup finely chopped nuts
1 8-ounce package cream cheese, softened
1 cup confectioners' sugar
1 8-ounce container frozen non-dairy whipped
    topping, thawed
2 packages (4 serving-size) instant lemon pudding and
    pie filling
2½ cups chilled milk

In a medium bowl combine flour and butter or margarine; mix well. Stir in nuts. Press mixture in a 13x9x2-inch baking pan. Bake in a 350-degree oven for 15 minutes or till lightly browned. Cool.

In a bowl blend cream cheese and confectioners' sugar till smooth. Fold in 1 cup whipped topping. Spread over cooled crust.

In a large mixing bowl beat pudding mix and milk until smooth and creamy. Spread over cream cheese layer. Cover with remaining whipped topping (2 cups). Cover pan and chill for at least 4 hours. Makes 15 servings.

Variation:

Chocolate Square Gems

Prepare recipe for Lemon Square Gems except — substitute 2 packages instant chocolate pudding and pie filling for lemon.

In most recipes walnuts and pecans are interchangeable. To measure, pack nuts lightly into measuring cup and level off.

SKILLET CUSTARD

Try this one when heating the oven is inefficient or impractical. You may never BAKE another custard.

2 eggs
3 tablespoons sugar
1½ cups milk, scalded
1 teaspoon vanilla
⅛ teaspoon salt
Nutmeg

In a quart measuring utensil or bowl beat eggs till evenly blended. Beat in sugar. Slowly add scalded milk, beating with a fork. Stir in vanilla and salt.

Divide mixture evenly among four 6-ounce custard cups. Sprinkle tops lightly with nutmeg. Place in a heavy 10-inch skillet with a tight-fitting cover. Add hot water to within ½-inch of top of cups. Heat just to simmering. Reduce heat and cover skillet. Simmer for 12 to 15 minutes or until custards are set. DO NOT let water boil!

Immediately remove custard cups from water and cool slightly on a wire rack. Refrigerate. Serve cold. Makes 4 servings.

Variation:

Caramel Custards

Prepare custard as recipe directs except — reduce sugar to 2 tablespoons. Place 1 tablespoon caramel ice cream sauce in bottom of each custard cup. Fill with egg mixture. Omit nutmeg and cook as directed.

❖ ❖

Too much heat will cause a custard to curdle. Use a double boiler for a custard sauce. Baked custards should be placed in a pan with about 1-inch cold water.

❖ ❖

SUZANNE'S TRIFLE

Everyone's favorite and "I suspect you will want a second help-
ing" of this simple, yet elegant dessert. A delicious ending to a
heavy meal!

Filling:
 ½ 9-inch white angel food cake, torn into 1-inch pieces
  (4 to 5 cups)
 ½ cup strawberry jam or raspberry preserves
 1 16-ounce can sliced peaches, drained
 2 tablespoons dark rum (optional)
Custard Topping:
 1¼ cups milk
 1 egg
 ⅓ cup sugar
 3 tablespoons cornstarch
 ¼ teaspoon salt
 2 tablespoons milk
 1 tablespoon butter
 1 teaspoon vanilla
 ½ cup sliced pecans
  Whipped cream

To assemble Trifle, arrange half of cake pieces in a 2-quart glass
serving bowl. Spread with half of jam. Arrange half of peach
slices atop. (If very thick, cut slices in half lengthwise.) Sprinkle
with 1 tablespoon rum, if desired. Repeat with remaining cake
pieces, jam, peaches and rum.

To prepare Custard Topping, in a saucepan bring milk to just
below boiling point over low heat. In mixing bowl beat egg, sugar,
cornstarch, salt and 2 tablespoons milk. Gradually stir in hot milk.
Return mixture to saucepan and cook, stirring constantly, over

Never eat a custard mixture that has been held overnight with-
out refrigeration.

low heat till mixture thickens. Cool slightly; pour warm custard over filling. Sprinkle pecans atop.

Cover and chill thoroughly in refrigerator. To serve, spoon into dessert dishes and top with whipped cream. Makes 8 servings.

CUSTARD SAUCE

Let 'em eat cake; I'll eat the sauce.

1½ cups milk
2 eggs (see note)
3 tablespoons sugar
⅛ teaspoon salt
1 teaspoon vanilla
1 teaspoon butter

Heat milk in the top of a double boiler until tiny bubbles appear around the edge. Remove from heat.

In a medium bowl or 1-quart measuring utensil beat eggs lightly; stir in sugar and salt. Gradually add hot milk, stirring constantly with a wooden spoon.

Return mixture to top of double boiler and place over hot, NOT BOILING, water. Cook, stirring constantly, for about 5 minutes or until mixture coats a metal spoon.

Remove from heat and pour mixture into medium bowl; set in a larger bowl of cold water to hasten cooling. Stir in vanilla and butter. Chill 4 hours before serving over sweetened fresh fruits or angel cake slices. Makes 1½ cups.

Note:

4 egg yolks may be substituted for 2 eggs.

Custard mixtures are very perishable. Cook; cover and store in the refrigerator — no longer than 48 hours.

FUDGE SAUCE

Smooth and chocolate-y!

1 1-ounce square unsweetened chocolate
6 tablespoons hot water
1 tablespoon butter
⅛ teaspoon salt
1 cup sugar
3 tablespoons light corn syrup
1 teaspoon vanilla

In a small saucepan combine chocolate, hot water, butter and salt. Place over low heat and stir constantly until chocolate and butter melt.

Add sugar and corn syrup; stir until sugar dissolves. Bring mixture to a boil over medium-low heat. Simmer gently for 5 minutes, stirring occasionally to prevent scorching. Remove from heat and stir in vanilla. Serve warm over ice cream or cake. Makes 1 cup.

HARD SAUCE

An Indian Pudding's companion!

½ cup butter or margarine
1⅔ cups sifted confectioners' sugar
2 tablespoons light cream
1 teaspoon vanilla

In small bowl cream butter or margarine till soft. Gradually blend in sugar, cream and vanilla. Pack into a small loaf pan. Cover and freeze. To serve, cut into slices.

OLD-FASHIONED BERRY SAUCE

Created with good eating in mind!

2 cups fresh or frozen blueberries, raspberries, sliced
strawberries or a combination of berries

½ cup water
1 tablespoon cornstarch
2 tablespoons water
¼ cup sugar
2 teaspoons lemon juice

In a saucepan combine berries and ½ cup water; heat until berries begin to wilt.

Dissolve cornstarch in 2 tablespoons cold water; add to berries with sugar. Cook and stir until mixture is clear and slightly thickened. Stir in lemon juice. Serve warm or cold over ice cream or wedges of sponge cake. Makes 2 cups.

VANILLA SAUCE

Creamy and rich!

1 cup sugar
½ cup butter or margarine
½ cup light cream
1½ teaspoons vanilla
Dash nutmeg

In a saucepan combine sugar, butter or margarine and cream. Place over low heat, stirring occasionally, for 10 to 15 minutes or till slightly thickened. Stir in vanilla and nutmeg. Serve hot over puddings, apple desserts or ice cream. Refrigerate and reheat any remaining sauce. Makes 1½ cups.

Variation:

Butterscotch Sauce

Follow recipe for Vanilla Sauce except — use 1 cup packed brown sugar for white sugar and omit nutmeg.

Chapter 10

Pies, flaky and tender, picture-pretty and people-pleasing, are an all-time, all-occasion and all-American dessert.

Pie, as it is known today, is a food tradition with Yankee roots. In an attempt to stretch her sparse food supply, a thrifty New England housewife discovered that a round, shallow pan required less filling than a deep dish. Soon "pyes" were almost daily fare and, in some instances, consumed at every meal. We are indebted to Martha Washington, however, for having advanced the art of preparing fruit and custard "pyes."

The pie you bake is only as good as the crust. It must be flaky, fork-tender and golden brown; it must complement the filling. The flavor and texture may be varied with the type of fat; vegetable shortening and lard are popular choices.

Pies, whether single or double crust, need a raised, fluted or shaped edge to give them a professional touch. Customize your creation with a fluting to suit your fancy: plain, fork-pressed or scalloped. Then, add a slit or two in the top crust to allow the steam to escape while the pie bakes.

Besides the traditional favorites which make use of our wonderful indigenous foods, this treasury of temptations comprises a variety of pies with cosmopolitan appeal. Whether you bake a Perfect Apple Pie to satisfy the soul of a loved one or prepare an impressive Chocolate Angel Strata to soothe your creative instincts, may your diners sing praises for your pastry-making skills!

Pies & Pastry

BLUEBERRY CRUMB PIE

Take a ready-made shell from the freezer and marvel at the ease in preparing this Down East delight. The bottom crust is pastry; the top, a crumbly topping. Inside, everyone's favorite — little gems of goodness . . . either fresh or frozen!

> Pastry for single-crust pie
> 4 cups fresh or frozen blueberries
> ½ cup sugar
> 2½ tablespoons quick-cooking tapioca or 4 tablespoons all-purpose flour
> ½ teaspoon cinnamon
> 1 tablespoon lemon juice
> 1 tablespoon butter
> ½ cup sugar
> ⅓ cup all-purpose flour
> ¼ cup butter or margarine
> Dash salt
> Vanilla ice cream

Prepare pastry for single-crust pie. Fit into a 9-inch pie plate. Flute edges high. DO NOT prick.

Place half of berries in pastry-lined pie plate. Mix together ½ cup sugar, tapioca or flour, and cinnamon; sprinkle half of the mixture over berries in pie plate. Add remaining berries and cover with remaining tapioca mixture. Drizzle with lemon juice and dot with butter.

To make crumb topping, combine ½ cup sugar, ⅓ cup flour, ¼

To prevent a single crust from shrinking, bake-blind. Fit a 12-inch square of aluminum foil into unbaked pastry. Spread 1½ cups of dry beans or lentils over foil. Bake 8 minutes. Remove foil and beans and return pastry to oven to finish baking. Store beans in a jar in the cupboard and save exclusively for this purpose. Don't try to cook them!

❖ ❖

cup butter or margarine and a dash of salt; blend till crumbly. Spread evenly over berries.

Bake in a 375-degree oven for 40 to 45 minutes or till golden brown. If necessary, wrap strips of aluminum foil around edge of pie to prevent over-browning. Serve slightly warm or cold with a scoop of vanilla ice cream. Makes 6 to 8 servings.

Pastry needs a hot oven to make it flaky and tender and to set bottom crust quickly. Glass or enamel pans are good choices.

CARROT PIE

"C'mom eat your carrots!" No amount of cajoling worked on getting a five year old to eat cooked carrots until — "Mommie, if you make this pie, I'll eat my carrots EVERY day!"

Pastry for single-crust pie
1½ cups mashed cooked carrot
¾ cup sugar
½ teaspoon cinnamon
½ teaspoon ginger
½ teaspoon salt
2 eggs
1½ cups milk
1 tablespoon butter, melted

Prepare pastry for single-crust pie. Fit into a 9-inch pie plate. Flute edge high. DO NOT prick.

In a large mixing bowl combine carrot, sugar, cinnamon, ginger and salt; mix thoroughly. Beat in eggs, milk and melted butter. (Or, place all ingredients in blender container. Cover and blend until mixture is smooth.) Pour mixture into pastry-lined pie plate.

Bake in a 375-degree oven for 50 to 55 minutes or till knife inserted near center comes out clean. Serve slightly warm or cold with a dollop of whipped cream, if desired. Makes 6 to 8 servings.

CHEESECAKE PIE

From the Governor's wife! Try this one when you hanker for cheesecake and time in the kitchen is precious.

1 cup graham cracker crumbs
3 tablespoons butter or margarine, melted
¾ pound (12 ounces) cream cheese, softened
2 eggs
⅓ cup sugar
2 tablespoons lemon juice
2 teaspoons grated lemon peel
½ teaspoon vanilla
   Dash salt
⅔ cup dairy sour cream
1 tablespoon sugar
½ teaspoon vanilla
   Fresh or frozen strawberries

In small mixing bowl combine cracker crumbs and butter or margarine; blend well. Press mixture evenly and firmly against bottom and sides of a 9-inch pie plate.

In large mixing bowl beat cream cheese until fluffy. Add eggs, ⅓ cup sugar, lemon juice and peel, ½ teaspoon vanilla and salt. Beat until smooth. Pour mixture into crust. Bake in a 325-degree oven for 25 to 30 minutes or until set. Cool for 10 minutes.

Combine sour cream, 1 tablespoon sugar and ½ teaspoon vanilla; blend well. Spread over pie; return to oven for 10 minutes longer. Cool on wire rack. Chill in refrigerator for several hours or overnight. Decorate with fresh strawberries or spread a spoonful of thawed, frozen berries over each serving. Makes 6 to 8 servings.

CHERRY PIE

A homespun favorite flavored with memories: our backyard with a cherry tree laden with fruit and a flock of robins eager to share the bounty!

¾ to 1 cup sugar
2 tablespoons all-purpose flour

2 tablespoons quick-cooking tapioca
¼ teaspoon cinnamon
4 cups pitted fresh sour pie cherries
   Pastry for lattice-top pie
4 or 5 drops almond extract
1 tablespoon butter
   Vanilla ice cream

In a large mixing bowl combine sugar, flour, tapioca and cinnamon; add cherries and toss lightly to coat with mixture.

Prepare pastry for lattice-top pie. Fit half into a 9-inch pie plate. DO NOT prick. Fill with cherry mixture. Sprinkle with almond extract and dot with butter.

Cover with lattice top. Seal and flute edges high. Brush strips with milk. Bake in a 400-degree oven for 40 to 50 minutes or till bubbly and nicely browned. Serve warm with vanilla ice cream. Makes 6 to 8 servings.

Variation:

Canned Cherries In A Pie

Follow recipe for Cherry Pie except — use one 16-ounce can sour pie cherries, undrained, omit flour and reduce tapioca to 1½ tablespoons. Pour mixture into an 8-inch pastry-lined pie plate; cover with a lattice top and bake at 400 degrees for 30 to 35 minutes. Makes 6 servings.

❖ ❖

To make an even layer on bottom and sides of a 9-inch crumb crust, set an 8-inch pie plate on top of crumbs and press firmly.

❖ ❖ ❖ ❖ ❖ ❖ ❖ ❖

To prevent juice from bubbling out and over, and pie edge from over-browning, wrap a wet 1-inch strip of cotton fabric around edge of fruit pies. Remove after pie is baked.

❖ ❖

CHOCOLATE ANGEL STRATA

An elegant dessert with layers — pastry, meringue, chocolate and whipped cream — and "everyone fighting for a sliver."

> **Pastry for single-crust pie**
> **2 egg whites**
> **¼ teaspoon salt**
> **¼ teaspoon cinnamon**
> **½ teaspoon vinegar**
> **½ cup sugar**
> **1 cup (6-ounce pkg.) semi-sweet chocolate morsels**
> **¼ cup water**
> **2 egg yolks**
> **1 cup whipping cream**
> **¼ cup sugar**
> **¼ teaspoon cinnamon**

Prepare pastry for single-crust pie. Fit into a 9-inch pie plate. Trim and flute edge. Prick bottom and sides with a fork. Bake in a 425-degree oven for 12 to 15 minutes or till golden.

Meanwhile, in medium bowl combine egg whites, salt, cinnamon and vinegar. Beat till soft mounds form. Gradually add ½ cup sugar, beating till meringue stands in stiff, glossy peaks. Spread over bottom and sides of baked pie shell. Bake at 325 degrees for 15 to 18 minutes or till golden. Cool.

In small bowl combine chocolate morsels and water; melt over hot water. Remove from heat; stir in slightly beaten egg yolks. Spread 3 tablespoons of mixture over meringue. Chill remaining chocolate mixture.

In chilled bowl combine whipping cream, ¼ cup sugar and cinnamon; beat till stiff. Spread half over chocolate mixture.

For perfect chocolate curls, shave chocolate with a vegetable peeler into long thin strips.

Fold reserved chocolate mixture into remaining whipped cream. Carefully spread over whipped cream layer in pie shell. Chill in refrigerator for at least 4 hours before serving. Garnish with semi-sweet chocolate curls, if desired. Makes 6 to 8 servings.

CRAZY CUSTARD PIE

It's crazy — no mixing, no rolling and no shaping. This pie makes its own crust!

½ cup butter or margarine, melted (1 stick)
3 eggs
¾ cup sugar
⅔ cup shredded coconut
½ cup all-purpose flour
¼ teaspoon salt
¼ teaspoon nutmeg
1 teaspoon vanilla
2 cups milk

In blender container combine butter or margarine, eggs, sugar, coconut, flour, salt, nutmeg, vanilla and milk. If container will not hold all of mixture, add only as much milk as it will hold. Blend on high speed, stopping blender occasionally to stir, for 1 minute. Stir in remaining milk. (Or beat in a large bowl with hand beater for 2 minutes.)

Pour mixture into a buttered deep 9x1¼-inch pie plate. Bake in a 325-degree oven for 45 to 50 minutes or till knife inserted 1-inch from center comes out clean. Cool on wire rack. Serve with a dollop of whipped cream, if desired. Refrigerate leftovers. Makes 6 to 8 servings.

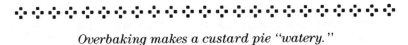

Overbaking makes a custard pie "watery."

DATE PIE

*A recipe from Mama. It's sweetened naturally with dates . . .
and very rich. Serve in small slices!*

> **Pastry for single-crust pie**
> **1 cup (8-ounce pkg.) snipped pitted dates**
> **½ cup water**
> **1 tablespoon butter or margarine**
> **2 tablespoons all-purpose flour**
> **1 tablespoon sugar**
> **¼ teaspoon salt**
> **1½ cups milk**
> **2 eggs**

Prepare pastry for single-crust pie. Fit into a 9-inch pie plate.
Flute edge high. DO NOT prick.

In medium saucepan combine dates and water. Cook over low
heat, stirring frequently, till dates are soft. Add butter or margarine; mix well. Cool. Stir in flour, sugar and salt.

In medium bowl combine milk and eggs; beat well. Add to date
mixture; mix thoroughly. Pour mixture into pastry-lined pie
plate.

Bake in a 400-degree oven for 15 minutes. Reduce heat to 350
degrees and bake for 25 to 30 minutes longer or till no imprint
remains when lightly touched in center with fingertip. Serve cold
with a dollop of whipped cream, if desired. Makes 8 servings.

FRENCH BERRY PIE

*When is a recipe rated GOOD? At our house, it is when the fam-
ily asks for seconds. I feel confident that your family will judge
this recipe as GOOD, perhaps Better. It's irresistibly good . . . and
possibly the Best berry pie you'll ever taste!*

> **1 3-ounce package cream cheese, softened**
> **3 tablespoons light cream or dairy sour cream**
> **1 9-inch baked pie shell**
> **1 quart fresh strawberries, raspberries or blueberries,
> rinsed and hulled, if necessary**

½ cup sugar
3 tablespoons cornstarch
½ cup water
1 tablespoon lemon juice
¾ cup whipping cream
2 tablespoons confectioners' sugar

In small bowl blend together cream cheese and cream or sour cream until smooth. Spread over bottom of pie shell.

Mash enough berries to measure 1 cup. In saucepan mix together sugar and cornstarch. Stir in water, lemon juice and mashed berries. Cook over low heat, stirring constantly, until thick and clear. Cool 10 minutes.

Meanwhile, arrange remaining berries, stem end down, over cream cheese in pastry shell. (Halve large strawberries.) Pour cooked mixture over berries. Chill for 3 hours or till set.

In chilled bowl beat whipping cream and confectioners' sugar until stiff. Spread a ring of whipped cream around outside edge of pie. Makes 6 to 8 servings.

HARVEST PIE

A fall feast! It's tart and picture-pretty with apples, cranberries and nuts peeking through a lattice crust.

½ cup sugar
2 tablespoons all-purpose flour
¼ teaspoon cinnamon
¼ teaspoon salt
1 teaspoon grated orange peel
⅓ cup honey
1 tablespoon butter or margarine
3 cups diced pared tart apple (3 medium)
2 cups fresh or frozen cranberries
½ cup coarsely chopped nuts
   Pastry for lattice-top pie
   Vanilla ice cream

In a large saucepan combine sugar, flour, cinnamon, salt, orange peel, honey and butter or margarine. Cook, stirring constantly, for 2 minutes or till sugar dissolves.

Add apple and cranberries. Bring mixture to a boil; cook, stirring occasionally, for 2 or 3 minutes or till cranberries begin to burst. Remove from heat and stir in nuts. Set aside.

Prepare pastry for lattice-top pie. Fit half into a 9-inch pie plate. DO NOT prick. Fill with cranberry mixture. Cover with lattice top. Seal and flute edges. Brush strips with milk; sprinkle with sugar.

Bake in a 400-degree oven for 35 to 40 minutes or till crust is golden brown and filling is bubbly. Cool on a wire rack. Serve warm with vanilla ice cream. Makes 6 to 8 servings.

When a recipe calls for grated lemon or orange peel, thoroughly wash the fruit before grating.

HEAVENLY PIE

No misnomer this pie. Your guests will agree, "It's heavenly!" and worth your effort.

> 1 cup sugar
> ¼ teaspoon cream of tartar
> 4 egg whites
> 4 egg yolks
> ½ cup sugar
> 3 tablespoons lemon juice
> 1 tablespoon finely grated lemon peel
> 1 pint whipping cream (see note)

Sift together 1 cup sugar and cream of tartar. Beat egg whites until stiff but not dry. Gradually add sugar mixture, beating until smooth and glossy. Spread meringue on bottom and sides of a 9- or 10-inch well-greased pie plate, hollowing out center and being careful not to spread too close to the rim. Bake in 275-degree oven for 1 hour. Cool.

In upper part of double boiler, beat egg yolks slightly; stir in ½ cup sugar, lemon juice and peel. Cook over hot water, stirring constantly, until very thick (about 8 to 10 minutes). Remove from heat. Cool.

Whip cream until stiff. Fold half into lemon-egg mixture. Fill meringue shell. Spread remaining cream atop filling. Chill 24-hours before serving. Makes 6 to 8 servings.

Note:
For best results, thoroughly chill mixing bowl and beaters before whipping cream!

MUD PIE

A native shares a popular Southern dessert — a rich freezer pie that's a winner with chocolate enthusiasts!

1½ cups fine chocolate wafer crumbs
¼ cup butter or margarine, melted
1 quart coffee ice cream
1 square (1 ounce) unsweetened chocolate
2 tablespoons butter or margarine
¾ cup confectioners' sugar
Dash salt
⅓ cup light cream or evaporated milk
¼ teaspoon vanilla

In medium bowl combine 1¼ cups of the wafer crumbs and ¼ cup melted butter or margarine; mix well. Press evenly and firmly against bottom and sides of an ungreased 9-inch pie pan. Chill until firm. Set aside remaining ¼ cup crumbs. Soften ice cream slightly; spoon into chilled crust. Freeze.

In top of double boiler combine chocolate, butter or margarine, confectioners' sugar, salt and light cream or evaporated milk; mix well. Simmer over hot water for 30 minutes, stirring occasionally. Add vanilla.

Drizzle hot sauce over top of ice cream. Sprinkle with reserved crumbs. Serve immediately or return to freezer. Garnish with a dollop of whipped cream and slivered almonds, if desired. Makes 6 to 8 servings.

PERFECT APPLE PIE

A favorite with my "apple-holics!" Bet yours will like it, too. Choose a variety of apple that suits your fancy.

Pastry for double-crust pie
2 pounds tart cooking apples
½ cup sugar
2 tablespoons all-purpose flour
1 teaspoon cinnamon
¼ teaspoon nutmeg
¼ teaspoon salt
1 tablespoon butter or margarine

Prepare pastry for double-crust pie. Fit half into a 9-inch pie plate. DO NOT prick. Set aside.

Pare apples; quarter, core and thinly slice to make about 5½ cups. In a large mixing bowl combine sugar, flour, cinnamon, nutmeg and salt. Add sliced apples and toss gently to coat with mixture.

Fill pastry-lined pie plate with apple slices, heaping up apples in center of pie. Dot with butter or margarine.

Cover with top crust, pressing edges together. Seal by pressing with a fork or fluting with fingers. Cut slits or make a design in top crust to allow steam to escape. Sprinkle lightly with sugar, if desired.

Bake in a 400-degree oven for 50 to 55 minutes or until crust is a deep golden brown and apples are tender. Serve warm or cold with a slice of cheese or a scoop of vanilla ice cream, if desired. Makes 6 to 8 servings.

PISTACHIO ICE CREAM PIE

This recipe traveled a circuitous route before finding my kitchen. Consisting of instant pudding mix, milk and ice cream, this easy freezer pie makes a refreshing, light dessert.

1 package (4 serving-size) instant pistachio pudding
   and pie filling
1 cup chilled milk
1 quart vanilla ice cream, slightly softened

1 9-inch graham cracker crust
1 cup whipped cream or frozen non-dairy whipped topping, thawed

In deep mixing bowl combine dry pudding mix and milk. Beat
at medium speed of electric mixer for 2 minutes or until thoroughly blended. Fold in softened ice cream. Turn mixture into
graham cracker crust. Cover loosely with aluminum foil; freeze for
several hours or till firm.

Remove from freezer 10 minutes before serving. Top each serving with a dollop of whipped cream or topping. Garnish with additional graham cracker crumbs, if desired. Makes 6 to 8 servings.

RASPBERRY BAVARIAN PIE

*A true Bavarian does not include egg whites — only whipped
cream. To avoid leftovers, some cooks whip and add the egg
whites. Others, however, make a meringue shell rather than a pastry crust.*

Pastry for single-crust pie
½ cup sugar
1 envelope or 1 tablespoon unflavored gelatin
½ cup milk
3 egg yolks
1 tablespoon lemon juice
1 cup puréed raspberries or strawberries
¾ cup whipping cream
2 tablespoons confectioners' sugar

Prepare pastry for single-crust pie. Fit into a 9-inch pie plate.
Flute edge; prick pastry with a fork. Bake in a 425-degree oven
for 12 to 15 minutes or till golden. Cool.

In top of double boiler combine sugar, gelatin and milk. Heat
over simmering water until steaming hot.

In medium bowl beat egg yolks slightly. Gradually mix a small
amount of hot milk mixture into yolks, stirring constantly. Return
to saucepan; cook and stir for 3 to 5 minutes or until thickened
and no raw taste of egg remains. Remove from heat and stir in
lemon juice and puréed berries. Chill in refrigerator, stirring occa-

sionally, until mixture mounds when dropped from a spoon.

In chilled bowl combine whipping cream and confectioners' sugar. Beat until firm peaks form. Fold whipped cream into raspberry mixture. Spoon into baked pastry shell. Chill till firm, at least 4 hours. Top with additional whipped cream and garnish with raspberries, if desired. Makes 6 to 8 servings.

To prevent meringue from shrinking during baking, spread meringue to the edge of pie crust.

When cutting a meringue-topped pie, dip the knife in water to prevent the meringue from sticking to the knife.

RHUBARB MERINGUE PIE

A recipe from Grandma's! It's beautiful with a flaky crust holding a rhubarb-custard filling and a fluffy meringue.

Pastry for single-crust pie
3 egg yolks
½ cup light cream or half-and-half
1 cup sugar
3 tablespoons all-purpose flour
¼ teaspoon salt
¼ teaspoon nutmeg
3 cups unpeeled rhubarb cut in ½-inch lengths
3 egg whites
¼ teaspoon cream of tartar
⅓ cup sugar

Prepare pastry for single-crust pie. Fit into a 9-inch pie plate. Flute edge high. DO NOT prick.

In large mixing bowl beat yolks till thick. Blend in cream or half-

and-half. Combine 1 cup sugar, flour, salt and nutmeg; add to egg mixture and beat until smooth. Add rhubarb; stir to coat with egg mixture. Pour mixture into pastry-lined pie plate.

Bake in a 425-degree oven for 10 minutes. Reduce heat to 350 degrees and continue to bake for 30 to 35 minutes or till center is set.

Meanwhile, in small bowl beat egg whites with cream of tartar till frothy. Gradually beat in ⅓ cup sugar; continue beating until stiff peaks form. Spread meringue over filling, sealing to edge of crust. Continue baking at 350 degrees for 15 minutes or till meringue is golden brown. Makes 6 to 8 servings.

SPRING RHUBARB PIE

One of our springtime favorites and so-o-o easy! This single-crust pie with its tart filling and crumb topping is a perfect ending to your Memorial Day cook-out!

    1 egg
    ¾ cup sugar
    ¼ cup all-purpose flour
    ½ teaspoon nutmeg
    4 cups unpeeled rhubarb cut in ¾-inch lengths
       Pastry for single-crust pie
    ½ cup sugar
    ⅓ cup all-purpose flour
    ¼ teaspoon salt
    ¼ cup butter or margarine

In large mixing bowl beat egg lightly. Stir in sugar, flour and nutmeg. Add rhubarb; toss to coat with egg mixture. Set aside.

Prepare pastry for a single-crust pie. Fit into a 9-inch pie plate. Flute edge high. DO NOT prick. Fill crust with rhubarb mixture.

In small bowl mix together ½ cup sugar, ⅓ cup flour and salt. Cut in butter or margarine till mixture is crumbly. Spread evenly over rhubarb.

Bake in a 425-degree oven for 20 minues. Reduce heat to 350 degrees and bake for 20 minutes longer or till rhubarb is tender and topping is golden brown. Serve warm or cold. Makes 6 to 8 servings.

SOUTHERN PECAN PIE

The specialty of a Georgia cook to her Yankee friends. Pecan-addicts are sure to find it pleasing to the bite!

Pastry for single-crust pie
3 eggs
1 cup dark corn syrup
⅓ cup sugar
⅓ cup packed brown sugar
¼ teaspoon salt
1 teaspoon vanilla
⅓ cup butter, melted
1 cup coarsely broken pecans

Prepare pastry for a single-crust pie. Fit into a 9-inch pie plate. Flute edge high. DO NOT prick.

In a large mixing bowl beat eggs till light. Add corn syrup, sugars, salt and vanilla; beat well. Stir in melted butter and pecans. Pour mixture into pastry-lined pie plate.

Place in a 425-degree oven. Immediately reduce heat to 350 degrees and bake for 45 minutes or till firm. (Filling will not be as firm in center as around edge.) Serve with a dollop of whipped cream, if desired. Freezes beautifully. Makes 8 servings.

GRAHAM CRACKER CRUST

Press crumbs firmly with the back of a spoon or by setting an 8-inch pie plate inside the larger one. Incidentally, the omission of sugar is intentional; this cook relies on the pie filling to satisfy her "sweet tooth."

1¼ cups finely crushed graham cracker crumbs
  (16 squares)
¼ cup butter or margarine, melted

In small bowl combine crumbs and butter or margarine; blend thoroughly. Press mixture firmly and evenly against bottom and sides of a 9-inch pie plate, building up slightly around rim.

Bake in a 350-degree oven for 5 to 8 minutes or till lightly browned. Cool on wire rack before filling.

SINGLE-CRUST PASTRY

Pastry like grandma made.

1 cup all-purpose flour
½ teaspoon salt
⅓ cup vegetable shortening or lard
3 tablespoons cold water, approx.

In medium mixing bowl sift together flour and salt. Using a pastry blender, cut in shortening or lard until mixture resembles coarse crumbs. Add water, a tablespoon at a time, until all the dry mixture is moistened. Gather up pastry and form into a ball.

Roll out on a lightly floured surface to a ⅛-inch thickness. Fit loosely in bottom of a 9-inch pie plate and gently pat out any air pockets. Trim pastry 1 inch beyond rim of plate. Fold excess under to build up edge. Flute.

Unbaked Pastry Shell:
Fill as desired and bake following directions stated in recipe.

Baked Pastry Shell:
Prick bottom and sides with a fork. Bake in a 425-degree oven for 12 to 15 minutes or till a light golden brown.

Or, line pastry with a 12-inch circle of aluminum foil; fill with 1½ cups dry beans. Bake in a 425-degree oven for 7 minutes; carefully remove foil and beans. Return shell to oven and bake 6 to 8 minutes longer or till golden.

❖ ❖

"Bake-blind" means to bake a pastry shell before a filling is added.

❖ ❖ ❖ ❖ ❖ ❖ ❖ ❖

For a golden brown crust on a double-crust pie, lightly brush top of unbaked pie with milk or cream. DO NOT brush fluting!

❖ ❖

DOUBLE-CRUST PASTRY

For a deep golden crust, lightly brush the top crust — but not the edges — with milk or cream before the pie goes into the oven. Sprinkle a little sugar on fruit pies.

2 cups all-purpose flour
1 teaspoon salt
⅔ cup vegetable shortening or lard
6 tablespoons cold water, approx.

In a large mixing bowl sift together flour and salt. Using a pastry blender, cut in shortening or lard until mixture resembles coarse crumbs. Add water, a tablespoon at a time, until all the dry mixture is moistened. Gather up pastry and form into a ball. Divide in half.

Roll out ½ on a lightly floured surface to a ⅛-inch thickness. Fit loosely in bottom of a 9-inch pie plate; gently pat out any air pockets. Trim pastry even with rim of plate.

Roll out second half for top crust. Cut 2 or 3 slits near center of pastry for steam to escape.

Fill pie with desired filling. Cover with top crust, allowing a 1-inch overhang. Fold overhang under bottom crust. Seal by pressing firmly over rim of plate. Flute or press edges with a fork. Bake as directed in recipe.

LATTICE-TOP PASTRY

Prepare pastry for double-crust pie except — allow a ½-inch overhang on bottom crust.

Roll out top crust to make a 12-inch circle. With a pastry wheel or knife cut into ¾-inch strips. Interweave strips across top of pie to make a lattice design: lay 5 strips at ¾-inch intervals over top. Place 5 more strips at right angles, interweaving crossing strips.

Trim strips even with bottom crust. Fold bottom up over strips to build up edge. Seal by pressing firmly over rim of plate. Flute. Bake as directed in recipe.

Cooking Notes

Chapter 11

Cakes are for special occasions and, at our house, the occasion generally means someone is celebrating a birthday! The choice is personal — both in flavor and shape, but the "big surprise" is never revealed until it is time to blow out the candles.

Cake-making, an expression of nostalgic tastes of days gone by, doesn't have to be difficult or time-consuming. Tender and moist with a fine, delicate crumb and delicious flavor, cakes have universal appeal.

When I was growing up, cake was our family dessert almost every supper . . . nothing elaborate, just a simple yellow sheet cake with a fluffy frosting. Sometimes the choice was chocolate, another time, peanut butter; occasionally, only a dusting of confectioners' sugar gleamed the top. Nearly every day after school my younger sister and I made the family dessert. I measured and added the ingredients; Lorraine beat the batter — by hand. And to make it a family affair, our brothers provided the cheers!

I must admit, even today, taking a cake fresh from the oven is my crowning glory — whether it's a Norwegian Gold Cake or a simple jelly roll. Successful cake-making, of course, depends on several factors: careful measurements, proper selection of pans and baking just the right length of time.

You will find in this sampling a cake to glamorize your special celebrations: birthdays, picnics and holidays — and a frosting to complement each creation. Perhaps while sifting through our recipes, thoughts of a baker's long-ago success will stir on your memories, too!

Cakes & Frostings

BEST WHITE FRUITCAKE

A fruitcake, light in color and worthy of its name — and sharing! It keeps well for at least a month; freeze for longer storage.

2 cups (1 pound) diced mixed candied fruits and peels
2 cups golden raisins
½ cup (4 ounces) snipped pitted dates
½ cup (4 ounces) candied cherries, halved
½ cup (4 ounces) diced candied pineapple
1 cup coarsely chopped nuts
2 cups sifted all-purpose flour
2 teaspoons baking powder
½ teaspoon salt
½ cup margarine
1 cup sugar
5 eggs
¼ cup unsweetened pineapple juice or light rum

In a large bowl combine mixed fruits, raisins, dates, cherries, pineapple and nuts. Sift together flour, baking powder and salt; sprinkle ½ cup over fruit mixture, mixing well.

In a large mixing bowl cream margarine and sugar till light. Add eggs, one at a time, beating well after each addition.

Add sifted dry ingredients alternately with pineapple juice or rum to creamed mixture. Beat until smooth. Blend in fruit mixture; mix well. Turn into a well-greased 9-inch tube pan, filling ¾ full. Or, divide batter evenly between 2 well-greased 9x5x3-inch loaf pans.

Bake in a 275-degree oven about 2½ hours for tube pan and 2 hours for loaf pans or till wooden pick inserted in center comes out clean. Cool in pan for 10 minutes. Loosen around edges with a metal spatula and turn out onto a wire rack. Glaze. Cool completely before wrapping or storing. Makes 1 tube fruitcake or 2 loaves.

Nut meats may be frozen up to 2 years at zero degrees. To freeze, pack nut meats in air-tight containers or plastic bags.

DARK FRUITCAKE

This old recipe has withstood the test of time. It makes a dark, moist cake and is a favorite among the relatives.

2 cups (1 pound) diced mixed candied fruits and peels
2 cups (1 pound) snipped pitted dates
1½ cups (8 ounces) seedless raisins
1 cup (8 ounces) candied cherries, halved
½ cup (4 ounces) diced candied pineapple
1 cup coarsely chopped nuts
2 cups sifted all-purpose flour
1 teaspoon soda
1 teaspoon cinnamon
½ teaspoon allspice
¼ teaspoon cloves
¼ teaspoon salt
½ cup shortening
1 cup sugar
3 eggs
½ cup molasses
½ teaspoon vanilla or orange extract
½ cup buttermilk

In a large bowl combine mixed fruits, dates, raisins, cherries, pineapple and nuts. Sift together flour, soda, spices and salt; sprinkle ½ cup over fruit mixture, mixing well.

In a large mixing bowl cream shortening and sugar till light. Add eggs, one at a time, beating well after each addition. Stir in molasses and flavoring.

Add sifted dry ingredients alternately with buttermilk to creamed mixture. Beat until smooth. Blend in fruit mixture; mix well. Turn into a well-greased 10-inch tube pan, filling ⅔ full. Or, divide batter between 2 well-greased 9x5x3-inch loaf pans.

When baking fruitcakes, place a pan with a 1-inch depth of water on bottom rack to make them moist and have greater volume.

Bake in a 275-degree oven about 2½ hours for tube pan and 2 hours for loaf pans or till wooden pick inserted in center comes out free of batter. Cool in pan for 10 minutes. Loosen around edges and turn out onto a wire rack. Glaze. Cool completely before wrapping or storing. Makes 1 tube fruitcake or 2 loaves.

GLAZE FOR FRUITCAKE

Fruitcakes take a shine to it!

⅓ cup light corn syrup
¼ cup unsweetened pineapple or orange juice

In a small saucepan combine corn syrup and pineapple or orange juice. Over medium-high heat bring to a rolling boil. Remove from heat and brush mixture over top and sides of warm fruitcake using a pastry brush. Decorate top with candied cherries and nuts. Allow glaze to set.

Bring remaining glaze to a rolling boil; brush second coat on fruitcake. Allow to dry completely before wrapping or storing. Makes enough glaze to double-coat 1 tube fruitcake or 2 loaves.

PETITE FRUITCAKES

Tiny gems with dates, nuts and an orange glaze are moist and delicious . . . and for folks who don't like traditional fruitcakes!

½ cup butter or margarine, softened (1 stick)
1 cup sugar
2 eggs
1 cup finely snipped pitted dates
½ cup chopped nuts
1 tablespoon grated orange peel
2 cups sifted all-purpose flour
1 teaspoon soda
½ teaspoon salt
⅔ cup buttermilk or soured milk
6 to 8 candied cherries, sliced
   Orange Glaze (recipe follows)

In a large mixing bowl cream butter or margarine and sugar till light. Add eggs; beat until fluffy. Stir in dates, nuts and orange peel.

Sift together flour, soda and salt. Add sifted dry ingredients to creamed mixture alternately with buttermilk or soured milk, beating well after each addition. Fill greased 2-inch muffin cups ⅔ full. Garnish tops with a slice of candied cherry.

Bake in a 375-degree oven for 15 to 18 minutes or till golden brown or till a wooden pick inserted in center comes out clean. Remove from pan to cooling rack. Brush while warm with Orange Glaze. Cool completely before storing. Makes 4 dozen petite cakes.

Orange Glaze

¼ cup sugar
2 tablespoons orange juice
2 teaspoons grated orange peel

In a small saucepan combine sugar, orange juice and peel. Heat, stirring constantly, until mixture comes to a boil.

APPLE KNOBBY CAKE

A family favorite from the kitchen of a good country cook! The batter is stiff, but apples make it a moist cake and unlike most, the flavor improves overnight.

¼ cup butter or margarine, softened
1 cup sugar
1 egg
1 teaspoon vanilla
1 cup sifted all-purpose flour
½ teaspoon baking powder
½ teaspoon soda
½ teaspoon salt
½ teaspoon cinnamon
½ teaspoon nutmeg
3 cups diced pared apples
¼ cup chopped nuts

In large mixing bowl cream butter or margarine and sugar till light and fluffy. Add egg and vanilla; beat well.

Sift flour, then measure. Resift together with baking powder, soda, salt and spices; add to creamed mixture. Beat until smooth. Stir in apples and nuts.

Pour batter into greased 8-inch square baking pan. Bake in a 350-degree oven for 40 to 45 minutes or till tester inserted in center comes out clean. Serve with ice cream or whipped cream, if desired. Makes 8 or 9 servings.

BUNNY'S CARROT CAKE

A festive cake with carrot, coconut and pineapple to make it moist and nuts to give it crunch. Spread with a cream cheese icing, it is even more special!

    3 eggs
    1½ cups sugar
    1¼ cups cooking oil
    1 teaspoon vanilla
    2 cups sifted all-purpose flour
    2 teaspoons cinnamon
    1 teaspoon soda
    1 teaspoon salt
    2 cups finely grated carrot
    1 cup well-drained crushed pineapple
    1 cup shredded coconut
    1 cup chopped nuts
       Sifted confectioners' sugar

In large mixer bowl combine eggs, sugar, cooking oil and vanilla. Beat at medium speed of electric mixer for 2 minutes.

Sift together flour, cinnamon, soda and salt; gradually add to egg mixture, beating until smooth. Fold in carrot, pineapple, co-

All recipes in the Sampler are written and tested with large eggs.

conut and nuts.

Turn batter into greased and floured 10-inch tube pan. Bake in a 325-degree oven for 1 hour and 15 minutes or till tester inserted in center comes out clean. Cool cake in pan on wire rack for 10 minutes. Remove from pan and cool completely. Sprinkle sifted confectioners' sugar over top of cake. Makes 12 to 15 servings.

Note:

If desired, cake may be baked in a greased and floured 13x9x2-inch baking pan in a 325-degree oven for 1 hour or till done. Cool in pan on wire rack.

CHOCOLATE BROWNIE CAKE

Within 60 minutes this cake evolves from the inspirational stage to the serving table. Says a former first lady, "it goes together easily, makes a large batch and always makes a hit!"

    2 cups sifted all-purpose flour
    2 cups sugar
    ½ cup butter or margarine (1 stick)
    ½ cup shortening
    1 cup water
    ¼ cup unsweetened cocoa
    ½ cup buttermilk
    1 teaspoon soda
    ¼ teaspoon salt
    2 eggs
    1 teaspoon vanilla
    Chocolate Joy Icing (recipe on page 272)

In large mixing bowl combine flour and sugar. Set aside. In saucepan combine butter or margarine, shortening, water and cocoa. Bring to a boil. Pour chocolate mixture over flour-sugar mixture; blend well.

Add buttermilk, soda, salt, eggs and vanilla. Beat, scraping sides of bowl, until thoroughly mixed. Batter is thin. Pour batter into greased and floured 15x10x1-inch jelly roll pan. Bake in a 400-degree oven for 20 minutes or until no imprint remains when lightly touched on top. Cool cake in pan on wire rack for 5 minutes. Frost while still hot with Chocolate Joy Icing. Makes 20 to 24 servings.

CHOCOLATE DATE CAKE

Without this recipe, no collection is complete. It's a winner from a dear friend, noted for her cooking ability.

    1 cup snipped pitted dates
    1 square (1 ounce) unsweetened chocolate
    1 teaspoon soda
 1½ cups boiling water
    ¾ cup shortening
    1 cup sugar
    2 eggs
 1½ cups sifted all-purpose flour
    ½ teaspoon salt
    ¼ cup sugar
    1 cup semi-sweet chocolate morsels
    ½ cup coarsely chopped nuts

In small bowl combine dates, chocolate and soda; pour boiling water over, stirring to melt the chocolate. Cool.

In large mixing bowl cream shortening and 1 cup sugar until light and fluffy; add eggs, one at a time, beating well after each addition. Sift together flour and salt; add alternately with date mixture to creamed mixture. Stir until blended. Spread batter in a greased and floured 13x9x2-inch baking pan.

Sprinkle batter evenly with remaining sugar, chocolate morsels and nuts. Bake in a 325-degree oven for 40 to 45 minutes or till wooden pick inserted in center comes out free of batter. Cool cake in pan on wire rack. Cut in pan. Makes 16 servings.

Note:

If desired, place batter in 2 greased and floured 9-inch round cake pans. Bake 30 to 35 minutes or till done. Serve in wedges, topped with a dollop of whipped cream.

A cake is baked if: (1) a wooden pick inserted in center of cake comes out free of batter, (2) no imprint remains when center of cake is lightly touched with a finger, or (3) the cake shrinks away from side of pan.

CHOCOLATE LAYER CAKE

A tender, fine-textured cake which is warmly received by my chocolate lovers!

1¾ cups sifted cake flour
1½ cups sugar
¾ teaspoon soda
¾ teaspoon salt
½ cup shortening
1 cup buttermilk
2 eggs
2 squares (2 ounces) unsweetened chocolate, melted and cooled
Velvet Frosting (recipe on page 274)

Sift flour, sugar, soda and salt together into a large mixing bowl. Add shortening and ¾ cup of the buttermilk. Beat, by hand or at medium speed of electric mixer, for 2 minutes.

Add remaining buttermilk, eggs and melted chocolate. Beat for 2 minutes longer, scraping sides and bottom of bowl frequently. Divide batter between 2 greased and floured 9-inch round cake pans.

Bake in a 350-degree oven for 25 to 30 minutes or till wooden pick inserted in center of cake comes out clean. Remove from oven to wire rack. Cool in pan for 5 minutes. Turn out onto rack to cool completely. Frost with Velvet Frosting or as desired. Makes one 2-layer cake.

To substitute all-purpose flour in recipes calling for cake flour, use ⅞ cup all-purpose flour for every 1 cup cake flour.

Make pan-coat to grease and flour pans in one step. Combine ½ cup vegetable shortening and ¼ cup all-purpose flour; mix well. Use generously to grease and flour cake pans or muffin cups. Store extra pan-coat in a covered jar on the pantry shelf.

GOLDEN LAYER CAKE

A heavenly cake with a magical ingredient — BUTTERMILK!

½ cup shortening
1 cup sugar
2 eggs
1 teaspoon grated lemon peel
1 teaspoon vanilla
2 cups sifted cake flour
1 teaspoon baking powder
¾ teaspoon soda
¼ teaspoon salt
1 cup buttermilk
Lemon Filling (recipe on page 271)
Fluffy White Frosting (recipe on page 273)

In large mixing bowl cream shortening and sugar till light and fluffy. Add eggs, one at a time, beating well after each addition. Stir in lemon peel and vanilla.

Sift together flour, baking powder, soda and salt. Add to creamed mixture alternately with buttermilk, beginning and ending with flour. Beat well after each addition. Turn batter into 2 greased and floured 9-inch round cake pans.

Bake in a 350-degree oven for 25 minutes or till cake shrinks away from sides of pan and no imprint remains when lightly touched in the center. Cool 5 minutes before removing from pans to wire racks. Cool completely. Put layers together with Lemon Filling and frost with Fluffy White Frosting. Makes one 2-layer cake.

HAZEL'S NUT CAKE

A one-egg cake, light in texture and big in flavor.

½ cup shortening
1 cup sugar
1 egg
2 cups sifted cake flour
3 teaspoons baking powder
¾ teaspoon salt

    1 cup milk
    1 teaspoon vanilla
    ¾ teaspoon lemon extract
    1 cup chopped nuts
    Butter Frosting (recipe on page 271)

In a large mixing bowl cream shortening and sugar till light and fluffy. Add egg; beat until smooth.

Sift together flour, baking powder and salt; add to creamed mixture alternately with milk and flavorings. Beat well after each addition. Fold in ¾ cup of the chopped nuts.

Turn batter into a greased and floured 9-inch square baking pan. Bake in a 350-degree oven for 35 to 40 minutes or till wooden pick inserted in center comes out free of batter. Cool in pan on wire rack. Frost with Butter Frosting and sprinkle with remaining ¼ cup chopped nuts. Makes 8 or 9 servings.

NORWEGIAN GOLD CAKE

Don't disguise the flavor of this unusual cake with a frosting. It's wonderful plain, with a scoop of ice cream or fresh fruit; but a whipped cream icing is fine for birthday celebrations. You will note a method so different: creaming butter with the flour!

    1 cup butter or margarine
    1½ cups all-purpose flour
    5 eggs
    1⅓ cups sugar
    1½ teaspoons baking powder
    ½ teaspoon salt
    1 teaspoon almond extract

In large mixer bowl combine butter or margarine and flour. Cream on low spead of mixer for 5 minutes.

Add eggs, one at a time, beating well after each addition. Scrape sides and bottom of bowl often.

Add sugar, baking powder, salt and almond extract. Beat for 2 minutes at low speed of mixer. Pour batter into ungreased 10-inch tube pan. Bake in a 325-degree oven for 1 hour or until the cake springs back and leaves no imprint when lightly touched on top. Invert pan; cool for 20 minutes. Remove from pan and finish cooling cake on wire rack. Sprinkle with confectioners' sugar, if desired. Makes 12 to 15 servings.

OLD-FASHIONED JELLY ROLL

The cake I remember from childhood! Spread with your favorite preserve; ours is spread with homemade chokecherry jelly.

1 cup sifted all-purpose flour
1 cup sugar
1 teaspoon baking powder
¼ teaspoon salt
3 eggs
1 teaspoon vanilla
3 tablespoons cold water
Sifted confectioners' sugar
⅔ cup apple jelly

In large mixing bowl sift together flour, sugar, baking powder and salt. Add eggs and vanilla. Beat at low speed of mixer until moistened, scraping bowl constantly. Beat at medium speed for 3 minutes, scraping bowl occasionally. Stir in water.

Spread batter evenly in greased and lightly floured 15x10x1-inch jelly roll pan. Bake in a 375-degree oven for 15 to 20 minutes or till cake springs back when lightly touched.

Loosen cake from sides of pan; immediately turn out onto towel generously sprinkled with confectioners' sugar. Starting with narrow edge roll up cake and towel together. Cool ½ hour on wire rack.

Unroll. Stir jelly to soften; spread over cake, leaving a ½-inch rim. Roll up cake. Wrap in wax paper. Makes 10 slices.

Variation:

Adrienne's Blueberry Roll

Prepare recipe for Old-Fashioned Jelly Roll. Bake and roll up as recipe directs. Omit jelly and spread Blueberry Filling (recipe follows) over unrolled cake; reroll and wrap in wax paper. Refrigerate at least 1 hour. Serve in slices with a dollop of sweetened whipped cream. Makes 10 servings.

Blueberry Filling

½ cup sugar
2 tablespoons cornstarch
2 tablespoons lemon juice
1 teaspoon vanilla
2 cups fresh or frozen blueberries

In a saucepan mix together sugar and cornstarch; stir in lemon juice and vanilla. Add blueberries. Cook over low heat, stirring frequently, until mixture thickens. Cool.

PERFECT POUND CAKE

An all-time favorite that needs no icing. Wonderful with fresh fruit!

⅔ cup butter or margarine
1¼ cups sugar
   Grated peel and juice of ½ lemon
½ cup milk
2¼ cups sifted cake flour
1¼ teaspoons salt
1 teaspoon baking powder
3 eggs

Combine butter or margarine and sugar in large mixer bowl. Cream together at medium speed of mixer until light and fluffy. Stir in lemon peel and juice. Add milk; mix just enough to break up creamed mixture.

Sift together flour, salt and baking powder. Add to creamed mixture; at low speed, mix until smooth. Add eggs, one at a time, beating well after each addition and scraping sides of bowl often. Beat 1 minute longer.

Turn batter into a greased and floured 9x5x3-inch loaf pan. Bake in a 300-degree oven for 1 hour and 15 minutes or until no imprint remains when gently pressed. Cool on wire rack 10 minutes before removing from pan. Cool completely before wrapping. If desired, sifted confectioners' sugar may be sprinkled over top. Makes 1 loaf.

SPANISH BAR

*From a cook who says this raisin-and-spice loaf is "the same
kind of cake that my father had been buying for his (bag) lunches
for years. It was sold, individually wrapped, either as a small
cake or as a thick slice."*

    1 cup packed brown sugar
    1 cup seedless raisins
    1¼ cups water
    ½ cup shortening
    1 teaspoon cinnamon
    ½ teaspoon nutmeg
    ½ teaspoon allspice
    1 tablespoon molasses
    2 cups sifted all-purpose flour
    1 teaspoon baking powder
    1 teaspoon soda
    ½ teaspoon salt
    Lemon Frosting (recipe on page 273)

In a large saucepan combine brown sugar, raisins, water, shortening, spices and molasses. Over medium heat bring to a slow boil;
simmer, uncovered, for 5 minutes. Cool.

Sift together flour, baking powder, soda and salt; add to raisin
mixture. Beat well. Turn mixture into a greased and floured
9x5x3-inch loaf pan.

Bake in a 350-degree oven for 50 to 55 minutes or till wooden
pick inserted in center of loaf comes out free of batter. Remove
pan from oven to cooling rack. Cool for 10 minutes. Remove cake
from pan and cool completely before slicing. If desired, frost with
Lemon Frosting. Makes 1 loaf.

SUGAR CUPCAKES

*This recipe goes together with such speed you may never use
another cake mix. As a basic cake, it is the beginning of many
happy endings!*

    ½ cup butter or margarine, softened
    1 cup sugar

2 eggs
½ teaspoon vanilla
1½ cups sifted cake flour
1¼ teaspoons baking powder
¼ teaspoon salt
⅓ cup milk

In large mixing bowl cream butter or margarine and sugar till light and fluffy. Add eggs, one at a time, beating well after each addition. Stir in vanilla.

Sift together flour, baking powder and salt; add to creamed mixture alternately with milk, beginning and ending with flour mixture. Beat after each addition until smooth.

Turn batter into 16 greased or paper-lined cupcake sections, filling each ½ full. Bake in a 375-degree oven for 18 to 20 minutes or till tester comes out free of batter. Remove cupcakes to cooling rack; when completely cooled, frost as desired. Makes 16 cupcakes.

Variations:

Boston Cream Pie

Prepare recipe for Sugar Cupcakes except — pour batter into greased and floured 9-inch round layer pan. Bake in a 350-degree oven for 25 to 30 minutes. Cool cake in pan on wire rack for 5 minutes. Remove from pan and cool completely.

Split cake in crosswise halves. Spread Custard Topping (from Trifle recipe on page 230) over lower half. Cover with top half. Frost with ½ recipe Velvet Frosting (recipe on page 274). Makes 6 to 8 servings.

Pineapple Upside-Down Cake

3 tablespoons butter or margarine
⅓ cup packed brown sugar
1 20-ounce can crushed pineapple, drained
Whipped cream

Melt butter or margarine in large skillet with oven-proof handle or a 2-inch deep, 9-inch round baking pan. Add brown sugar, stirring till sugar dissolves. Stir in crushed pineapple.

Prepare recipe for Sugar Cupcakes except — carefully pour

batter over pineapple in skillet or pan. Bake in a 350-degree oven for 30 minutes or till wooden pick inserted in center comes out clean. Let stand 5 minutes, then invert onto heat-proof serving plate. Remove skillet or pan after a few seconds. Serve warm with a dollop of whipped cream. Makes 8 servings.

Quick Twinkle Dessert

Twinkle Filling (recipe follows)
1 cup whipping cream
2 tablespoons confectioners' sugar
½ teaspoon vanilla

Prepare recipe for Sugar Cupcakes (recipe on page 268) as directed except — pour batter into a greased and floured 9-inch square baking pan. Bake in a 350-degree oven for 30 minutes or till a wooden pick inserted in the center comes out clean. Let cake stand in pan on wire rack for 5 minutes. Remove from pan and cool completely. Cut cake in half crosswise.

Return bottom half to pan. Cover with Twinkle Filling. Place top half of cake over filling.

In chilled bowl combine chilled whipping cream, confectioners' sugar and vanilla. Beat until stiff. Spread on top of cake. Chill for several hours or overnight. If desired, garnish each serving with maraschino cherry slice and chopped nuts. Makes 9 servings.

Twinkle Filling

2½ tablespoons all-purpose flour
½ cup milk
¼ teaspoon salt
½ teaspoon vanilla
½ cup sugar
½ cup butter or margarine

In small saucepan blend together flour and milk. Cook, stirring constantly, till mixture comes to a boil and thickens. Cook 1 minute longer. Remove from heat and cool.

Stir in salt and vanilla. Beat till fluffy. Add sugar and butter or margarine, one at a time, beating well after each addition.

LEMON FILLING

To spread between layers of cake. If filling is too soft, refrigerate till set.

½ cup sugar
2 tablespoons cornstarch
⅛ teaspoon salt
½ cup water
¼ cup lemon juice
1 tablespoon grated lemon peel
1 tablespoon butter or margarine

In medium saucepan mix together sugar, cornstarch and salt. Stir in water, lemon juice and peel. Over medium heat, bring mixture to a boil, stirring constantly. Boil for 1 minute. Remove from heat and stir in butter or margarine. Cool. Makes 1 cup.

To plump raisins, cover with very hot tap water. Allow to soak for 3 to 5 minutes. Drain and pat dry.

BUTTER FROSTING

It's made rich with butter and cream.

¼ cup butter or margarine, softened
1½ cups sifted confectioners' sugar
½ teaspoon vanilla
2 tablespoons light cream, approx.

In medium bowl cream butter or margarine; gradually blend in half the sugar. Stir in vanilla. Add remaining sugar and enough cream to make a spreading consistency; beat till smooth. Frosts one 9-inch square cake.

CHOCOLATE JOY ICING

A layer of fudge on a cake!

¼ cup butter or margarine
3 tablespoons unsweetened cocoa
¼ cup milk
2½ cups sifted confectioners' sugar
¼ teaspoon salt
1 teaspoon vanilla
½ cup chopped nuts

In saucepan combine butter or margarine, cocoa and milk. Bring to a boil, stirring constantly. Remove from heat. Stir in confectioners' sugar, salt and vanilla; beat smooth. Stir in nuts. Frosts Chocolate Brownie Cake or 16 cupcakes.

To snip marshmallows, use kitchen shears dipped in cold water.

To snip pitted dates, use kitchen shears dipped in cold water.

CREAM CHEESE ICING

Smooth and creamy — try it on your vegetable cakes!

1 3-ounce package cream cheese, softened
2 tablespoons butter or margarine, softened
2 cups sifted confectioners' sugar
1 teaspoon vanilla

In medium bowl combine cream cheese and butter or margarine; beat till light and fluffy. Add confectioners' sugar, beating until smooth. Stir in vanilla. Spread on cake. Makes frosting for 1 pan Pumpkin Bars or top of one 13x9x2-inch cake.

LEMON FROSTING

Tangy with a citrus flavor. ✓

2½ tablespoons butter or margarine
1½ cups sifted confectioners' sugar
1 teaspoon grated lemon peel
1½ to 2 tablespoons lemon juice

In a medium bowl cream butter or margarine till light. Blend in confectioners' sugar and lemon peel. Beat in enough lemon juice to make a spreading consistency. Beat smooth. Spread over top of cake. Makes enough for a 9-inch square cake.

7-MINUTE BROWN SUGAR FROSTING

Delightful . . . with chocolate cake.

2 tablespoons cold water
1 egg white
1 cup packed brown sugar
⅛ teaspoon salt
1 teaspoon vanilla

Place water, egg white, brown sugar and salt in upper part of double boiler. Beat ½ minute with a rotary egg beater or at low speed of electric mixer to blend.

Place over boiling water. (Keep the water boiling in lower part of double boiler, but water should NOT touch top of pan.) Beat the mixture with electric or rotary beater steadily and continuously for 7 minutes or till frosting forms stiff peaks. DO NOT OVER-COOK! Remove from heat. Add vanilla. Beat until thick enough to spread. Frosts tops and sides of one 2-layer cake.

Variation:

Fluffy White Frosting

Substitute 1 cup granulated sugar for brown sugar and use 3 tablespoons cold water. Add ⅛ teaspoon cream of tartar or 1 tablespoon light corn syrup.

VELVET FROSTING

Smooth and velvety — just like its name!

1 cup (6-ounce pkg.) semi-sweet chocolate morsels
½ cup dairy sour cream
1 teaspoon vanilla
¼ teaspoon salt
2¼ cups sifted confectioners' sugar

In medium bowl melt chocolate morsels over hot, not boiling water; remove from heat. Blend in sour cream, vanilla and salt. Gradually add confectioners' sugar, beating till smooth. Frosts two 8- or 9-inch round cakes or 16 cupcakes.

Invert cakes baked in tube pans to prevent them from losing volume while cooling!

For perfect, thin slices, chill fruitcakes before slicing.

Cooking Notes

Chapter 12

"Be sorry for people
Whoever they are
Who live in a house
With no cookie jar."

Cookie-making is the fun aspect of baking! It's reminiscent of home and hearth. Certainly not a necessity, but to me, a kitchen with a cookie jar generates warmth and good feelings.

Cookies bring to mind some delicious memories of childhood days. There were brown sugar cut-outs, appropriately decorated for all the holidays and family celebrations, old-fashioned molasses cookies rolled with love for everyday enjoyment, and a variety of drop delights for filling the cookie jar. Our pantry was stocked with childhood goodies.

The old-time flavors of grandma's cookies don't have to be just a memory. With no special culinary skills required — either in mixing or baking — there's no limit to the treasures even the most novice baker can make right at home.

Among the recipes in this section are the family favorites, both yours and ours, plus a few heirlooms. Included are an assortment of bars, both plain and fancy, and a variety of drop, shaped, filled, rolled and refrigerator cookies. Don't overlook the Pecan Balls for your holiday baking, nor the Oatmeal Chippers for stocking the cookie jar. Oh, yes, whoopie pies — both chocolate and molasses — are certainly worthy of someone's admiration. May they all gladden the hearts of your loved ones just as they have those dear to me!

Cookies & Bars

AUNT MARION'S BROWN SUGAR COOKIES

A crisp, old-time cookie filled with raisin-and-brown-sugar goodness. Use golden raisins when possible.

½ cup butter or margarine, softened
1 cup packed brown sugar
1 egg
½ teaspoon vanilla
1¼ cups all-purpose flour
½ teaspoon soda
¼ teaspoon salt
½ cup golden raisins

In mixing bowl cream butter or margarine and sugar until light and fluffy. Add egg and vanilla; beat thoroughly.

Sift together flour, soda and salt. Stir into creamed mixture; mix well. Stir in raisins.

Drop by rounded teaspoonfuls onto lightly greased cookie sheet, spacing 2-inches apart. Bake in a 350-degree oven for 12 to 14 minutes or till golden brown. Remove from cookie sheet; cool on wire rack. Makes 2½ dozen.

CHOCO-BRAN CRISPS

Combine two popular pantry shelf ingredients — chocolate morsels and bran cereal — for a crisp, textured cookie. It's another family favorite!

1 cup butter or margarine, softened
1½ cups sugar
2 eggs
1 teaspoon vanilla
1 cup bran cereal
1 cup (6-ounce pkg.) semi-sweet chocolate morsels
2 cups all-purpose flour
½ teaspoon soda
½ teaspoon salt

In mixing bowl beat butter or margarine and sugar until light

and fluffy. Add eggs and vanilla; beat well. Stir in bran and chocolate morsels.

   Sift together flour, soda and salt. Add to creamed mixture; mix
well. Drop by level tablespoonfuls 3 inches apart onto ungreased
cookie sheet. Bake in a 350-degree oven for 12 to 15 minutes or till
golden brown. Remove from cookie sheet to cooling rack. Makes 4
dozen cookies, 2½-inches in diameter.

   *Select baking sheets with little or no sides so cookies bake evenly
and quickly. Shiny light metal or teflon-coated pans give best results.*

CHOCOLATE CRINKLES

*Chill the dough; roll into balls, then confectioners' sugar for
perfectly round, crisp cookies. Chocoholics love 'em!*

   ½ **cup butter or margarine, softened**
   1⅔ **cups sugar**
    2 **eggs**
    2 **teaspoons vanilla**
    2 **squares (2-ounces) unsweetened chocolate, melted
      and cooled**
    2 **cups all-purpose flour**
    2 **teaspoons baking powder**
   ½ **teaspoon salt**
   ⅓ **cup milk**
   ½ **cup chopped nuts**
      Sifted confectioners' sugar

   In mixing bowl beat butter or margarine and sugar until light
and fluffy. Add eggs and vanilla; beat well. Blend in chocolate.

   Sift together flour, baking powder and salt; blend into creamed
mixture alternately with milk. Stir in nuts. Cover and chill at least
3 hours.

Roll into 1-inch balls . . . then roll in confectioners' sugar. Place 3 inches apart on lightly greased cookie sheet. Bake in a 350-degree oven for 15 minutes or till cookies are lightly browned around edges. Remove from pan to cooling rack. If desired, sift confectioners' sugar over tops of warm cookies. Makes 4 dozen.

Preheat oven to correct temperature before placing cookies in.

KRIS KRINGLES

A nut-crusted goodie topped with a candied cherry half to leave for Santa's snack . . . thanks to another good cook with Maine roots.

½ cup butter or margarine, softened
¼ cup sugar
1 beaten egg yolk
1 tablespoon grated orange peel
1 teaspoon grated lemon peel
1 teaspoon lemon juice
1 cup sifted cake flour
⅛ teaspoon salt
1 slightly beaten egg white
½ cup finely chopped nuts
9 candied cherries, halved

In mixing bowl beat butter or margarine and sugar until light and fluffy. Add egg yolk, orange peel, lemon peel and lemon juice; beat thoroughly. Stir in cake flour and salt. Cover and chill dough until firm.

Roll into ½-inch balls. Dip each ball in egg white . . . then roll lightly in nuts. Place on ungreased cookie sheet and press half of a candied cherry in center of each cookie. Bake in a 325-degree oven for 20 minutes, or until delicately browned. Remove from cookie sheet; cool on wire rack. Makes 1½ dozen.

MOLASSES CRINKLES

*A spicy-crisp molasses cookie that's sure to please your family
. . . and worthy of three stars in this cook's opinion.*

¾ **cup butter or margarine, softened**
1 **cup packed brown sugar**
1 **egg**
¼ **cup molasses**
2¼ **cups all-purpose flour**
2 **teaspoons soda**
¼ **teaspoon salt**
1 **teaspoon cinnamon**
1 **teaspoon ginger**
½ **teaspoon cloves**
   Granulated sugar

In mixing bowl beat butter or margarine and brown sugar until
light and fluffy. Add egg and molasses; beat well.

Sift together flour, soda, salt, cinnamon, ginger and cloves. Add
to creamed mixture; mix well. Cover and chill dough.

Roll into 1-inch balls . . . then roll in granulated sugar. Place 3
inches apart on lightly greased cookie sheet. Sprinkle each cookie
with 2 or 3 drops of water or coffee to produce a crackled surface.
Bake in a 350-degree oven for 10 to 12 minutes, or until set but
not hard. Remove from cookie sheet; cool on wire rack. Makes 4
dozen.

*When baking two pans of cookies at a time, switch pans once
during baking to brown cookies evenly.*

*Allow 2 inches between pan edges for circulation of heat and
even browning.*

OATMEAL CHIPPERS

An oatmeal and spice cookie — popular for stocking the cookie jar!

> 1 cup butter or margarine, softened
> 1 cup packed brown sugar
> 1 cup sugar
> 2 eggs
> 1 teaspoon vanilla
> 2 cups all-purpose flour
> 1 teaspoon soda
> 1 teaspoon salt
> 1 teaspoon cinnamon
> 1 teaspoon nutmeg
> 2 cups quick-cooking or old-fashioned rolled oats
> 1 cup (6-ounce pkg.) semi-sweet chocolate morsels
> 1 cup chopped nuts

In mixing bowl beat butter or margarine and sugars until creamy. Add eggs and vanilla; beat well.

Sift together flour, soda, salt, cinnamon and nutmeg. Add to creamed mixture, mixing thoroughly. Stir in rolled oats, chocolate morsels and nuts.

Drop by rounded teaspoonfuls, spacing 2-inches apart, onto lightly greased cookie sheet. Bake in a 350-degree oven for about 12 minutes or till lightly browned. Remove from pan to cool on wire rack. Makes 6 dozen.

PECAN BALLS

A devoted grandmother says, "This is my family's favorite recipe!" It's easy to taste why; they are sensational . . . with real butter. You may wish to reroll in confectioners' sugar just before serving.

> ½ cup butter or margarine, softened (1 stick)
> 3 tablespoons packed brown sugar
> 1 cup all-purpose flour
> ¼ teaspoon salt

1 teaspoon vanilla
1 cup finely chopped pecans (see note)
Confectioners' sugar

In a medium bowl cream butter or margarine and sugar till light and fluffy. Sift together flour and salt; add to creamed mixture, stirring to thoroughly blend. Stir in vanilla and pecans; mix well. Form into 1-inch balls. Place on ungreased cookie sheet. Bake in a 325-degree oven for 20 minutes or until golden brown. Cool slightly. While warm, roll cookies in confectioners' sugar. Cool completely on a wire rack before storing in an airtight container. Makes 2 dozen.

Note:
    One cup chopped walnuts or almonds may be used in place of pecans.

SADIE'S HERMITS

An old-time cookie dough shaped into logs and baked, then sliced. A taste of yesteryear . . . thanks to a childhood friend who shares her mother's recipe!

    ¼ cup shortening
    1 cup sugar
    1 egg
    ¼ cup molasses
    1 cup seedless raisins (see note)
    2¾ cups all-purpose flour
    2 teaspoons soda
    ½ teaspoon salt
    ½ teaspoon cinnamon
    ½ teaspoon nutmeg
    ¼ cup cold water or cold coffee

    In large mixing bowl cream shortening and sugar till light. Add egg; beat well. Stir in molasses and raisins.
    Sift together flour, soda, salt and spices. Add to creamed mixture alternately with cold water or coffee, mixing well after each addition. Chill dough. (If well covered, dough will keep in refrigerator for several days. Fresh cookies on a moment's notice!)

Divide dough into 3 equal portions. Roll each out on a lightly floured surface to a 14x10-inch rectangle. Starting at narrow end, roll up jelly-roll fashion into a log 1-inch in diameter. Place on a lightly greased cookie sheet, separating logs so they do not touch during baking. Sprinkle sugar over tops.

Bake in a 350-degree oven for 15 to 18 minutes or till no imprint remains when lightly touched with finger. DO NOT OVERBAKE! Cut into desired widths. Cool hermits on wire rack. Store in airtight container. Makes 3 to 4 dozen.

Note:

    1 cup finely snipped dates may be substituted for raisins.

SOUR CREAM COOKIES

A cookie developed through trial and error to use sour cream and seeded raisins . . . and awfully good.

    ½ cup butter or margarine, softened
    1½ cups sugar
    2 eggs
    ½ cup dairy sour cream
    1 teaspoon vanilla
    2½ cups all-purpose flour
    ½ teaspoon baking powder
    ½ teaspoon soda
    ½ teaspoon salt
    1 cup seeded or seedless raisins

In large mixing bowl cream butter or margarine and sugar until light and fluffy. Add eggs; beat well. Blend in sour cream and vanilla.

Sift together flour, baking powder, soda and salt. Stir into creamed mixture; mix thoroughly. Stir in raisins. Drop rounded teaspoonfuls of dough onto lightly greased cookie sheet, spacing 3-inches apart.

Bake in a 350-degree oven for 12 to 15 minutes or till golden. DO NOT OVERBAKE! Remove from cookie sheet to wire rack. Cool completely. Store in an airtight container. Makes 4 dozen.

WHOOPIE PIES

These puffy cookies, paired with a fluffy filling, move fast with kids of all ages. A reliable recipe with a lot of mileage!

⅔ cup shortening
1¼ cups sugar
2 eggs
2½ cups all-purpose flour
½ cup unsweetened cocoa
1¼ teaspoons soda
½ teaspoon salt
¼ teaspoon cream of tartar
1 cup milk
1½ teaspoons vanilla
Creme Filling (recipe follows)

In a large mixing bowl cream shortening and sugar till light and fluffy. Add eggs; beat well.

Sift together flour, cocoa, soda, salt and cream of tartar. Combine milk and vanilla. Add sifted dry ingredients to creamed mixture alternately with milk mixture. Beat just until smooth.

Drop by rounded tablespoons 2 inches apart on lightly greased cookie sheet, keeping cookies uniform in size for easy pairing. Bake in a 375-degree oven for 10 to 12 minutes or till no imprint remains when top is lightly touched. Remove from cookie sheet to cool on wire rack. When completely cool, sandwich 2 cookies with a rounded spoonful of Creme Filling. Wrap each "pie" individually in wax paper. Makes 2 dozen.

Creme Filling

3 cups sifted confectioners' sugar
½ cup shortening
½ cup marshmallow creme
½ teaspoon salt
3 tablespoons milk
1 teaspoon vanilla

In bowl combine sugar, shortening, marshmallow creme, salt, milk and vanilla. Beat smooth with electric mixer. If necessary, blend in a little additional milk, a teaspoon at a time, to make filling smooth and spreadable.

MOLASSES WHOOPIE PIES

"Terrific," says a mother, "for folks who love whoopie pies, but are sensitive to chocolate." Without the filling, these are a soft, tender molasses cookie.

½ cup butter or margarine, softened (1 stick)
¾ cup sugar
2 eggs
⅔ cup molasses
2¾ cups all-purpose flour
1 teaspoon soda
½ teaspoon salt
1¼ teaspoons cinnamon
½ teaspoon ginger
½ cup milk
Ginger Cream Filling (recipe follows)

In mixing bowl beat butter or margarine with sugar until light. Add eggs and beat until very light. Stir in molasses.

Sift together flour, soda, salt, cinnamon and ginger. Add to creamed mixture alternately with milk; beat just until smooth. Cover and chill for 1 hour.

Drop by rounded tablespoons 2 inches apart on lightly greased cookie sheet. Try to keep the cookies uniform in size for easy pairing. Bake in a 375-degree oven for 10 minutes or till surface springs back when gently pressed. Remove from cookie sheet; cool on wire rack. When completely cool, sandwich 2 cookies with a rounded tablespoon of Ginger Cream Filling. Wrap each "pie" individually in wax paper. Makes 2 dozen.

Grease baking sheet ONLY when stated in the recipe.

Ginger Cream Filling

½ cup butter or margarine, softened
3 cups sifted confectioners' sugar
1¼ teaspoons ginger
2 or 3 tablespoons milk
¼ cup molasses

Beat butter or margarine with sugar and ginger until creamy. Gradually beat in milk and molasses until smooth and spreadable.

GRAMMIE'S ROLLED MOLASSES COOKIES

An heirloom from grandmother's house. Hers were rolled — large and round, thick and crisp with sugar sprinkled atop — and the perfect companion to a glass of cold goat's milk which she always offered and, of course, never was refused!

⅔ cup shortening
½ cup sugar
1 cup molasses
1 teaspoon vanilla
3½ cups all-purpose flour
2 teaspoons soda
½ teaspoon salt
1 teaspoon ginger
½ teaspoon cinnamon
¼ teaspoon cloves
½ cup buttermilk or cold coffee

In a large mixing bowl cream shortening and sugar till light. Stir in molasses and vanilla.

Sift together flour, soda, salt and spices; add alternately with buttermilk or coffee to creamed mixture. Mix well. Cover and chill for several hours or overnight.

Roll out dough on a lightly floured surface to ¼-inch thickness. Cut with round cutter. Place on an ungreased cookie sheet. Bake in a 375-degree oven for 8 to 10 minutes or till no imprint remains when lightly touched. Remove from cookie sheet to cool on a wire rack. Makes about 6 dozen cookies, 2½-inches in diameter.

OLD-FASHIONED ROLLED SUGAR COOKIES

A crisp, rolled cookie with a hint of nutmeg. Says a young mother, "A sugar cookie without crumbs!" — perfect for the children's hour.

½ cup butter or margarine, softened
1 cup sugar
1 egg
1 teaspoon vanilla
2⅔ cups all-purpose flour
1 teaspoon baking powder
½ teaspoon soda
½ teaspoon salt
¼ teaspoon nutmeg
½ cup dairy sour cream

In mixing bowl beat butter or margarine and sugar till light and fluffy. Stir in egg and vanilla; beat well.

Sift together flour, baking powder, soda, salt and nutmeg. Add sifted dry ingredients to creamed mixture alternately with sour cream; mix well after each addition. Cover and chill.

Roll out on lightly floured surface to ¼-inch thickness. Cut into desired shapes with cookie cutters. Place on an ungreased cookie sheet. Bake in a 400-degree oven for 10 to 12 minutes or till golden. Remove from cookie sheet to wire rack. Makes 40 to 50 cookies.

Variation:

Chocolate Cookies

Melt 1-ounce unsweetened chocolate; cool. Blend into creamed mixture before adding dry ingredients.

Store crisp cookies in a loosely covered container.

PEANUT BUTTER PILLOWS

Another good recipe from a senior citizen! A younger cook, experimenting with the recipe, made this suggestion: tuck milk chocolate morsels inside the "pillows" and convert them into peanut butter cup pillows.

½ cup butter or margarine, softened
½ cup sugar
½ cup creamy peanut butter
¼ cup light corn syrup
1 tablespoon milk
1½ cups all-purpose flour
½ teaspoon soda
¼ teaspoon salt
  Additional creamy or crunchy peanut butter or milk
  chocolate morsels

In a large mixing bowl cream butter or margarine, sugar and peanut butter till light and fluffy; add corn syrup and milk.

Sift together flour, soda and salt; add to creamed mixture. Blend thoroughly.

Place dough on a large sheet of wax paper. Knead dough briefly; then shape into an 8x2-inch log. Wrap and chill till firm.

Cut into thin slices — no more than ¼-inch thick. Place half of the slices on lightly greased baking sheets, spacing 2 inches apart. Dot each slice with 1 teaspoon peanut butter or milk chocolate morsels. Cover with another cookie slice; press edges to seal. Don't worry about the cracks on top.

Bake in a 350-degree oven for 12 to 15 minutes or till golden brown. Remove from cookie sheet to wire rack. Cool completely. Makes about 1½ dozen.

Store soft cookies in a closely covered container to prevent them from drying out.

SAND COOKIES

A tender, butter-rich refrigerator cookie made crunchy with nuts. Bet you don't stop with one!

1½ cups butter or margarine, softened (3 sticks)
1½ cups sugar
1½ teaspoons vanilla
3 cups all-purpose flour
1 teaspoon soda
1 cup finely chopped nuts

In large mixing bowl cream butter or margarine and sugar till light and fluffy. Stir in vanilla.

Sift together flour and soda; add to creamed mixture, stirring to combine mixtures. Stir in nuts. Gather dough into a ball with hands and divide into 4 equal portions.

Shape each portion on a lightly floured surface into a 6-inch roll. Wrap in wax paper or aluminum foil, securing ends. Chill in refrigerator for several hours or overnight. (Dough will keep up to a week in the refrigerator or may be frozen for up to 6 months.)

To bake, cut in ¼-inch slices. Place on ungreased cookie sheet, spacing 1 inch between cookies. Bake in a 350-degree oven for 10 to 12 minutes or till lightly browned. Remove cookies to wire rack to cool. Each roll makes 2 dozen tea-size cookies.

WHIRLIGIGS

Peanut butter and melted chocolate are partners for this two-tone slice and bake cookie.

½ cup butter or margarine, softened
½ cup sugar
½ cup packed brown sugar
½ cup creamy peanut butter
1 egg
1¼ cups all-purpose flour
½ teaspoon soda
½ teaspoon salt

1 cup (6-ounce pkg.) semi-sweet chocolate morsels, melted

In mixing bowl cream butter or margarine, sugars and peanut butter till light and fluffy. Add egg; beat well.

Sift together flour, soda and salt; stir into creamed mixture, blending well. Chill for easier handling, if desired.

Roll out dough between two pieces of wax paper to a 12x18-inch rectangle. Spread melted chocolate to within 1 inch of edges. Roll up, jelly-roll fashion, starting with 18-inch side. Wrap; chill roll until chocolate hardens enough to slice. Cut into ¼-inch slices. If necessary, shape into circles with fingers. Place on ungreased cookie sheet. Bake in a 350-degree oven for 8 to 10 minutes or until light brown. Gently remove from cookie sheet to wire rack. Cool. Makes about 6 dozen.

APRICOT-OATMEAL BARS

A tangy apricot filling sandwiched between the goodness of rolled oats. A combination of dried fruits — prunes, raisins, figs and apricots — is good, too!

1 cup snipped dried apricots
2 tablespoons packed brown sugar
1 cup water
1 teaspoon lemon juice
½ cup shredded coconut
½ cup all-purpose flour
½ teaspoon salt
½ teaspoon soda
1 cup quick-cooking or old-fashioned rolled oats
½ cup packed brown sugar
⅓ cup butter or margarine, melted

In saucepan combine apricots, 2 tablespoons brown sugar, water and lemon juice. Cook and stir over low heat until mixture thickens. Stir in coconut. Cool.

In mixing bowl sift together flour, salt and soda. Stir in rolled oats and ½ cup brown sugar. Blend in melted butter or margarine until mixture resembles coarse crumbs.

Press half of crumb mixture in an 8-inch square baking pan. Spread apricot filling evenly over crumb base. Cover with remaining crumb mixture, pressing lightly.

Bake in a 350-degree oven for 25 to 30 minutes or until lightly browned. Cool in pan on wire rack. Cut into bars. Makes 2 dozen.

To measure brown sugar, pack firmly in a measuring utensil. When removed, the sugar should retain the shape of the utensil.

CHEESECAKE COOKIES

Cheesecake-addicts — Beware! These super-easy, super-delicious bars are irresistible.

1 cup all-purpose flour
⅓ cup packed brown sugar
⅓ cup butter or margarine
½ cup finely chopped pecans
1 8-ounce package cream cheese, softened
¼ cup sugar
1 egg
2 tablespoons milk
1 tablespoon lemon juice
½ teaspoon vanilla

In medium mixing bowl, sift together flour and brown sugar. Cut in butter or margarine till mixture forms fine crumbs; stir in pecans. Reserve 1 cupful for topping. Press remaining mixture into buttered 8-inch square pan. Bake in a 350-degree oven for 12 to 15 minutes or till lightly browned.

Stir cream cheese to soften. Add sugar and beat until smooth. Add egg, milk, lemon juice and vanilla; beat well. Spread mixture over partially baked crust. Top with reserved crumb mixture. Return to 350-degree oven for 20 to 25 minutes or until filling is set. Cool in pan on wire rack; cut. Store in refrigerator and serve cold. These freeze beautifully. Makes 16 cookies.

CHOCODILES

A big batch of bars with travel-well qualities — perfect for picnics and bag lunches!

2½ cups all-purpose flour
1¼ cups packed brown sugar
1 cup butter or margarine, softened
⅓ cup crunchy peanut butter
¼ teaspoon salt
1 egg yolk, beaten
1 teaspoon vanilla
1 cup (6-ounce pkg.) semi-sweet chocolate morsels
½ cup crunchy peanut butter
1½ cups crispy corn or rice cereal

In large mixing bowl combine flour, brown sugar, butter or margarine, ⅓ cup peanut butter and salt. Mix until mixture resembles coarse crumbs. Stir in egg yolk and vanilla, mixing well. Press mixture firmly into an ungreased 15x10x1-inch jelly roll pan.

Bake in a 325-degree oven for 25 to 30 minutes or till crust is golden and no imprint remains when lightly touched. Cool while making topping.

Melt chocolate morsels over hot water. Remove from heat and stir in peanut butter. Add cereal and mix till evenly coated. Spread over warm crust. Let stand at room temperature until chocolate hardens. Cut into bars. Makes 3 dozen.

Store brown sugar in an airtight container to prevent it from drying out!

CHOCOLATE BROWNIES

Corn syrup and cooking oil make an old favorite moist and yummy . . . a winner for a teenager in a brownie contest!

    2 eggs
    1 cup sugar
    ⅔ cup cooking oil
    2 tablespoons light corn syrup
    1 teaspoon vanilla
    ¾ cup all-purpose flour
    6 tablespoons unsweetened cocoa
    ½ teaspoon baking powder
    ¼ teaspoon salt
    ½ cup chopped nuts

In large mixing bowl beat eggs; gradually add sugar, beating till light and fluffy. Stir in cooking oil, corn syrup and vanilla.

Sift together flour, cocoa, baking powder and salt. Add to creamed mixture and mix well. Stir in nuts. Spread batter in a greased and floured 9-inch square baking pan. Bake in a 325-degree oven for 30 minutes or till brownies start to pull away from sides of pan. DO NOT OVERBAKE! Cool in pan on rack. Cut into bars. Makes 16 brownies.

DANISH BARS

This tri-layered bar, consisting of a buttery crust, coconut filling and orange icing with a hint of almond, is ideal party fare. A kitchen-tested recipe from a home economist.

    ⅓ cup butter or margarine
    1 cup all-purpose flour
    2 tablespoons sugar
    2 eggs
    ½ cup packed brown sugar
    ½ teaspoon salt
    ¾ cup shredded coconut
    ½ cup chopped nuts
      Orange Icing (recipe follows)

In small mixer bowl, cut butter or margarine into flour and sugar until mixture is coarse and crumbly. Press into ungreased 9-inch square baking pan. Bake in a 350-degree oven for 12 to 15 minutes, or till set but not brown.

In same mixer bowl, combine eggs, brown sugar and salt. Mix at low speed until well blended. Stir in coconut and nuts. Spread over partially baked crust. Bake at 350-degrees for 20 to 25 minutes. Cool in pan on wire rack. Frost with Orange Icing. Cut. Makes 16 bars.

Orange Icing ✓

1½ cups sifted confectioners' sugar
2 tablespoons butter or margarine, softened
5 teaspoons orange juice
¾ teaspoon almond extract

Measure all ingredients into small mixing bowl. Beat until smooth.

JANE'S MARBLE SQUARES

Try this one when there is no time to fill the cookie jar . . . it's a chocolate chip cookie dough spread in a pan!

½ cup butter or margarine, softened (1 stick)
½ cup packed brown sugar
¼ cup sugar
1 egg
1 teaspoon vanilla
1 cup plus 2 tablespoons all-purpose flour
½ teaspoon soda
½ teaspoon salt
½ cup coarsely chopped nuts
1 cup (6-ounce pkg.) semi-sweet chocolate morsels

In mixing bowl combine butter or margarine and sugars; beat until light and fluffy. Add egg and beat well. Stir in vanilla.

Sift together flour, soda and salt; add to creamed mixture. Mix well. Stir in nuts.

Spread batter in a greased and floured 13x9x2-inch baking pan; sprinkle chocolate morsels evenly over top. Place in a 375-degree oven for 2 minutes. Remove from oven and run a knife zigzag-fashion through batter to create a marble appearance.

Return pan to oven and continue to bake for 12 to 14 minutes or till golden brown. Cool in pan on wire rack. Cut into desired shapes. Makes 2 dozen.

For baking bars, select a pan with 1½-inch sides. If using a glass utensil, reduce oven temperature by 25 degrees.

JELLY MERINGUE BARS

A three-layered bar consisting of a shortbread crust, jelly center and meringue topping changes flavor and color with the selection of jelly. Perfect for showing off your finest homemade preserves!

½ cup confectioners' sugar
1 cup all-purpose flour
½ cup butter or margarine
2 egg yolks
⅔ cup jelly (apple, currant, grape or strawberry)
2 egg whites
½ cup sugar
¼ teaspoon cinnamon
½ cup finely chopped nuts

Sift, then measure confectioners' sugar. In medium bowl combine confectioners' sugar, flour and butter or margarine. Mix until well blended. Stir in egg yolks. Press mixture in bottom of lightly greased 13x9x2-inch baking pan. Flatten with hand or spatula. Bake in a 350-degree oven for 10 minutes.

Stir jelly to soften; set aside. Beat egg whites until stiff. Gradually add sugar and cinnamon; beat until smooth and glossy. Fold in nuts.

Remove crust from oven and spread with jelly. Carefully spread meringue topping over jelly. Return pan to 350-degree oven for 25 minutes or till delicately browned. Cool in pan on wire rack. Cut into desired shapes. Makes 2 dozen.

To prevent bars from drying out, keep tightly covered. Store in their pan with a piece of aluminum foil over the top or place in a container with a tight-fitting cover.

LUSCIOUS LEMON SQUARES

A bar with a refreshing lemon filling baked on a crisp short-bread crust. Tastes especially good the next day!

    1 cup all-purpose flour
    ½ cup butter or margarine
    ¼ cup confectioners' sugar
    2 eggs
    1 cup sugar
    ½ teaspoon baking powder
    ¼ teaspoon salt
    2 tablespoons lemon juice
    1 teaspoon grated lemon peel

In medium bowl thoroughly blend flour, butter or margarine and confectioners' sugar. Press evenly in ungreased 9-inch square baking pan. Bake in a 350-degree oven for 20 minutes.

In mixing bowl combine eggs, sugar, baking powder, salt, lemon juice and lemon peel; beat for 3 minutes or until light and fluffy. Pour over hot crust. Bake at 325-degrees for 25 minutes or until no imprint remains when lightly touched. Cool in pan on wire rack. Carefully cut into squares with a sharp knife. Makes 16 squares.

MAYBELLE'S CONGO BARS

Shh! The secret for making this popular bar moist and light came from a knowledgeable baker: bake in a s-l-o-w oven. A favorite with teenagers!

> ¾ cup butter or margarine
> 2¼ cups packed brown sugar
> 3 eggs
> 2¾ cups all-purpose flour
> 2½ teaspoons baking powder
> ½ teaspoon salt
> 2 cups (12-ounce pkg.) semi-sweet chocolate morsels
> 1 cup coarsely chopped nuts

In large saucepan melt butter or margarine over low heat. Remove pan from heat and add brown sugar; mix well. Cool. Add eggs, one at a time, beating well after each addition.

Sift together flour, baking powder and salt; add to sugar mixture and mix well. Stir in chocolate morsels and nuts. Spread batter evenly in greased 15x10x1-inch jelly roll pan. Bake in a 250-degree oven for 1 hour or until wooden pick inserted near center comes out clean. Cool in pan on wire rack. Cut when almost cool. Makes 3 dozen bars.

Store spices in a cool, dry place away from heat. Ground spices are seldom at their best after one year.

MELT-AWAY BARS

A buttery-crusted bar made glamorous for the holidays with colored sugar and chopped nuts. Colorful!

> 1 cup butter or margarine, softened
> 1 cup sugar

1 egg yolk
1 teaspoon vanilla
2 cups all-purpose flour
½ cup chopped nuts
1 egg white
½ cup chopped nuts
  Colored sugar

In large mixing bowl cream butter or margarine and sugar. Blend in egg yolk and vanilla. Stir in flour, mixing thoroughly. Add ½ cup nuts. Spread dough evenly in ungreased 15x10x1-inch jelly roll pan.

In small bowl beat egg white till frothy; spread over dough. Sprinkle with ½ cup nuts and colored sugar, if desired.

Bake in a 350-degree oven for 25 to 30 minutes or till crust is golden. Cool slightly before cutting into bars. Makes 40 bars.

PUMPKIN BARS

A moist, old-fashioned cake-like bar made special with a cream cheese icing. Says the cook sharing the recipe, "They move fast!"

4 eggs
1⅔ cups sugar
1 cup cooking oil
1 16-ounce can solid pack pumpkin or 2 cups cooked pumpkin
2 cups all-purpose flour
2 teaspoons baking powder
2 teaspoons cinnamon
1 teaspoon soda
1 teaspoon salt
¾ cup raisins
½ cup chopped nuts
  Cream Cheese Icing (recipe on page 272)

In large mixing bowl beat eggs till light and fluffy. Add sugar, cooking oil and pumpkin; beat thoroughly.

Sift together flour, baking powder, cinnamon, soda and salt; add to pumpkin mixture, beating till thoroughly blended. Stir in raisins and nuts.

Pour batter into greased and floured 15x10x1-inch jelly roll pan. Bake in a 350-degree oven for 25 to 30 minutes or till tester inserted in center comes out free of batter. Cool in pan on wire rack. Frost with Cream Cheese Icing. Makes 3 dozen.

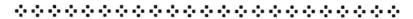

Butter gives cookies and bars a richer flavor than shortening.

SCOTCH SHORTBREAD

An authentic recipe from a Scotsman. "The rice flour gives the shortbread crispness as it cools," but cornstarch is a substitute.

> 1 cup butter, softened
> ½ cup sugar
> 1½ cups all-purpose flour
> ½ cup rice flour or cornstarch

In a large mixing bowl cream butter till light and fluffy. Add sugar; mix thoroughly.

Sift together flour and rice flour or cornstarch; add to creamed mixture; blend thoroughly. Chill.

Turn out onto lightly floured surface. Press with the hand into 2 circles, ½-inch thick. Place each on an ungreased cookie sheet. Flute to form a scalloped edge; prick all over with a fork. Sprinkle lightly with confectioners' sugar, if desired.

Bake in a 300-degree oven for 45 to 50 minutes or till golden. (Shortbread should NOT be brown.) Cool in pan. Cut into small pieces as it is very rich. Makes about 2 dozen pieces.

Variation:

Shortbread Cookies

Roll dough out on a lightly floured surface to ⅓ to ½-inch thickness. Cut into fancy shapes with cookie cutters. Place on un-greased cookie sheet. Bake at 300 degrees for 20 to 25 minutes. Cool on wire rack.

SUGARED DATE SQUARES

An old-fashioned, date-studded cake-like bar with a subtle fla-vor of spices and a sprinkling of sugar for a glistening top. The recipe is from a grandmother's kitchen!

½ cup butter or margarine, softened (1 stick)
1 cup sugar
2 eggs
1½ cups all-purpose flour
½ teaspoon soda
½ teaspoon cinnamon
½ teaspoon nutmeg
¼ teaspoon cloves
⅛ teaspoon salt
1 cup finely snipped pitted dates

In mixing bowl cream butter or margarine and sugar till light and fluffy. Add eggs, one at a time, beating well after each addi-tion.

In second bowl sift together flour, soda, cinnamon, nutmeg, cloves and salt. Stir in snipped dates. Add flour mixture to creamed mixture; mix well.

Spread batter in greased and floured 9-inch square baking pan. Sprinkle top lightly with sugar. Bake in a 350-degree oven for 25 to 30 minutes or till tester comes out free of batter. Cool in pan on wire rack. Cut. Makes 16 squares.

Hardened brown sugar may be softened by heating in a slow (250-degree) oven. Handle while warm as brown sugar becomes even harder if allowed to cool!

❖❖ ❖❖ ❖❖ ❖❖ ❖❖ ❖❖ ❖❖ ❖❖ ❖❖ ❖❖ ❖❖ ❖❖ ❖❖ ❖❖ ❖❖ ❖❖

THURLIE'S TOFFEE SQUARES

Says the cook who totes these to family gatherings, "They are a favorite of home economists!" They are with this one!

1½ cups all-purpose flour
½ cup butter or margarine, softened
¼ cup packed brown sugar
½ teaspoon salt
¼ teaspoon soda
3 tablespoons milk
½ cup chopped nuts
¾ cup butter or margarine
¾ cup packed brown sugar
¾ cup semi-sweet or milk chocolate morsels

In a mixing bowl combine flour, ½ cup butter or margarine, ¼ cup brown sugar, salt, soda, milk and chopped nuts; blend together until crumbly. Press mixture firmly in an ungreased 13x9x2-inch baking pan. Bake in a 350-degree oven for 15 to 20 minutes or till golden brown. Prick crust generously with a fork.

In a saucepan combine remaining butter or margarine and brown sugar. Bring to a boil, stirring constantly, over low heat; boil for 3 minutes. Pour over crust. Bake at 375 degrees for 5 minutes. Remove from oven and cool on a rack for 5 minutes.

Sprinkle chocolate morsels evenly over top; let stand until chocolate is softened. Spread smooth with a metal spatula to frost squares. Cool. Cut into 32 pieces.

Cooking Notes

Chapter 13

New Englanders take pride in preserving our culinary heritage; "stocking up" is a tradition we cherish. Many women — and men — continue to pack the pantry with home-preserved fruits and vegetables to add zest and interest to year-round meals.

Newcomers to the art of food preservation will find that preserving the harvest provides a great deal of personal accomplishment as well as pleasure to the palate. The satisfaction one gets from opening a jar of home-canned food in the middle of the winter makes the time and labor seem very worthwhile.

In colonial days homemakers "put down" pickles in stone crocks and "put up" relishes and preserves in glass jars. Paraffin wax was used as a sealing agent for fruit and vegetable preserves. But times have changed and so have canning procedures! Heat processing is recommended for all home-canned preserves and pickle products to insure a good seal and prevent spoilage.

This section boasts an assortment of recipes for jellies and jams, pickles and relishes. All contain enough acid so they may be safely processed in a boiling-water-bath canner.

Many of the recipes — Apple Butter and Pioneer Corn Relish — are the treasures from grandmother's kitchen; others, such as Fresh Strawberry Jam, are updated versions with contemporary appeal. Whether you preserve Nature's bounty for economy or sheer love of the art, may this activity bring you — the serious cook — an immeasurable amount of joy and satisfaction!

Pickles & Preserves

A GUIDE TO FOOD PRESERVATION

There are no shortcuts in home canning and perfect results cannot be expected with less than perfect procedures. Airtight containers, proper processing and adequate heat penetration are the only SAFE procedures.

As for canning low-acid foods, which includes all vegetables except tomatoes, DON'T — unless you have a pressure canner. These vegetables must be processed at 10 pounds pressure and 240 degrees.

A boiling water bath reaches only 212 degrees — or boiling at sea level, which is ineffective for destroying bacteria. This method is recommended ONLY for acidic foods — fruits, tomatoes and some pickled vegetables.

To process in a boiling water bath, you will need a canner or kettle large enough to allow 2 inches above jars or water depth plus another 2 inches for boiling during processing; a rack to hold jars ½-inch above the bottom and a cover so water can be kept at a good rolling boil.

If you cold-pack jars — that is, fill with uncooked food — the water in the canner should be just hot when the jars are added. If the food is hot-packed — cooked or heated before putting in jars — the water may be boiling. Add water to a depth of 1 to 2 inches above tops of jars. Bring water to a boil; start processing time at this point!

At the end of the processing time, set jars in an upright position on a folded cloth or rack away from a draft. Allow 1-inch space between jars and do not cover. Cool.

Following the cooling process, check seals on all jars. Any unsealed jar should be refrigerated for immediate use. Reprocessing unsealed jars is not recommended.

Wipe jars with a clean, damp cloth and label with date and name of product. Store in a cool, dark and dry place where there is no danger of freezing.

The chief concern with home-canning, of course, is safety; but if you use a little common sense and follow directions, there should be no spoilage.

Here are some additional hints to insure success in preserving food.

1. Select produce in prime condition at peak flavor. Choose fruits and vegetables of the same size so heat penetration during processing will be equal.

2.   Wash the produce in cold water to remove all soil. Once you begin to process fresh food, work rapidly with small quantities at a time.

3.   Use PURE granulated salt. The bag will be marked for canning and pickling purposes. Although uniodized table salt may be satisfactory when used for seasoning ONLY, it could leave a sediment in the bottom of the jar; iodized table salt is NOT recommended as it may discolor foods.

4.   Select a high-grade vinegar of 4 to 6 percent acidity — either cider or white vinegar. Generally, the flavor of cider vinegar is preferable, however.

5.   Use white sugar unless the recipe calls for brown sugar or a darker colored pickle is desired.

6.   Use fresh spices for the best flavors. Ground spices darken the pickle and old spices give a musty flavor.

7.   Glass, pottery or enamel containers are recommended for soaking pickles; enamel pots are recommended for cooking.

8.   Check all jars and closures for cracks, nicks or rust. Discard any with defects.

9.   Wash jars in hot, soapy water and rinse thoroughly. Fill completely with boiling water until you are ready to fill with food. Wash lids and keep in water until ready to use.

10.   Fill jars to within ½-inch of top. Wipe rim free of seeds or pulp.

APPLE BUTTER

A taste from the good old days. It's spicy with a not-too-sweet flavor. Spread it on freshly baked bread or toast, blend with peanut butter for a super filling between crackers or serve as a meat condiment.

6 pounds unpared tart apples (see note)
2 cups pure apple juice or apple cider
5 cups sugar
1 tablespoon cinnamon
1 teaspoon cloves
½ teaspoon allspice

Wash and quarter apples. Place in a heavy kettle. Add juice or cider. Cook, covered, over low heat until soft, stirring occasionally. Cool slightly; press through a coarse sieve or food mill to remove skins and seeds. Measure amount of pulp; place in kettle. To each cup of pulp, add ½ cup sugar. Stir in spices.

Simmer over low heat for 2 hours or until apple butter is thick and spreadable, stirring frequently. Watch carefully as mixture scorches easily.

Remove from heat and ladle into clean, hot jars, leaving a ½-inch headspace. Adjust lids. Process in a boiling water bath for 10 minutes. Butter thickens as it cools. Makes about 5 pints.

Note:

When using crab apples, substitute water for apple juice or cider.

CHOKECHERRY JELLY

A bit of nostalgia in every spoonful! Wild cherries produce a flavor unequaled in commercial jellies. If the consistency is thinner than you expect, it makes a wonderful sauce to pour over vanilla ice cream.

- 4 quarts chokecherries
- 2 cups water
- 4 cups chokecherry juice
- 1 1¾-ounce package dry fruit pectin
- 5 cups sugar

Remove leaves and large stems from cherries. Wash and drain. Place in a large kettle; add water. Bring to a boil. Cover and simmer for 15 minutes or till soft, stirring occasionally.

Place cooked cherries in a dampened jelly bag or muslin-lined colander. Do not squeeze bag nor let tip touch extracted juice. Allow to stand until all juice has been extracted.

Measure the amount of juice and continue on to second step; or, cover the juice tightly and refrigerate — up to several days — until ready to make jelly.

In a heavy 8- to 10-quart kettle combine juice and pectin, stirring to dissolve. Bring quickly to a high boil, stirring occasionally. Stir in sugar and bring to a high rolling boil — a boil that cannot be stirred down. Boil hard for 1 minute, stirring constantly.

Remove from heat. Skim off foam with a metal spoon. Immediately pour into clean, hot jars with 2-piece screwband lids, leaving a ¼-inch headspace. Adjust lids. Process in a boiling water bath for 5 minutes. Cool. Store in a cool, dark place. Makes 6 half pints.

FRESH STRAWBERRY JAM

A spread for the calorie-counters! Unflavored gelatin acts as a thickening agent and helps retain the fresh natural flavor of the berries. It's stored in the refrigerator.

4 cups washed and hulled strawberries, sliced
½ cup sugar
2 tablespoons lemon juice
1 envelope unflavored gelatin
½ cup cold water

In medium saucepan combine strawberries, sugar and lemon juice. Heat mixture 5 minutes, crushing berries slightly. Bring to a boil; boil rapidly, stirring constantly, for 3 minutes.

In small bowl sprinkle gelatin over water. Add to mixture and heat, stirring till gelatin dissolves, about 3 minutes.

Let jam stand for 5 minutes, skimming off foam with a spoon. Pour into clean, hot jars. Cover and cool slightly. Store in refrigerator. Use within 3 or 4 weeks or freeze for longer storage. Makes 2 half pints.

MOCK RASPBERRY JAM

You're in for a surprise with this recipe. It combines ripe tomatoes and raspberry-flavored gelatin for a delightful preserve. We like it!

4 cups peeled and quartered, firm ripe tomatoes
1 6-ounce package raspberry-flavored gelatin
1 tablespoon blackberry-flavored gelatin (for color)
3½ cups sugar

Chop tomato pulp into small pieces; place in a large saucepan. Add NO WATER! Bring to a boil over medium-low heat; boil, stirring frequently, for 15 minutes.

Add dry gelatin and sugar; mix well. Bring mixture back to a boil. Cook for 10 minutes or until mixture starts to thicken slightly. Watch carefully as mixture scorches easily!

Ladle into clean, hot jelly jars with 2-piece screwband lids, leaving a ½-inch headspace. Adjust lids. Process in a boiling water bath for 10 minutes. Makes 6 half pints.

RHUBARB JAM

A foolproof method for making a batch of jam. No commercial pectin is needed!

5 cups unpeeled rhubarb cut into ½-inch lengths
1 8-ounce can crushed pineapple in juice
4 cups sugar
1 3-ounce package strawberry- or raspberry-flavored gelatin

In a large, heavy saucepan combine rhubarb and pineapple. Add sugar; mix thoroughly. Let stand 30 minutes.

Bring mixture slowly to a boil. Reduce heat. Cook for 15 minutes or till mixture thickens slightly; stir frequently to prevent sticking. Remove from heat; add dry gelatin, stirring till thoroughly dissolved. Ladle into clean, hot jars, leaving a ½-inch headspace. Adjust lids. Process in a boiling water bath for 10 minutes. Makes 6 half pints.

BEET RELISH

A tasty way to use the last of the harvest!

1 quart peeled and chopped cooked beets
1 quart finely chopped cabbage
1 medium onion, peeled and chopped
1 teaspoon pure salt
2 cups cider vinegar

1 cup sugar
1 tablespoon prepared horseradish
¼ teaspoon cayenne pepper

Chop beets and cabbage or put through food grinder; combine beets, cabbage and onion in a large bowl, sprinkle with salt.

In a large saucepan bring vinegar to a boil. Add sugar, horseradish and cayenne pepper, stirring till sugar is dissolved. Add vegetable mixture. Bring to a boil. Reduce heat and simmer until clear, about 15 minutes; stir frequently. Ladle into clean, hot jars, leaving a ½-inch headspace. Adjust lids. Process in a boiling water bath for 15 minutes. Makes about 4 pints.

Don't take shortcuts or experiment in home canning.

CUCUMBER AND CARROT RELISH

A sweet relish that "you can eat right out of the jar," says the donor of this recipe.

3½ cups coarsely ground unpared cucumber (4 to 6)
1½ cups finely ground carrot (6 medium)
1 cup finely ground onion
2 tablespoons pure salt
2½ cups sugar
1½ cups cider vinegar
1½ teaspoons celery seed
1½ teaspoons mustard seed

Prepare vegetables. Combine cucumber, carrot and onion in a large bowl; stir in salt. Let stand for 3 hours. Drain thoroughly; discard liquid.

In a large kettle combine sugar, vinegar, celery seed and mustard seed. Bring mixture to a boil. Add drained vegetables. Simmer, uncovered, for 20 minutes. Stir occasionally. Ladle into clean, hot jars, leaving a ½-inch headspace. Adjust lids. Process in a boiling water bath for 10 minutes. Makes 3 pints.

JOYCE'S CUCUMBER RELISH

Combine a surplus of cucumbers with a little Yankee ingenuity and what do you get? For a frugal, young homemaker the result was a super relish . . . one of our most requested recipes!

6 large cucumbers
2 large onions
¼ cup pure salt
2 cups sugar
2 cups cider vinegar
½ cup sugar
¼ cup all-purpose flour
1 tablespoon turmeric
1 tablespoon mustard seed
1 tablespoon celery seed
¼ cup cider vinegar

Pare cucumbers; discard seeds and inner pulp. Put flesh through food chopper using coarse blade to make about 12 cups.

Peel onions and grind coarsely to make about 2 cups. Combine cucumber and onion; sprinkle with salt. Cover with cold water and let stand overnight. Drain; rinse with cold water. Drain thoroughly.

In a large kettle bring 2 cups each of sugar and vinegar to a boil. Add drained vegetables and bring back to a boil. Simmer, uncovered, for 20 minutes or just till tender. Stir occasionally. DO NOT boil!

Combine ½ cup sugar, flour, turmeric, mustard seed and celery seed; mix in vinegar to make a smooth paste. Add to cucumber mixture, stirring constantly, over low heat until thickened. Ladle into clean, hot jars, leaving ½-inch headspace. Adjust lids. Process in a boiling water bath for 5 minutes. Makes 6 pints.

Use only jars made for home canning! Do NOT reuse sealing lids!

PIONEER CORN RELISH

An old-time condiment to make when there's a summer bounty!

18 to 20 medium ears fresh corn, husks and silk
   removed
 3 large sweet red peppers, seeded and diced (2 cups)
 3 large green peppers, seeded and diced (2 cups)
 3 stalks celery, chopped (2 cups)
 1 cup chopped onion
1¼ cups sugar
 3 cups vinegar
 4 teaspoons pure salt
 2 teaspoons celery seed
 3 tablespoons all-purpose flour
 1 tablespoon dry mustard
 1 teaspoon turmeric
 ¼ cup cold water
 ½ cup vinegar

Cook corn in boiling salted water for 5 minutes; plunge into cold water to cool rapidly. Cut (don't scrape) corn from cob to make about 8 cups.

In a large kettle combine peppers, celery, onion, sugar, 3 cups vinegar, salt and celery seed. Bring mixture to a boil; cook, uncovered, for 5 minutes.

In small bowl combine flour, dry mustard and turmeric; add water to make a smooth paste. Stir in remaining ½ cup vinegar. Add to kettle; cook, stirring, till mixture comes to a boil and thickens. Add corn. Bring back to a boil, stirring frequently, to prevent scorching; cook for 5 minutes.

Ladle hot relish into clean, hot jars, leaving a ½-inch headspace. Adjust lids. Process in a boiling water bath for 15 minutes. Makes 6½ pints.

Heat processing is recommended for all pickle products!

KATHY'S ZUCCHINI RELISH

This tried-and-true favorite of many cooks makes worthwhile use of Nature's bounty. If the zucchini is young and tender, just cut off the blossom and stem ends and put the whole squash through the food chopper using a coarse blade. Pare mature zucchini, discarding seeds and inner pulp; use only the flesh.

> 10 cups ground unpared zucchini
> 4 cups ground onion
> 5 tablespoons pure salt
> 4½ cups sugar
> 2¼ cups white vinegar
> 1 green pepper, seeded and finely chopped
> 1 sweet red pepper, seeded and finely chopped
> 1 tablespoon nutmeg
> 1 tablespoon dry mustard
> 1 tablespoon turmeric
> 1 tablespoon cornstarch
> 2 teaspoons celery salt

Prepare vegetables. Combine zucchini, onion and salt in a large bowl; mix well. Let stand 8 hours, or overnight. Drain. Rinse in cold water; drain thoroughly.

In a large kettle combine sugar, vinegar, chopped peppers, nutmeg, dry mustard, turmeric and cornstarch. Add zucchini mixture. Bring to a boil. Simmer, uncovered, for 30 minutes. Stir occasionally. Ladle into clean, hot jars, leaving a ½-inch headspace. Adjust lids. Process in a boiling water bath for 5 minutes. Makes 7 pints.

GOLDEN GLOW PICKLES

Mama's favorite! Try to keep the pieces uniform for even cooking and don't overcook. This is a crisp pickle.

> 5 quarts prepared ripe cucumbers
> 2 medium onions, peeled and chopped
> 2 sweet red peppers, seeded and diced
> ½ cup pure salt
> 5 cups packed brown sugar

4 cups cider vinegar
1 tablespoon turmeric
1 teaspoon mustard seed

To prepare cucumbers, pare and cut in half lengthwise. Remove seeds and pulp; discard. Cut firm white inner rind into ¾-inch pieces.

In large bowl combine cucumbers, onions and red peppers. Sprinkle with salt; stir slightly to mix. Let stand overnight. Drain. Rinse in cold water. Drain well.

In a large kettle mix together brown sugar, vinegar, turmeric and mustard seed. Bring mixture to a boil. Add drained vegetables. Bring back to a boil. Reduce heat and simmer, uncovered, for 20 minutes or till transparent but still crisp. Stir occasionally.

Ladle into clean, hot jars, filling to within ½-inch of top. Adjust lids. Process in a boiling water bath for 10 minutes. Makes about 8 pints.

GREEN TOMATO SLICES

A traditional Saturday night supper on the farm: baked beans, brown bread and green tomato slices!

2½ quarts green tomatoes, cut in ¼-inch slices
2 cups thinly sliced onions
¼ cup pure salt
2 tablespoons mixed pickling spices
1½ cups packed brown sugar
1½ cups cider vinegar

Alternate layers of tomato and onion slices in a large glass bowl. Sprinkle with salt and add cold water to cover. Let stand 12 hours or overnight. Drain thoroughly, discarding liquid.

Tie pickling spices in a small cloth bag and place in a large kettle; add brown sugar and vinegar. Bring mixture to a boil, stirring to dissolve sugar. Add drained vegetables. Cook slowly, uncovered, for 30 minutes or until tomatoes are just tender.

Pack loosely in clean, hot jars; fill with liquid to within ½-inch of top. Adjust lids. Process 5 minutes in a boiling water bath. Makes 3 pints.

MUSTARD PICKLES

A family treasure that has stood the test of time!

2 quarts green tomatoes, cut into large chunks
2 quarts small cucumbers, unpared and cut into chunks
2 quarts small white pickling onions, peeled
1 large cauliflower, broken into flowerets
½ cup pure salt
6 tablespoons all-purpose flour
2 tablespoons dry mustard
1 tablespoon turmeric
½ cup vinegar
2 quarts vinegar
2 cups sugar

Prepare vegetables and arrange in layers in a large bowl. Sprinkle with salt and add cold water to cover. Allow to stand overnight; drain thoroughly.

In a large kettle combine flour, dry mustard and turmeric; add ½ cup vinegar, making a smooth paste. Stir in remaining vinegar and sugar. Cook and stir till mixture thickens. Add drained vegetables and slowly bring to the boiling point. Cook just till vegetables are tender, stirring frequently to prevent scorching. DO NOT OVERCOOK. Vegetables should not be mushy.

Pack in clean, hot jars, leaving a ½-inch headspace. Adjust lids. Process in a boiling water bath for 10 minutes. Makes 8 to 10 pints.

OLD-FASHIONED SOUR PICKLES

An heirloom recipe! They are worth the 14-day wait.

Cucumbers, about 3 inches long
1 tablespoon sugar
1 tablespoon pure salt
1 tablespoon dry mustard
1 cup cider vinegar

Wash cucumbers and wipe dry. Pack loosely in two clean, hot

pint jars. In saucepan combine sugar, salt and dry mustard; blend well. Stir in vinegar. Bring mixture to a boil, stirring constantly.

Pour over cucumbers, filling jars to within ½-inch of top of rim. Remove air bubbles, adding more liquid if needed. Adjust lids. Process in a boiling water bath for 15 minutes, timing as soon as jars are placed in boiling water. Cool completely. Turn jars over daily for next 14 days. Ready to eat after 2 weeks. Makes 2 pints.

SHERRY'S CUCUMBER PICKLES

"My favorite!" says the cook sharing this recipe.

4 quarts thinly sliced unpared cucumber
6 medium onions, peeled and thinly sliced
½ cup pure salt
2 trays ice cubes
3 cups cider vinegar
2 cups sugar
2 tablespoons mustard seed
2 teaspoons celery seed
1 teaspoon turmeric

Prepare vegetables. Combine cucumbers and onions in a large bowl. Sprinkle with salt. Cover with ice cubes. Let stand 3 hours or until ice melts. Drain thoroughly.

In large kettle combine vinegar, sugar, mustard seed, celery seed and turmeric; blend thoroughly. Add vegetables. Bring just to the boiling point, but DO NOT boil! Simmer, uncovered, for 10 minutes, turning vegetables over occasionally. Pack loosely in clean, hot jars, leaving a ½-inch headspace. Adjust lids. Process in a boiling water bath for 10 minutes. Makes 6 pints.

Pure granulated salt, which contains no iodine, is recommended for ALL canning and pickling purposes. It is available in most supermarkets.

VIOLA'S SPANISH PICKLES

A zesty green tomato relish for hot dogs and hamburgers.

  1 peck green tomatoes, thinly sliced
12 large onions, peeled and thinly sliced
  1 cup pure salt
  2 quarts cider vinegar
  6 cups packed brown sugar
12 green peppers, seeded and diced
  6 sweet red peppers, seeded and diced
  6 cloves garlic, peeled and minced
  2 tablespoons dry mustard
  2 tablespoons ground ginger
  1 tablespoon pure salt
  1 tablespoon celery seed
  1 tablespoon whole cloves
  2 inches stick cinnamon

Prepare tomatoes and onions; alternate layers in a large earthenware bowl. Sprinkle each layer with salt. Let stand for 12 hours or overnight. Drain. Rinse in cold water and drain thoroughly, discarding liquid.

In large kettle combine vinegar, brown sugar, diced peppers, garlic, dry mustard, ginger, 1 tablespoon salt and celery seed. Tie whole cloves and stick cinnamon in a small cloth bag and add to kettle; bring mixture to a boil. Add drained vegetables. Bring back to a boil. Simmer, stirring frequently, for 1 hour or till tomatoes are transparent. Remove spice bag.

Pack pickles loosely in clean, hot jars, leaving a ½-inch headspace. Adjust lids. Process in a boiling water bath for 10 minutes. Makes about 8 pints.

ZUCCHINI PICKLE SLICES

A bread-and-butter pickle made from zucchini.

  2 quarts thinly sliced small, unpared zucchini
2½ cups thinly sliced onion
  ¼ cup pure salt
  2 cups cider vinegar

1 cup sugar
1½ teaspoons celery seed
½ teaspoon turmeric
½ teaspoon dry mustard

In large bowl combine zucchini and onion slices. Sprinkle with salt. Cover with cold water and let stand for 2 hours. Drain. Rinse with cold water and drain thoroughly.

In large saucepan combine vinegar, sugar, celery seed, turmeric and dry mustard. Bring mixture to a boil; cook for 2 minutes. Add zucchini and onions, stirring gently to mix. Remove from heat; cover. Let stand for 1 hour.

Bring vegetable mixture back to a boil. Cook gently, uncovered, for 5 minutes. Stir occasionally. Ladle into clean, hot jars, adding liquid to within ½-inch of top. Adjust lids. Process in a boiling water bath for 10 minutes. Makes 3½ pints.

GREEN TOMATO MINCEMEAT

My family's favorite filling for the holiday turnovers. It makes a delightful pie, too!

6 pounds green tomatoes
6 pounds tart apples, pared and cored
2 medium oranges, unpeeled
1 small lemon, unpeeled
1 cup ground suet
5 cups packed brown sugar
1 cup vinegar
1 tablespoon ground cinnamon
2 teaspoons ground nutmeg
2 teaspoons pure salt
1 teaspoon ground cloves

Finely chop tomatoes and apples or put through food grinder using coarse blade to make about 3 quarts each. Drain well.

Wash and quarter oranges and lemon. Put through food grinder using fine blade; discard seeds but reserve all juices. Finely grind suet.

Combine prepared tomatoes, apples, orange and lemon peel and pulp and suet in a large heavy kettle. Add brown sugar, vinegar, cinnamon, nutmeg, salt and cloves; mix well.

Bring mixture to a boil, stirring frequently. Reduce heat and simmer, uncovered, 2 to 2½ hours or till mixture thickens slightly. Stir frequently to prevent sticking. Watch carefully towards end of cooking process as mixture scorches easily.

Pack hot mixture into clean, hot pint jars, leaving ½-inch headspace. Adjust lids. Process in a boiling water bath for 25 minutes. Makes 9 to 10 pints.

CHILI SAUCE

A condiment from yesteryear to spice up a hamburger!

    5 pounds ripe tomatoes
    4 medium onions
    2 medium green peppers
    2 medium sweet red peppers
    2 stalks celery
    1 cup cider vinegar
    ⅔ cup packed brown sugar
    2 teaspoons pure salt
    1 teaspoon ground nutmeg
    ½ teaspoon ground cinnamon
    ¼ teaspoon ground cloves
    ¼ teaspoon pepper

Peel, core and quarter tomatoes to make 2 quarts. Peel and finely chop onions to make 2½ cups. Remove seeds and membranes from green and red peppers; finely chop peppers and celery to make 1 cup each.

In a large kettle combine tomatoes and chopped vegetables. Add vinegar, brown sugar, salt, nutmeg, cinnamon, cloves and pepper; mix well.

Bring mixture to a boil, stirring frequently, over high heat. Reduce heat and simmer, stirring occasionally, 3 to 4 hours or until of desired consistency. Watch carefully towards end of cooking process as mixture scorches easily.

Ladle into clean, hot jars, leaving a ½-inch headspace. Adjust lids and process in a boiling water bath for 5 minutes. Makes 4 pints.

PRESERVING TOMATOES

*Because tomatoes have a high acid content, they may be proc-
essed in a boiling water bath. The acid content, nevertheless,
varies among varieties, soil conditions and climate. To correct
the acid level, lemon juice is added. Salt, on the other hand, is
added for flavor, not as a preservative. Omit for persons on low-
sodium diets.*

**3 medium tomatoes weigh approximately 1 pound
2½ to 3 pounds fresh tomatoes yield 1 quart canned tomatoes**

Canning Tomatoes

Select firm ripe tomatoes. Wash carefully and drain. Let tomatoes stand in boiling water for about 15 seconds or just until the
skins begin to crack. Remove with a slotted spoon and plunge
tomatoes into cold water. Remove skins and cut out stems.
Quarter tomatoes and place in a large saucepan. Add NO WATER!
Bring tomatoes to a boil, stirring. Pack boiling tomatoes in clean,
hot jars. Use the handle of a wooden spoon to release trapped air
bubbles. Fill to within ½-inch of top.

Add ½ teaspoon salt (for flavor only!) and 1 tablespoon bottled
lemon juice to each pint; 1 teaspoon salt and 2 tablespoons lemon
juice to each quart. Wipe rim and outer threads with a clean,
damp cloth. Adjust lids. Process in a boiling water bath for 35
minutes for pints; 45 minutes for quarts.

Freezing Tomatoes

Wash, scald and peel firm ripe tomatoes. Remove stem ends
and cut into quarters. Simmer, covered, 10 to 20 minutes or just
until tender. Cool quickly by placing pan of tomatoes in cold
water. Ladle into freezer containers, leaving a 1-inch headspace.
Seal, date the contents and freeze. Store in freezer no longer than
8 months to one year.

Or, wash firm ripe tomatoes. Peel, stem and pack whole in
freezer containers, leaving a 1-inch headspace. Seal, date and
freeze.

TOMATO JUICE

Select firm ripe tomatoes. Wash and remove stem ends. Peeling is optional; quarter or cut into chunks. Add NO WATER!

Simmer, stirring frequently, 5 to 10 minutes or just till soft and juicy. Put through a sieve or food mill. Add ½ teaspoon salt to each pint of juice and 1 teaspoon to each quart.

To process:

Reheat strained, seasoned juice to boiling. Fill clean, hot jars, leaving a ½-inch headspace. Adjust lids. Process in a boiling water bath for 35 minutes for pints and quarts.

To freeze:

Pour strained, seasoned juice into freezer containers, leaving a 1-inch headspace. Seal, date and freeze.

FREEZING FIDDLEHEADS

Unless you know where fiddleheads grow, you had better purchase them at a market. Folks who "fiddlehead" are rather secretive about sharing their spots, so don't even bother to ask!

Shake fiddleheads gently to rid them of brown flakes; wash thoroughly.

Place clean fiddleheads in a blanching basket. Lower basket into blancher or kettle filled with 1 gallon of boiling water. Cover. Heat for 2 minutes. Place fiddleheads in iced water to stop cooking; cool for 5 minutes.

Spread greens on a screen (similar to window screen) and allow to air dry. Pack in freezer containers or in plastic bags, expelling as much air as possible. Cover containers or close bags with twist-ties. Date contents and freeze.

Cooking Notes

Chapter 14

The choices in our final chapter have little in common with one another — except good eating! Including appetizers, beverages and confections, all recipes were selected with an eye to their taste, appearance and appeal. While this assemblage does not necessarily claim a New England heritage, it does reflect the diversity and generosity of regional cooks.

You will find an array of hors d'oeuvres or appetizers in order to appeal to all appetites. Some, such as Olive Savories, stimulate the taste buds, while others, Sweet and Sour Beef Balls, for instance, serve as more substantial fare.

In the collection of beverage recipes are make-ahead mixes for personal enjoyment, and party punches for receptions and holiday gatherings. While it is difficult to estimate the amount of punch to make, the general rule is to allow two or three drinks per guest.

Among the recipes with a sweet touch are the old favorites — Candied Apples and Molasses Popcorn Balls — to warm the hearts of younger folks and a few newer versions, such as Easy Pralines, which are sure to win rave reviews at money-raising events.

As you turn the pages of our people-pleasers, you will find special treats for just about any occasion. None is difficult to make and many recipes claim foolproof results. But don't wait for a celebration to enjoy them. Show someone you really care — TODAY!

Potpourri

Continued

ARTICHOKE APPETIZERS

Wonderfully easy — a delectable hors d'oeuvre from a Southern hostess!

    2 6-ounce jars marinated artichoke hearts
    1 small onion, peeled and finely chopped
    1 clove garlic, peeled and minced
    4 eggs
    ¼ cup fine dry bread crumbs
    ¼ teaspoon salt
    ⅛ teaspoon pepper
    ⅛ teaspoon oregano
    ⅛ teaspoon bottled hot pepper sauce
    2 cups (8-ounce pkg.) shredded Cheddar cheese
    2 tablespoons snipped fresh parsley

Drain artichokes, reserving liquid from one jar; discard liquid from second jar. Chop artichokes; set aside.

Place reserved artichoke liquid in small skillet; add onion and garlic. Cook and stir until onion is transparent.

In medium bowl beat eggs until frothy. Add bread crumbs, salt, pepper, oregano and hot pepper sauce. Stir in cheese, parsley, chopped artichokes and onion mixture. Turn into buttered 11x7x1½-inch baking pan.

Bake in a 350-degree oven for 30 minutes or until center is set. Remove pan from oven to wire rack. Let cool completely in pan. Cut into small squares.

When ready to serve, reheat squares in a 325-degree oven for 10 to 12 minutes. Serve skewered with wooden picks. Makes about 60 squares.

CRABBIES

For the cocktail hour — a crabmeat-cheese filling spread on English muffins and broiled to a golden goodness!

1 6- or 6½-ounce can crabmeat or 1 cup fresh crabmeat
1 5- or 6-ounce jar process cheese spread
2 tablespoons mayonnaise
½ teaspoon seasoned salt
½ teaspoon Worcestershire sauce
6 English muffins

Drain crabmeat; remove cartilage and flake. Set aside. In small mixing bowl combine cheese, mayonnaise, salt and Worcestershire sauce; mix to blend. Stir in crabmeat.

Split each English muffin in half crosswise. Divide crab mixture evenly among halves. Cut each half into 4 strips. Arrange crabbies on an ungreased baking sheet. Place 3 or 4 inches from heating element. Broil for 4 to 5 minutes or until bubbly and golden brown. Or, freeze Crabbies. Just before serving, remove from freezer to baking sheet. Broil until topping bubbles. Makes 48 appetizer servings.

Variation:

Shrimpies

Follow recipe for Crabbies except — substitute shrimp for crabmeat.

OLIVE SAVORIES

A favorite with guests — make in advance for the cocktail hour!

    1 10-ounce jar Spanish olives
    2 cups (8-ounce pkg.) shredded sharp Cheddar cheese
       (room temperature)
    ½ cup butter or margarine, softened
    1 cup all-purpose flour
    1 teaspoon paprika
    ¼ teaspoon salt
      Dash pepper

Drain olives; set aside. In medium bowl mash cheese until smooth. Add butter or margarine; blend thoroughly. Sift together flour, paprika, salt and pepper; add to cheese mixture. Mix well.

Encase each olive in 1 teaspoon cheese mixture by rolling in palm of hands. Place on ungreased baking sheet. Bake in a 400-degree oven for 10 to 12 minutes or until delicately brown. Makes 5 dozen.

PARMESAN APPETIZERS

Savory cheese sticks for your next party!

    ¼ cup butter or margarine
    1 cup grated Parmesan cheese
    1 cup all-purpose flour
    ½ cup dairy sour cream
    1 tablespoon caraway seed
    1 slightly beaten egg white

In medium bowl stir butter or margarine to soften. Beat in cheese till light and fluffy. Add flour alternately with sour cream; blend until smooth. Stir in caraway seed. Chill dough for at least 2 hours.

Divide dough in half. Roll half on a lightly floured board or canvas to a 12x6-inch rectangle. Using a pastry wheel cut into ½x6-inch strips. Brush tops of strips with egg white. Twist each strip in opposite directions. Place on a lightly greased baking sheet, firmly

pressing ends against pan. Repeat with remaining dough.
Bake in a 350-degree oven for 12 to 15 minutes or till golden.
Remove from baking sheet to wire rack. Cool. Makes 4 dozen.

PARTY CHICKEN WINGS

*Drumettes are chicken wings with the tips removed. You may
buy packaged drumettes or whole wings and make your own.
Marinate the drumettes the day prior to your party and bake just
before the guests arrive!*

       24 chicken drumettes
        1 chicken-flavored bouillon cube
        1 tablespoon butter or margarine
       ½ cup hot water
        3 tablespoons honey
        2 tablespoons lemon juice
        2 tablespoons soy sauce
        2 tablespoons dry sherry
        1 tablespoon salad oil
        1 teaspoon salt
       ⅛ teaspoon dry mustard
       ⅛ teaspoon curry powder
        1 clove garlic, peeled and minced

Place wing pieces in a shallow glass dish or plastic bag. In small
bowl combine bouillon cube, butter or margarine and hot water,
stirring till bouillon dissolves. Add remaining ingredients. Pour
mixture evenly over chicken, turning wing pieces to coat completely. Cover dish or twist-tie bag and refrigerate for overnight.
Turn wings over occasionally.
Arrange chicken in a greased shallow baking dish. Bake in a
350-degree oven for 50 to 60 minutes or till golden brown and fork-
tender. Baste several times with marinade. Makes 24 pieces.

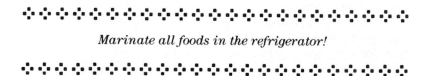

Marinate all foods in the refrigerator!

SARDINE SURPRISES

Admittedly, out comes the dictionary each time I write the word "hors d'oeuvres;" but these little surprises are easier to make than spell.

  1 4-ounce can sardines packed in oil
  Pastry for single-crust pie
  Lemon juice or mustard

 Drain and halve sardines; pat dry on paper toweling. Prepare pastry for a single-crust pie. Roll out on a lightly floured surface to a ⅛-inch thickness. Cut strips of pastry slightly wider than sardines. Place a sardine half on a strip of pastry. Sprinkle with a few drops of lemon juice or spread a dab of mustard atop each sardine. Cut off enough pastry to encase filling. Dampen edges with milk; fold pastry over so edges meet. With fork tines press edges together to seal; brush tops lightly with milk. Prick tops 2 or 3 times with the tip of a sharp knife.

 Place, a few inches apart, on an ungreased baking sheet. Bake in a 450-degree oven for 12 to 15 minutes or till deep golden brown. Remove from baking sheet with a wide spatula. Serve warm or cool and refrigerate until needed; then place on a baking sheet and reheat in a 350-degree oven for about 10 minutes. Makes about 12 appetizers.

SHRIMP-STUFFED MUSHROOMS

A prize-winning recipe created for a seafood contest.

  1 pound raw shrimp in shells or 1 cup cooked shrimp (see note)
 24 medium mushrooms (about 1 pound)
  ¼ cup butter or margarine
  2 cloves garlic, peeled and minced
  ½ cup light cream
  ½ cup soft bread crumbs
  ½ teaspoon salt
  ¼ teaspoon pepper
  1 tablespoon lemon juice

Shell and clean raw shrimp; pat dry. Cut into pieces. Wash mushrooms; remove stems and chop into small pieces; set aside. Simmer caps in boiling water for 2 minutes. Remove with a slotted spoon; drain on paper toweling.

Melt butter or margarine in a skillet; add shrimp, mushroom stems and garlic. Cook, stirring, for 2 minutes or till shrimp start to lose their glossiness. DO NOT OVERCOOK! Add cream and cook, stirring constantly, until mixture thickens. Remove from heat and stir in bread crumbs, salt and pepper.

Spoon mixture evenly into mushroom caps. Place in a shallow baking dish. Drizzle lemon juice over filling.

Bake, uncovered, in a 375-degree oven for 15 minutes or until lightly browned on top. Serve warm. Makes 24 appetizer servings.

Note:

    If using cooked shrimp, stir shrimp in with cream.

SWEET AND SOUR BEEF BALLS

One of my favorite recipes . . . perfect for parties or buffets. Serve these tiny beef balls in their piquant sauce for a no-fuss main dish for your family, too! They disappear fast.

    1 **pound lean ground beef**
    ½ **cup soft bread crumbs**
    ¼ **cup milk**
    ½ **teaspoon salt**
    Dash pepper
    ½ **cup catsup**
    2 **tablespoons packed brown sugar**
    1 **tablespoon vinegar**
    1 **tablespoon Worcestershire sauce**
    1 **small onion, peeled and finely chopped**

In mixing bowl combine ground beef, bread crumbs, milk, salt and pepper; mix well. Shape into 1-inch balls. Arrange on rack in broiler pan. Bake in a 350-degree oven for 10 minutes or until lightly browned.

Meanwhile, prepare sauce. In small bowl combine catsup, brown sugar, vinegar, Worcestershire sauce and onion; blend well.

Remove meatballs from broiler pan to 1½-quart baking dish; discard drippings. Pour sauce evenly over meatballs. Bake at 350 degrees for 20 minutes. Serve hot. Makes 30 meatballs.

DILLY DIP

A dip fast-to-fix for your vegetable sticks!

½ **cup mayonnaise**
½ **cup dairy sour cream**
1 **teaspoon lemon juice**
1 **teaspoon grated onion**
½ **teaspoon seasoned salt**
½ **teaspoon dry mustard**
½ **teaspoon dried dill weed**

In small bowl combine mayonnaise, sour cream, lemon juice, onion, salt, dry mustard and dill weed. Blend thoroughly. Chill. Use as a dip with broccoli, cauliflower, celery or carrot sticks. Or try it with fish! Makes 1 cup.

GREEN GODDESS CHEESE BALL

Serve either as a tasty cheese ball or delicious dip!

3 **8-ounce packages cream cheese, softened**
¾ **cup butter or margarine, softened**
1 **8-ounce bottle green goddess dressing**
1 **cup chopped nuts**

In large mixing bowl combine cream cheese and butter or margarine; beat till light and fluffy. Gradually add dressing; mix to blend. Chill until firm, at least 3 hours. Shape into 2 balls.

Spread chopped nuts in a shallow pan. Roll balls in nuts to coat evenly. Cheese balls may be stored in refrigerator for several days before serving. Serve with crackers. Makes 2 medium balls.

To serve as a dip: Blend together cream cheese, butter or margarine and dressing. Serve with vegetable dippers or potato chips. Makes about 4½ cups.

FROSTED SANDWICH LOAF

This triple-flavored loaf, consisting of chicken, ham and egg fillings, is perfect for parties and showers. Since unsliced bread is not always available, the recipe has been adapted to use a loaf of sliced sandwich bread. Frost with a cream cheese icing and transform it into a single loaf. Serve with potato chips and a relish tray.

Egg Salad Filling:
    4 hard-cooked eggs, coarsely chopped
    3 tablespoons mayonnaise
    2 teaspoons prepared mustard
    1 tablespoon finely chopped onion
    ½ teaspoon salt

Ham Filling:
    1½ cups ground cooked ham
    ½ cup mayonnaise
    1 teaspoon prepared mustard

Chicken Filling:
    1½ cups ground cooked chicken
    ¼ cup finely chopped celery
    ⅓ cup mayonnaise
    3 tablespoons pickle relish

    16 slices sandwich bread
    Soft butter or margarine

Frosting:
    1 8-ounce package cream cheese, softened
    ¼ cup light cream or milk

To prepare egg filling: In small bowl blend together eggs, mayonnaise, mustard, onion and salt. Chill.

To prepare ham filling: In a small bowl blend together ham, mayonnaise and mustard. Chill.

To prepare chicken filling: In small bowl blend together chicken, celery, mayonnaise and relish. Chill.

To prepare sandwich loaf: Remove crusts from bread. Lay a large piece of aluminum foil on a work surface; place four slices of bread together lengthwise, having each slice touch the next.

Spread with butter or margarine, then egg filling. Cover with four more slices of bread and butter tops. Spread with ham filling for second layer. Cover with four slices and butter tops. The chicken filling completes the layer. Butter last four slices and place buttered side down. Bring foil up and wrap around loaf. Chill.

To prepare frosting: In a small mixing bowl beat cream cheese and cream or milk till fluffy. Spread on sides and top of loaf. If desired, decorate top with olive slices, green pepper rings or wedges of hard-cooked egg. Wrap loosely in foil to prevent frosting from sticking to wrapper. Refrigerate.

To serve: Cut each slice into three sections, making a total of 12 slices about 1¼-inches wide. Makes one dozen servings.

Frozen rings of punch or fruit juice add flavor as they melt without diluting the punch. Hold a second ring in the freezer to replace melted one.

ICE RING

Adds a pretty touch to a punch bowl and keeps indefinitely in your freezer.

Water
5 or 6 large leaves, such as lemon or mint
1 lemon, cut into 4 slices
1 8-ounce can sliced pineapple, drained
4 strawberries
2 candied cherries, halved

Fill a 6-cup ring mold half full of water. Freeze until solid. Remove mold from freezer and place leaves over ice. Alternate lemon and pineapple slices over leaves. Place a strawberry on each pineapple ring and a cherry half on each lemon slice.

Carefully pour more water around fruit and leaves. Return to freezer. When frozen solid, add water to fill mold to rim. Freeze overnight or until needed.

To unmold, dip bottom of mold in cold water; turn out onto heavy-duty aluminum foil. Wrap ring securely and freeze until ready to serve. Float ring, fruit side up, in punch bowl. Makes 1 ice ring.

DOT'S STRAWBERRY PUNCH

The recipe for this popular summertime beverage is from a berry-addict who knows exactly when Nature's little gems are at their peak. "I can smell 'em," she boasts.

1 16-ounce package frozen sliced strawberries in syrup, partially thawed
½ cup sugar
3 6-ounce cans frozen lemonade concentrate, partially thawed
2 quarts ice water
1 32-ounce bottle gingerale, chilled
1 pint fresh strawberries

In container of electric blender combine strawberries in syrup and sugar. Cover and blend till smooth.

In punch bowl or large pitcher combine strawberry mixture and lemonade concentrate. Stir till lemonade is thawed. Stir in ice water. Refrigerate at least 30 minutes to blend flavors.

Before serving punch, add gingerale; mix well. Add ice or ice ring. Float fresh hulled strawberries on top of punch, if desired. Makes 32 4-ounce servings.

❖ ❖

All ingredients for preparing punch should be cold. When refrigerator space is limited, use an ice chest packed with ice cubes to chill the ingredients.

❖ ❖

FROSTY GOLDEN PUNCH

A light-colored banquet punch — tastes as good as it looks!

1 6-ounce can frozen lemonade concentrate
1 6-ounce can frozen orange juice concentrate
1 6-ounce can frozen limeade concentrate
4 cups cold water
1½ cups apricot nectar
½ cup lemon juice
2 quarts gingerale, chilled
1 quart lemon sherbet

In large pitcher or punch bowl combine frozen juice concentrates and cold water. Stir until juices are thawed and blended. Stir in apricot nectar and lemon juice. Chill.

Before serving punch, add gingerale; mix well. Float scoops of lemon sherbet on top of punch. Makes 32 ½-cup servings.

Beverages are a very important part of entertaining. Although the number of drinks consumed will depend on the type of beverage, the time of day, and the season, the general rule is to allow 2 or 3 servings per guest. Recipes in the Sampler are easily doubled or tripled for those special occasions.

HOLIDAY CRANBERRY PUNCH

To toast your holidays!

1 6-ounce can frozen orange juice concentrate
1 6-ounce can frozen lemonade concentrate
2 cups cold water
6 cups (48-ounce bottle) cranberry juice cocktail
1 quart gingerale
1 pint raspberry sherbet

In a large pitcher combine frozen juice concentrates and water. Stir until juices are thawed and blended. Mix in cranberry juice. Chill for several hours or overnight to blend flavors.

Just before serving, pour punch in a punch bowl. Add gingerale; mix well. Float scoops of sherbet atop punch. Makes 30 4-ounce servings.

SPARKLING FRUIT PUNCH

Perfect for an open house! Recipe is easily doubled or tripled.

1 6-ounce can frozen pink lemonade concentrate
1 6-ounce can frozen orange juice concentrate
1 6-ounce can frozen grape juice concentrate
4 cups cold water
1 46-ounce can fruit punch
1 quart gingerale
1 orange, thinly sliced
1 lemon, thinly sliced

In a large pitcher combine frozen juice concentrates and cold water. Stir until juices are thawed and blended. Stir in fruit punch. Chill for several hours or overnight to blend flavors.

Before serving punch, mix well; pour over ice ring in punch bowl. Add gingerale, mixing well. Garnish with orange and lemon slices. Makes 32 4-ounce servings.

PERCOLATOR PUNCH

A spicy beverage perked in a pot!

3 cups unsweetened pineapple juice
3 cups water
½ cup packed brown sugar
Dash salt
6 inches stick cinnamon, broken
1 tablespoon whole cloves
1½ teaspoons whole allspice

In 10-cup electric percolator combine pineapple juice, water, brown sugar and salt. Place cinnamon, cloves and allspice in percolator basket. Perk for 10 minutes. Remove basket and serve hot. Makes 12 4-ounce servings.

HOT MULLED CIDER

Use apple juice if you prefer, but don't forget the doughnuts!

> 2 quarts cider
> ½ cup packed brown sugar
> ¼ teaspoon salt
> 1 teaspoon whole allspice
> 1 teaspoon whole cloves
> 3 inches stick cinnamon

In a large saucepan combine cider, sugar and salt. Tie spices in a small piece of nylon or cheesecloth. Add to cider mixture. Slowly bring mixture to the boiling point. Reduce heat and simmer, covered, for 20 minutes. Remove spice bag. Serve hot with a slice of unpeeled apple floating on top. Makes eight 8-ounce servings.

RUSSIAN TEA

My favorite version of a popular mix; it requires but ½ cup sugar which is considerably less than most recipes. Try it for a refreshing, hot drink!

> 2 cups orange-flavored instant breakfast drink
> ½ cup instant tea
> ½ cup sugar
> 1 envelope (2-quart size) unsweetened lemonade mix
> 1 teaspoon cinnamon
> ½ teaspoon nutmeg
> ½ teaspoon cloves

In a large sifter combine all ingredients; sift into a large bowl. Stir until evenly blended. Place in a 1-quart jar or container with a tight-fitting lid. Store in a cool dry place.

To serve, place 2 heaping teaspoons of tea mix in a cup; add boiling water. Stir and enjoy! Makes approximately 50 servings.

HOT CHOCOLATE MIX

Kids love it! Mix with hot water . . . right out of the tap.

> **1 1-pound can instant chocolate-flavored drink mix**
> **1 6-ounce jar non-dairy cream powder**
> **½ cup confectioners' sugar**
> **1 8-quart package instant nonfat dry milk powder**

In a large sifter combine chocolate-flavored drink mix, non-dairy cream powder and confectioners' sugar; sift into large bowl or kettle. Blend in dry milk powder. Pour into a 1-gallon container with tight-fitting lid. Store in a cool dry place.

To serve, use ⅓ cup chocolate mix and 8-ounces hot water; mix well. Top with a marshmallow, if desired. Makes approximately 50 servings.

CANDIED APPLES

A sure-fire winner — popular with kids of all ages!

> **2 cups sugar**
> **1 cup water**
> **¼ teaspoon cream of tartar**
> **Few drops red food coloring**
> **10 to 12 small apples on wooden sticks**

In a large saucepan combine sugar and water, stirring till sugar dissolves. Boil, without stirring, to the hard crack stage — 290 degrees on a candy thermometer.

Or, test by dropping a little of the syrup into a cup of cold water. When syrup separates in threads (threads become brittle), the hard crack stage has been reached.

Remove pan from heat and place in an outer pan of boiling water to keep syrup from hardening. Add cream of tartar. Add food coloring, drop by drop, till mixture is bright red; stir as little as possible.

Holding each apple by the stick, dip quickly into hot syrup. Roll around till apple is completely coated. Place apples, without touching, on a buttered cookie sheet. Cool till firm. Makes 10 to 12 candied apples.

EASY PRALINES

"Great for the holidays," says the cook sharing the recipe. We agree. They're a melt-in-the-mouth confection and so-o-o easy to make!

> 12 whole graham crackers (24 squares)
> 1 cup butter or margarine (2 sticks)
> 1 cup packed brown sugar
> 1 cup coarsely chopped nuts

Line an ungreased 15x10x1-inch jelly roll pan with a single layer of graham crackers.

In a saucepan combine butter or margarine and brown sugar. Stirring constantly, cook over medium heat until mixture starts to boil around edge of pan. Cook for 2 minutes. Remove from heat.

Cool for 1 minute; stir in nuts. Pour mixture over crackers; spread to coat evenly. Bake in a 350-degree oven for 10 minutes. Remove from oven; cool in pan on wire rack. While warm, cut along perforations with a sharp knife. Store in an airtight container, separating layers with wax paper. These freeze well. Makes 48 pieces.

Hard shells may be easier to crack if nuts are soaked in water for several hours or overnight.

A large saucepan with a heavy bottom minimizes the chances of scorching and boil-overs.

FANTASY FUDGE

A foolproof recipe for the novice candy-maker. A quick-and-easy fudge made creamy without a thermometer.

- ¾ cup butter or margarine (1½ sticks)
- 3 cups sugar
- ⅔ cup (5⅓-ounce can) evaporated milk
- 2 cups (12-ounce pkg.) semi-sweet chocolate morsels
- 1 7-ounce jar marshmallow creme (1¾ cups)
- ½ cup chopped nuts
- 1 teaspoon vanilla

In a heavy 2½- to 3-quart saucepan melt butter or margarine; add sugar and evaporated milk. Stirring constantly, bring to a rolling boil over medium heat. Cook, stirring constantly, for 5 minutes. (Watch carefully to avoid scorching.)

Remove from heat. Add chocolate morsels; beat till melted. Stir in marshmallow creme, nuts and vanilla. Pour mixture into a buttered 13x9x2-inch baking pan. Cool. Cut into squares. Makes 4 dozen pieces.

GERT'S PEANUT BUTTER FUDGE

It's smooth and creamy — the easiest and tastiest you'll ever make!

- 2 cups sugar
- ¼ cup butter or margarine
- ½ cup milk
- 1 cup creamy or crunchy peanut butter
- 3 tablespoons marshmallow creme
- 1 teaspoon vanilla

In a heavy 2-quart saucepan combine sugar, butter or margarine and milk. Stirring constantly, bring to a rolling boil over medium heat. Cook, stirring, for 3 minutes.

Remove from heat. Add peanut butter, marshmallow creme and vanilla; mix well. Pour mixture into a buttered 8-inch square pan. Cool. Cut into squares. Makes 25 pieces.

PEANUT BUTTER CRISPS

These no-bake bars disappear fast! Separate layers with wax paper and carry them along in the picnic basket.

½ cup sugar
½ cup dark corn syrup
¾ cup creamy or crunchy peanut butter
1 teaspoon vanilla
2 cups crispy rice cereal

In large saucepan bring sugar and corn syrup to a boil over medium heat. Remove from heat. Add peanut butter and vanilla; stir until blended. Fold in rice cereal. Press mixture into a buttered 8-inch square baking pan. Cool slightly; cut into bars. Makes 18 bars.

PEANUT BUTTER CUPS

"My most favorite recipe," admits one cook; they are "fun to make and fun to give," says a second. For a professional touch, place them in petit fours cases.

1 cup fine graham cracker crumbs
1 cup sifted confectioners' sugar
1 cup creamy peanut butter
1 cup (6-ounce pkg.) semi-sweet chocolate morsels
1 cup (6-ounce pkg.) milk chocolate morsels
Petit fours cases

In a medium bowl combine graham cracker crumbs, confectioners' sugar and peanut butter; blend thoroughly. (The mixture will be dry.)

Using a rounded teaspoonful of mixture, press firmly and form into a ball. To have a perfectly shaped confection — flat on top with rounded edges — hold ball between thumb and forefinger of left hand; then rotate ball with thumb and forefinger of right hand. (Left-handed cooks should reverse directions.) Place in a petit fours case, leaving enough space around ball for chocolate coating.

Melt chocolate morsels in a small dish over hot, NOT BOILING, water, stirring till melted and smooth. Using a teaspoon, drop a small amount of melted chocolate onto peanut butter cups, spreading to cover tops and sides. Chill till firm. Makes about 80 confections.

Note:
> Best results are obtained when chocolate is melted in small batches — ½ cup at a time. Work with one batch while second batch melts.

PEANUT BUTTER OATMEAL DROPS

A candy substitute. Rolled oats give this no-bake confection chewiness.

> **2 cups sugar**
> **¼ cup unsweetened cocoa**
> **⅛ teaspoon salt**
> **½ cup butter or margarine (1 stick)**
> **½ cup milk**
> **½ cup crunchy peanut butter**
> **1 teaspoon vanilla**
> **3 cups quick-cooking rolled oats**

In 3-quart saucepan combine sugar, cocoa and salt. Stir in butter or margarine and milk. Bring to a boil over medium heat, stirring constantly. Simmer 2 minutes.

Remove from heat. Blend in peanut butter and vanilla then stir in rolled oats. Drop by teaspoonfuls onto wax paper-lined cookie sheet. Cool until firm. Makes 36 pieces.

For gift-giving, place individual candies in paper-wrappings; separate layers with wax paper.

Chocolate scorches easily even when combined with other ingredients. Keep the heat low!

WONDER FUDGE

This never-fail confection combines confectioners' sugar and crispy rice cereal for a not-too-sweet flavor.

> 1 cup (6-ounce pkg.) semi-sweet chocolate morsels
> ¼ cup butter or margarine
> ¼ cup light corn syrup
> 1 teaspoon vanilla
> 1½ cups sifted confectioners' sugar
> 2 cups crispy rice cereal

In 2-quart saucepan, combine chocolate morsels, butter or margarine, corn syrup and vanilla. Cook over low heat, stirring constantly, until mixture is smooth. Remove from heat.

Stir in confectioners' sugar. Add cereal, stirring until evenly coated. Press mixture into buttered 8-inch square baking pan. Refrigerate for 2 hours or till firm. Cut into squares. Makes 25 pieces.

POPCORN BALLS

A molasses-flavored corn ball from the good old days. Wrap each ball in a small plastic bag for hand-outs. "Kids can hold onto the bag and what they don't eat, they can return to the bag."

> 5 quarts popped corn (about 1¼ cups unpopped)
> 1 cup molasses
> ½ cup sugar
> ½ teaspoon salt
> 1 tablespoon butter or margarine

Pick over corn to remove any burned or unpopped kernels. Measure corn into large kettle.

In heavy 2-quart saucepan combine molasses, sugar, salt and butter or margarine. Stir to dissolve sugar, then bring mixture to a boil. Boil gently over medium heat, stirring occasionally so molasses doesn't burn. Cook until mixture registers 270 degrees on a candy thermometer (soft crack stage), or test by dropping a bit of the mixture in cold water (syrup separates into threads that are not brittle).

Pour mixture over popped corn. With a long-handled spoon gently mix to coat kernels. Butter hands lightly and shape corn into balls, 2½-inches in diameter. Wrap each ball in wax paper or place in a small plastic bag. Makes 18 popcorn balls.

RENA'S POPCORN BALLS

No boiling, no testing and no candy thermometer is needed for "the easiest popcorn balls ever." A native Texan says these were a favorite back in the days "when room mothers (at school) made treats for the holidays."

6 quarts popped corn (about 1½ cups unpopped)
½ cup butter or margarine (1 stick)
1 1-pound package (64 large) marshmallows
Red or green food coloring (optional)

Pick over corn to remove any burned or unpopped kernels. Measure corn into large kettle. DO NOT salt.

In a saucepan melt butter or margarine over low heat. Add marshmallows; heat, stirring constantly, till marshmallows melt and mixture is smooth. Remove from heat and tint to desired color with a few drops of food coloring.

Pour mixture over popped corn. Stir gently with a long-handled spoon until kernels are well-coated. Lightly butter hands and shape into balls, 2½-inches in diameter. Cool till firm.

Place each ball in a small plastic bag; close with a twist-tie. Makes 18 to 20 popcorn balls.

Variation:
Scotch-Nut Corn Balls

Follow recipe for Rena's Popcorn Balls except — reduce popped corn to 5½ quarts. Add 1 cup (6-ounce pkg.) butterscotch bits and 1 cup salted peanuts to popped corn.

To keep popcorn fresh, store kernels in the freezer.

ROASTED PUMPKIN SEEDS

A tasty treat for nibblers!

2 cups pumpkin seeds
2 tablespoons butter or margarine, melted
1 teaspoon seasoned salt

Remove seeds from fibrous portion of pumpkin. DO NOT wash. In medium bowl combine melted butter or margarine and salt. Add seeds; stir until seeds are evenly coated with mixture. Spread out in a shallow baking pan. Bake in a 250-degree oven for 1 hour or until seeds are crisp and brown. Stir occasionally for even browning. Makes 2 cups.

Variation:

Roasted Squash Seeds

Follow above recipe as directed except — substitute 2 cups squash seeds for pumpkin.

Watch carefully when toasting nuts; they burn easily.

SPICED PECANS

Nut lovers — Beware! These could be habit-forming!

2 cups pecan halves
¼ cup butter or margarine, melted
1 tablespoon garlic salt
1 teaspoon Worcestershire sauce
½ teaspoon Tabasco sauce

Place nuts in a shallow baking pan. Melt butter or margarine in a small saucepan; mix in garlic salt and sauces. Pour mixture over nuts; stir to coat nuts evenly.

Toast nuts in a 350-degree oven for 20 to 25 minutes, stirring occasionally for even browning. Cool. Store in an airtight container. Makes 2 cups.

ALL-SEASON SALT

The ingredients are universal for this simple, inexpensive seasoning.

    1¼ cups salt
     2 tablespoons black pepper
     2 tablespoons white pepper
     2 tablespoons sugar
     1 tablespoon paprika
     1 tablespoon celery salt
    1½ teaspoons garlic salt
    1½ teaspoons onion salt
    1½ teaspoons dry mustard

Combine all ingredients in a jar with a tight-fitting lid. Cover. Shake vigorously to thoroughly blend mixture. Store tightly covered. Makes 1¾ cups.

GRANOLA

A very sustaining cereal, consisting of rolled oats, sesame seeds and wheat germ, made right in your own kitchen.

     6 cups uncooked old-fashioned rolled oats
     ⅓ cup packed brown sugar
     ⅓ cup wheat germ
     ⅓ cup shredded coconut
     ¼ cup sesame seeds
     1 cup sunflower seeds
     1 cup seedless raisins
     ⅓ cup cooking oil
     ¼ cup honey
     1 teaspoon vanilla

Spread oats in a 15x10x1-inch pan or other large, shallow pan. Heat in a 325-degree oven for 10 minutes.

Stir in brown sugar, wheat germ, coconut, sesame seeds, sunflower seeds and raisins.

Combine cooking oil, honey and vanilla; pour over rolled oat mixture, mixing until dry ingredients are evenly coated. Bake in a 325-degree oven for 20 to 25 minutes; stir occasionally. Cool. Stir until crumbly. Store in a tightly-covered container in the refrigerator. Makes 9 cups.

HORSERADISH MUSTARD

A nice gift idea for a gourmet!

  2 onion-flavored bouillon cubes (see note)
1½ cups hot water
  4 teaspoons cornstarch
  4 teaspoons sugar
  4 teaspoons dry mustard
  2 teaspoons turmeric
  ½ teaspoon salt
  ¼ cup white vinegar
  4 teaspoons prepared horseradish
  2 egg yolks, slightly beaten

Dissolve bouillon in hot water. In saucepan combine cornstarch, sugar, dry mustard, turmeric and salt; blend well. Stir in vinegar and horseradish; slowly blend in bouillon mixture. Cook and stir over low heat until mixture thickens and bubbles.

Slowly stir a small amount of hot mixture into egg yolks in bowl. Return mixture to saucepan. Cook, stirring constantly, about 1 minute or till mixture comes just to a boil. Cool. Store tightly covered in the refrigerator. Makes 1½ cups.

Note:
When onion bouillon cubes aren't available, substitute 2 beef bouillon cubes.

Cooking Notes

Ingredient Equivalents

Beans, dry	1 pound	2 cups
	2 cups	6 cups, cooked
Butter or margarine	1 pound	2 cups
	1 stick	½ cup
	½ cup	8 tablespoons
Cheese		
American,		
Cheddar, Swiss	1 pound	4 cups shredded or cubed
	4 ounces	1 cup shredded or cubed
Cottage cheese	1 pound	2 cups
Cream cheese	8 ounces	1 cup
Parmesan, grated	3 ounces	1 cup
Chocolate		
cooking chocolate	1 ounce	1 square
morsels	6-ounce package	1 cup
Cream		
Sour cream	8 ounces	1 cup
Whipping	1 cup	2 cups whipped
Crumbs		
Dry bread	1 slice	¼ cup fine dry crumbs
Soft bread	1 slice	¾ cup soft crumbs
Cornflakes	2 cups cereal	½ cup crumbs
Eggs	1 large	3 tablespoons
	1 white	2 tablespoons
	1 yolk	1 tablespoon
Flour		
All-purpose	1 pound	3½ cups unsifted
	1 pound	4 cups sifted
Cake	1 pound	4½ cups sifted
Whole wheat	1 pound	3½ cups stirred

Ingredient Equivalents

Fruits, dried

Dates	1 pound	2 cups pitted
Prunes	1 pound	2½ cups
Raisins, seedless	1 pound	2¾ to 3 cups
Raisins, seeded	1 pound	2½ cups

Gelatin

unflavored	1 envelope	1 tablespoon

Lemon

	1 juiced	2 to 3 tablespoons
	1 grated	2 teaspoons peel

Milk

Evaporated (Whole or skim)	14 ounces	1¾ cups
	6 ounces	⅔ cup

Nuts

Pecans	1 pound unshelled	2 cups shelled
Walnuts	1 pound unshelled	2¼ cups shelled

Pasta

Macaroni	8 ounces	4 cups cooked
Noodles, broad	8 ounces	6 cups, uncooked
narrow	8 ounces	5 cups, uncooked
Spaghetti	8 ounces	4 to 5 cups cooked

Rice

Long-grain	1 pound	2 cups uncooked
	2 cups	6 cups cooked

Sugar

Confectioners'	1 pound	3⅓ cups unsifted
	1 pound	4 cups sifted
Brown	1 pound	2¼ cups packed
Granulated	1 pound	2¼ cups

Measurements

Dash = ⅟₁₆ teaspoon
3 teaspoons = 1 tablespoon
4 tablespoons = ¼ cup or 2 ounces
8 tablespoons = ½ cup or 4 ounces
16 tablespoons = 1 cup or 8 ounces
16 ounces = 1 pound

When measuring dry ingredients, use a dry measuring utensil of the exact capacity for which you wish to measure. Spoon the ingredients lightly into cup and level with a metal spatula.

8 fluid ounces = 1 cup or ½ pint
2 cups = 1 pint or 16 ounces
4 cups = 1 quart or 32 ounces
16 cups = 4 quarts or 1 gallon

When measuring liquids, use a glass measuring cup with graduated markings. Place on a level surface at eye level and fill to desired capacity.

A Guide to Interchanging Baking Utensils

When a recipe in the Sampler calls for a casserole, it does not mean that another type of utensil may not be used; but it may be necessary to adjust baking time and temperature when interchanging a shallow dish for a deep casserole.
Here are some interchangeable containers:

A 10x6x1½-inch baking dish for a 1½-quart casserole.
A 12x8x2-inch baking dish for a 2-quart casserole.
A 13x9x2-inch baking dish for a 3-quart casserole.

The term *baking dish* refers to a glass utensil; a *baking pan* is metal. Remember, a recipe stating a specific pan or dish means it has been tested using only the utensil stated. Although baking pans and dishes are interchangeable, be sure to reduce the oven temperature by 25 degrees when substituting glass for metal.

Also, if a cake recipe calls for a 13x9x2-inch baking pan, you may substitute two 9-inch round pans; or use two 8-inch round pans rather than one 12x8x2-inch baking pan.

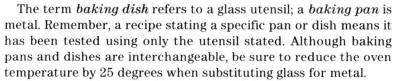

Average Can Sizes

The Sampler lists all canned goods by weight; yet knowing the corresponding measurement in cups is helpful. Also, since some cookbooks refer to canned goods by the number of the can, their equivalent is added for your convenience.

Can Size	Approximate weight or fluid measurement	Approximate number of cups
8-ounce	8 ounces	1 cup
12-ounce vacuum	12 ounces	1½ cups
#303	16 ounces	2 cups
#2	20 ounces	2½ cups
#2½	28 ounces	3½ cups
#3 cylinder	46 fluid ounces	5¾ cups
#10	106 ounces	13 cups

Note:
Due to the density of some foods, the net weight of one product may differ slightly from that of a second product in an identical can.

Glossary of Cooking Terms
Used in the Sampler

Beat — to mix thoroughly with a rapid over and over motion.

Blend — to mix or combine thoroughly two or more ingredients until smooth.

Boil — to bring a liquid to 212 degrees F. with constant bubbling.

Braise — to brown in fat; then cook gently, covered, in liquid.

Casserole — a container with a cover in which food is baked and then served.

Cream — to blend ingredients with a spoon or fork until soft and fluffy.

Dice — to cut into small cubes.

Dutch oven — a cooking utensil with a deep cooking capacity and a tight-fitting cover.

Grill — to cook by direct heat.

Marinate — to let a food stand in a seasoned mixture, usually an oil-acid combination, before cooking.

Mince — to cut or chop into very fine pieces.

Parboil — to cook partially in boiling water in preparation for further cooking.

Poach — to cook a food in simmering liquid.

Render — to melt animal fat until liquid portion can be removed.

Sauté — to cook lightly in a small amount of butter, margarine or other fat.

Scald — to bring milk or cream just below the boiling point so that tiny bubbles appear around edge of pan.

Shred — to cut or slice into very narrow strips.

Simmer — to cook in a liquid just below the boiling point.

Skillet — a frying pan.

Stir — to mix food with a circular motion.

Stock — a liquid from cooked meat or vegetables.

Index

356

363

Cooking Notes

JAN 2 1984	**DATE DUE**	
JAN 2 6 1985	APR 18 '92	OCT 1 4 2015
MAR 8 1985	DEC 15 '92	
MAR 2 9 1985	FEB 18 '93	
APR 2 4 1985	FEB 23 '93	WITHDRAWN
MAY 9 1985	OCT 26 '94	
OCT 2 2 1985	OCT 27 '94	
DEC 2 4 1985	DEC 29 '98	
JUL 1 6 1987	MAY 2 1 2003	
AUG 7 1987	NOV 2 4 2009	
SEP 13 1988	SEP - 5 2013	
JUL 30 '91